P9-DIE-003

Lincoln Christian College

CENTER FOR JUDAIC-CHRISTIAN STUDIES

There is no more rewarding or important task at hand for us as Christians than exploring the Hebrew heritage of our faith. To do so is to expand and enrich every dimension of our lives, to deepen our understanding and appreciation of Jesus, and to make us more informed and productive believers. Further, returning to the foundations of our faith opens us to a new respect for Jews, Judaism, and Israel.

The Center for Judaic-Christian Studies serves as an educational resource to the Christian community, publishing books and audio and video teaching tapes, and producing seminars, conferences, and television programs. The Center also sponsors and publishes the work of its research extension in Israel, the Jerusalem School for the Study of the Synoptic Gospels. By researching the Hebrew background of the Synoptic Gospels, this distinguished group of Jewish and Christian scholars is making dramatic new discoveries about the life and teachings of Jesus.

We welcome you to the adventure of discovering your biblical roots. Write and request a free copy of the Center's catalog of educational materials.

DWIGHT A. PRYOR, President
Center for Judaic-Christian Studies
P.O. Box 202707
Austin, Texas 78720

A Time to Speak

The Evangelical-Jewish Encounter

Edited by

A. James Rudin
Marvin R. Wilson

William B. Eerdmans Publishing Company
Grand Rapids, Michigan
and
Center for Judaic-Christian Studies
Austin, Texas

Copyright © 1987 by the Center for Judaic-Christian Studies
P.O. Box 202707, Austin, Texas 78720
Published by Wm. B. Eerdmans Publishing Co.
255 Jefferson Ave. S.E., Grand Rapids, Mich. 49503

All rights reserved
Printed in the United States of America

Library of Congress Cataloging-in-Publication Data

A Time to speak : the evangelical-Jewish encounter
edited by A. James Rudin, Marvin R. Wilson.
p.   cm.
Proceedings of the third national conference entitled Evangelicals and Jews:
coming of age, held at Gordon College, Wenham, Mass.,
Feb. 28, 29 and Mar 1, 1984.
Bibliography: p. 198.
ISBN 0-8028-0281-8
1. Evangelicalism — Relations — Judaism — Congresses.   2. Judaism-
Relations — Evangelicalism — Congresses.   I. Rudin, A. James (Arnold
James), 1934-   .   II. Wilson, Marvin R.
BR1641.J83T55   1987   261.2′6—dc19

Contents

v

75676

Foreword

The name of the conference on which the present volume is based was *Evangelicals and Jews: Coming of Age*. That designation might have been somewhat optimistic; only the next few years will tell. But in its literal and grammatical sense, the phrase is true: *"coming of age,"* not *"having come* of age." It is a statement of progress, not one of accomplishment. It makes no claim of achievement. At the same time, it is a statement of life. The dialogue between evangelicals and Jews is alive and well and ongoing. Having begun in 1975—if we take the date of the first national conference as the beginning of the dialogue—it continues, although it might at times have seemed to be somewhat frail.

Actually, the dialogue began long before 1975, but in small ways. A number of us, the most active being the late G. Douglas Young, took part in various kinds of conversation with Jewish leaders from the early 1950s. I cannot speak specifically for others, although there must be several score of them, but I can tell of my own involvement in such dialogue.

Having gone to a high school whose student body was between 90 and 95 percent Jewish, and years later having taken my doctorate at Dropsie College and having subsequently served as Professor of Old Testament at Fuller Theological Seminary, I was naturally interested in Jewish studies to a more-than-average degree. For my second doctoral degree I wrote a dissertation on the subject "A Preliminary Reconstruction of Judaism at the Time of the Second Temple in Light of the Published Qumran Materials." I must in honesty admit that when I had completed it I knew more about the Dead Sea scrolls than I did about Judaism—but I was at least well initiated into Judaism.

While I was teaching at Lafayette College in Easton, Pennsylvania, in the late forties, I was invited to speak at a local synagogue following the Friday evening service on the subject "The Fundamentals of Christianity." I chose as my two main points *revelation* (we believe that God makes himself and his will known to and through his chosen people) and *redemption* (we believe that God has been and is active for the deliverance of the world from the bondage of sin), and I built my presentation largely on portions of the Old Testament. The lengthy open discussion that followed demonstrated the great deal of interest the subject had aroused. I was encouraged to have more such discussions.

A few years later, after I had moved to California, I was invited to participate in the formation of a Jewish-Christian fellowship. According to the ground rules, the group was to consist only of lay persons (I was to be involved only for the formative meeting), and it was to avoid discussion of theological matters. It seemed to me that this was to deny any real significance to the fellowship: how could Christians and Jews come to know each other better if they could not discuss what made them Christians and Jews in the first place?

Another opportunity for dialogue came when I was invited to speak to a group of rabbis. From some of the reaction I saw that I was using words that aroused emotion in my audience, and I asked one of my rabbinic friends what I had said. Gradually I came to know that what I might say in all goodwill could very easily be misunderstood as prejudice or triumphalism, simply because I did not know the vocabulary to use. I had learned the first important rule of dialogue: both sides must know precisely what each means. That requires each of us to learn the vocabulary, the emotional hang-ups, the deep convictions of the other. We must avoid those things that bring dialogue to an unsatisfactory and early end.

In 1974 a group of clergymen made a pilgrimage. We were eleven Protestants, four Catholics, and three Jews, and we visited Rome, Geneva, and Jerusalem. It was the sort of rich experience that can develop only from living together and worshiping together for two weeks. We formed friendships that have lasted ever since. More significant is the fact that we came to understand each other and therefore to trust each other. True dialogue—particularly that which involves our deepest convictions—can exist only in an atmosphere of complete trust, when we know at last that no one is trying to change our minds for us and no one is trying to convert us.

On such a basis of mutual trust, a group of rabbis and professors from Fuller Seminary met once a month for a period of two years or so. Two of us, an evangelical and a rabbi, would prepare papers on a common subject, present them, and the group would have a hearty discussion. We were not nibbling at the fringes of our faith; we were involved in discussion of serious questions—questions that without complete trust would have divided us at once into hostile camps.

All these discussions, though, were at a strictly local level. In

1975 that changed. Sparked, I believe, by Rabbi Marc Tanenbaum and Dr. G. Douglas Young (although Rabbi A. James Rudin and Dr. Marvin R. Wilson were deeply involved), a conference was held in New York City, December 8 to 10, 1975, that included a number of Jewish and evangelical clergymen and scholars. Eighteen of us were given assigned subjects, one Jewish and one evangelical scholar for each subject, and we were to present these to the entire conference.

The general subjects were: Evangelical Christians and Jews Share Perspectives; The Messiah; The Meaning of Israel; Interpretation of Scripture; Responses to Moral Crises and Social Ferment; Religious Pluralism; and The Future. The conference organizers imposed no restrictions, either on the presentations or on the discussions that followed each presentation. At times the exchange of views became a bit heated. But trust and a desire to know each other's views prevailed. The first national conference was a remarkable success; the papers were later published in the volume *Evangelicals and Jews in Conversation on Scripture, Theology, and History* (Baker, 1978).

The second national conference was held in Deerfield, Illinois, December 9-11, 1980. The theme was "Evangelicals and Jews in an Age of Pluralism"; the format was similar to that of the first conference, but with one marked difference. Whereas the first conference began with an undercurrent of suspicion about each other's motives, the second conference was distinguished from the beginning by its trust and candor. The scholars who presented papers were interested not only in presenting their convictions without adulterating them in any way but also in learning more about the firmly held faith and cordial ethical practice of their counterparts. These essays were publshed in *Evangelicals and Jews in an Age of Pluralism* (Baker, 1984).

There were other conferences, some local, some regional. I have had the privilege of participating in a number of them, some of which involved Protestants from the broader spectrum beyond evangelicalism, some of which included Catholic scholars as well. It has been my experience without exception that such dialogues have always been conducted with great respect for the views of others. And so it should be. Truth is so large that none of us can comprehend it completely. Each of us can learn something about truth from what another has come to learn about truth.

So we come to the third national conference, held at Gordon College, Wenham, Massachusetts, on February 28 and 29 and March 1, 1984, the proceedings of which are found in the following pages. A study of the lists of participants at the three conferences will indicate that while a number of the original conferees were involved in one or both of the succeeding conferences, there are also additional names. It seems obvious that the circle is growing larger.

But the original vision has not been lost. The subjects range from basic theological matters, to the outworking of our faith in modern society, to understanding each other. Evangelicals and Jews attempt to define themselves, to express honestly how they perceive each other, to grapple with theological stereotypes of each other, and to discover where they are and whither they are going in this dialogue. We are truly *coming* of age!

The title of this volume is prophetic: *A Time to Speak: The Evangelical-Jewish Encounter.* With anti-Semitism on the rise again in the world (including in our own country) and with suspicion and ridicule increasingly expressed concerning the motives of evangelicals, it is indeed a time to speak. To speak with love and understanding. To demonstrate to an incredulous world that there are Jews and Christians who take scriptural teachings seriously and who seek to apply them sincerely in all areas of life. The authors of the following articles have spoken to each other, with mutual respect and love. Now they send their message to a wider audience through this publication.

It is fitting to express appreciation for the editorial work of Rabbi A. James Rudin and Dr. Marvin R. Wilson in putting together this volume, and gratitude to the William B. Eerdmans Publishing Company and the Center for Judaic-Christian Studies for publishing it. It is a valuable addition to the ongoing series of discussion between evangelicals and Jews.

WILLIAM SANFORD LASOR

Introduction*

For centuries, evangelical Christians and Jews have moved past (or away from) each other like the proverbial "ships in the night," never really encountering one another as vibrant and unique spiritual communities. But recently a fresh breeze has begun to stir on the American religious landscape. Increasingly, evangelicals and Jews are now meeting and entering into serious dialogue with an openness, understanding, and mutual respect rarely experienced before. And it is happening without compromising our deepest faith commitments.

The purpose of such dialogue is not to produce some symbiotic or syncretistic world body by melting down evangelical Christianity and Judaism to their lowest common denominators. Neither is the goal of such genuine dialogue to proselytize or convert the other community out of religious existence. Rather, it is a time for evangelicals and Jews alike to speak out boldly and honestly to each other, to come to know and understand each other as people and not as spiritual abstractions. Both groups are weary of being the victims of stereotypic caricatures and of viewing the respective beliefs and teachings of the other from a distance.

Early in 1984, Gordon College and the Interreligious Affairs Department of the American Jewish Committee cosponsored a conference that focused on the historical roots of evangelical Christianity and Judaism, and the impact of the pluralistic American experience on both groups. While candidly facing the profound theological differences that have separated us for nearly two thousand years, the conference participants sought new avenues of cooperation on contemporary issues of mutual concern.

Just prior to the meeting at Gordon College in Wenham, Massachusetts, we, as conference cochairpersons, jointly issued the "Conference Call" as a working document. We believe it can serve as the basis for constructive evangelical Christian–Jewish dialogue in the future:

1. We are united in a common struggle against anti-Semitism. We are outraged by the continued presence of this evil and pledge to work

*This Introduction is based on an article entitled "Judeo-Christian Values and Social Justice" that first appeared in *Eternity* (Sept. 1985): 57-59.

together for the elimination of anti-Semitism and all other forms of racism. We are committed jointly to educate this present generation and future generations about the unspeakable horror of the Holocaust.

2. We categorically reject the notion that Zionism is racism. Zionism, the Jewish people's national liberation movement, has deep roots in the Hebrew Scriptures, no less than in the painful history of the Jewish people.

3. We are committed to support Israel as a Jewish state, within secure and recognized borders. We also recognize that Palestinian Arabs have legitimate rights. We pledge our joint efforts in behalf of a just and lasting peace not only between Jews and Arabs but among all peoples of the Middle East.

4. No government is sacred, and no government's policies are beyond criticism. But we strongly object to the practice of holding Israel to a different standard of conduct and morality from that applied to all other nation-states, especially to those committed to Israel's destruction.

5. We affirm the eternal validity and contemporary relevance of the Hebrew Scriptures as a primary source of moral, ethical, and spiritual values. And we pledge to work together to uphold and advance these biblical values in our own society and throughout the world.

6. We pledge to uphold the precious value of religious pluralism in our society. We strongly condemn those who would use unethical, coercive, devious, or manipulative means to proselytize others. Witness to one's faith must always be accompanied with great sensitivity and respect for the integrity of the other person lest religious freedom and pluralism be threatened.

7. We will seek to overcome any popular stereotypes, caricatures, and images that may contribute to one faith community falsely perceiving the other. To further this end, we pledge to continue to examine the rich spiritual legacy that Judaism and evangelicalism hold sacred together as well as their profound differences of belief.

8. We share a common calling to help eliminate inhumanity and injustice among all humankind. We also jointly resolve to work together to prevent nuclear annihilation and to pursue the path of world peace.

9. We share a joint commitment to uphold the principle of separation of church and state in the United States.

10. We pledge to deepen our joint involvement in the struggle to achieve human rights and religious liberty for our coreligionists in the Soviet Union and elsewhere in the world.

This volume represents the fruits of the conference at Gordon College, and it is our hope that this book will spur new evangelical-Jewish dialogue. The questions found at the conclusion of each chapter are intended to serve as a useful catalyst to help prompt and achieve that end. Now that our two communities have learned to speak to one another in candid, and yet reconciling voices, it is also our hope that evangelical Christians and Jews will work together even more effectively in the future. Two thousand years of estrangement is long enough!

The editors wish to express their thanks to those who have rendered assistance in the preparation of this volume, especially Mary Jasper Cate, Celia Horowitz, and Florence Mordhorst for their secretarial skills. The editors also acknowledge the unfailing support and assistance of Dwight Pryor, president of the Center for Judaic-Christian Studies of Austin, Texas, and of Jon Pott, editor-in-chief of William B. Eerdmans Publishing Company.

A. JAMES RUDIN
MARVIN R. WILSON

Contributors

Thomas A. Askew, Professor of History, Gordon College, Wenham, Massachusetts

Judith H. Banki, Associate National Interreligious Affairs Director, American Jewish Committee, New York, New York

Herman J. Blumberg, Rabbi, Congregation Shir Tivka, Wayland, Massachusetts

David R. Blumenthal, Professor of Religion, Emory University, Atlanta, Georgia

Kenneth A. Briggs, Former Religion Editor, *The New York Times,* New York, New York

Henry L. Feingold, Professor of History, City University of New York, New York, New York

Vernon C. Grounds, President Emeritus, Conservative Baptist Theological Seminary, Denver, Colorado

Joshua O. Haberman, Rabbi, Washington Hebrew Congregation, Washington, D.C.

Alan F. Johnson, Professor of Biblical Studies and Christian Ethics, Wheaton College, Wheaton, Illinois

Walter C. Kaiser, Jr., Professor of Old Testament and Semitic Languages, Dean and Vice President of Education, Trinity Evangelical Divinity School, Deerfield, Illinois

Hillel Levine, University Professor, Boston University, Boston, Massachusetts

John N. Oswalt, Professor of Old Testament and Semitic Languages, Trinity Evangelical Divinity School, Deerfield, Illinois

David A. Rausch, Professor of Church History and Judaic Studies, Ashland College Theological Seminary, Ashland, Ohio

A. *James Rudin,* National Interreligious Affairs Director, American Jewish Committee, New York, New York

Timothy L. Smith, Professor of History and Director, Program in American Religious History, The Johns Hopkins University, Baltimore, Maryland

Robert Sternberg, Director of Holocaust Center, Jewish Federation of St. Louis, Missouri

Gordon Tucker, Dean of Rabbinical School, Jewish Theological Seminary of America, New York, New York

David F. Wells, Andrew Mutch Professor of Historical and Systematic Theology, Gordon-Conwell Theological Seminary, South Hamilton, Massachusetts

Marvin R. Wilson, Harold Ockenga Professor of Biblical Studies, Gordon College, Wenham, Massachusetts

1
Jews and Judaism: A Self-Definition

HERMAN J. BLUMBERG

I

The first responsibility in dialogue is to achieve an understanding of one's partner as that person chooses to be understood. Then stereotypes collapse, essential feelings are perceived, and avenues of communication are opened. Foundations for a bridge spanning the gulf between distant others are firmly established. It is in this spirit that I welcome the opportunity to discuss how I understand the terms *Jews* and *Judaism*.

For the Jew the task of self-definition was once relatively clear-cut. The entire Jewish community accepted the authority of sacred literature as interpreted by rabbis serving as teachers and judges. When it was necessary to fend off challenges to the authority of the system, Jews built walls to maintain their distinctiveness. Efforts by non-Jews to keep Jews separate and isolated also served to preserve the system.

Jewish law (Halakhah) considers anyone born of Jewish parents as a member of the "kingdom of priests, the holy nation" (Exod. 19:6), thereby obliged to observe the mitzvoth or religious imperatives. Halakhah further qualifies that a Jew is anyone born of a Jewish woman, thereby including the children issuing from the marriage of a non-Jewish man and a Jewish woman, but not the reverse. One born of a non-Jewish mother, whether the father is Jewish or not, is considered a Jew only following a conversion ritual that includes immersion *(tevilah)* and circumcision *(brit milah)* performed for the purpose of entrance into the Covenant of Abraham. Conversion for adults is preceded by a period of study and by examination for knowledge of Jewish practice, adherence to essential beliefs, and sincere intent in becoming part of the covenant community. Children are converted conditionally, subject to their assent at the age of maturity.

So much for the easy part of defining a Jew. With ghetto walls destroyed and the Jew permitted to move freely in the secular and Christian worlds, the task has become more difficult. After two hundred years of emancipation, after the tragedy of the Holocaust and the establishment of the State of Israel, we recognize a variety of situations in which Halakhah appears inadequate. Here are some of the issues with which contemporary Jewry has been struggling.

1. Thousands—no, tens of thousands—of individuals fail the standard established by Jewish tradition but nevertheless identify themselves as Jews. They live Jewish lives and share the destiny, responsibility, risks, and privileges of the Jewish people.

    There are Israelis who speak Hebrew, fight in the Israeli Defense Force, and build the land. They are, in fact, part of the Jewish nation, culturally and spiritually . . . but their mothers are not Jewish.

    There are Russian Jews in the United States and Israel who experienced all of the discrimination that follows from having *"ʿIvri"* stamped on their identity card—individuals who risked job and social status to leave the Soviet Union in order to live as Jews in freedom. But once outside the Soviet Union their status as Jews is questioned because of problems in the Jewishness of their maternal lineage.

2. We also are aware that during the Second World War the Nazis identified many individuals as Jews even though they fell far short of the Halakic definition; some identified actively as Christians. They were all murdered as Jews. How shall we consider them?

3. There is also a considerable community of men and women who have formally converted to Judaism under the auspices of the Conservative and Reform movements, but not in full accordance with Halakhah. They belong to synagogues and sometimes lead them, raise their children as Jews, and share in the behaviors and ways of the Jewish people. Yet some would question their status as Jews.

4. There is one final dimension to our discussion: Some are born as Jews and continue to identify as Jews, but profess Christianity, speaking of themselves as fulfilled Jews—Jews for Jesus. Where do they fit in?

All these questions occupy rabbis, synagogues, Jewish communities, the rabbinate in Israel, the Israeli government, and individuals who fit into one or another of these subgroups. Sometimes practical questions arise: membership in the synagogue; eligibility for bar/bat mitzvah; for wedding ceremonies recognized as Jewish by the Jewish community. In

Israel there are more technical issues regarding grounds for citizenship, laws of inheritance, and other matters of personal status. Always there is the tension between an individual's self-definition and commitments and the different, usually more stringent, standards of the community. Some of these issues have been addressed—in Israel and in diaspora—with varying levels of resolution. Let us return now to examine them.

Every Israeli identity card includes a classification of *le'um,* one's nationality or nationhood. Jewish law provides the standard for determining nationality, and attempts to admit secular definitions have been thwarted.

In 1968 Benjamin Shalit, a Naval officer, petitioned the Israeli Supreme Court to register his two sons, Israeli in every regard, but born of a non-Jewish mother, as Jews by nationality. The court urged that the government registrar accept the good faith declaration of the father and record the children as Jews. But strong public protest of this decision resulted in passage of a statute (1970) that reaffirmed Halakic authority in defining Jewish nationality. Of note is the fact that the law did not specify that conversion to Judaism must be conducted by Orthodox authorities. Thus, Reform and Conservative conversions performed outside the State of Israel are accepted *post facto,* although Orthodox religious groups continue to press for their exclusion and are held back only by the fragile nature of the political coalitions in which they participate.

This measure also specified that the non-Jewish spouse or children and grandchildren of Jews arriving in Israel with the Jewish family member receive all the rights afforded Jews, as defined by Jewish law, including automatic citizenship and other privileges connected with the Law of Return.[1] In this regard, recently the Central Conference of American Rabbis (CCAR), representing over one thousand Reform rabbis, spoke to the issue of defining a Jew. One of the hallmarks of Reform Judaism is the independence it assumes vis-à-vis the authority of Jewish law. The Reform rabbinate, responding to both the increased numbers of mixed marriages and the reality that the religious identity of the mother neither guarantees nor precludes a child being raised as a Jew, adopted the following policy: If one parent is Jewish (either mother or father) there is the "presumption of Jewish descent." This presumption should be established "through appropriate and timely public and formal acts of identification with the Jewish faith and People." Thus parents are obligated to

---

1. *Encyclopedia Judaica* 10:23.

demonstrate commitment to raise their child as a Jew via such public ceremonies as *brit milah* (circumcision), naming of the child in synagogue, bar/bat mitzvah, and confirmation. Moreover, parents and children are urged to adopt for themselves those mitzvoth which lead toward a positive and exclusively Jewish identity.[2]

A pattern for defining a Jew outside the framework of Jewish law begins to emerge: The Jew is one who actively accepts this identity for him/herself and expresses affiliation through life as a Jewish citizen of the State of Israel or within the ambiance of synagogue, and through Jewish holiday observances and life-cycle events.

It is important for observers of the Jewish community to realize that these new definitions derive not from individuals or from groups marginal to Jewish life, but from significant corporate bodies (the Supreme Court of the State of Israel and the Reform movement). Thus the inclination of individuals to identify as Jews is not a sufficient warrant for inclusion among the Jewish people. The force and authority of significant organized and accepted institutions in our community serves to confirm an individual's self-definition.

Are there any limits to the definition individuals or groups establish? In one sense the statement of the Reform rabbis, while motivated by the desire to be inclusive, defines an outer limit that may be helpful to both Jews and non-Jews faced with evaluating numbers of Jews who have established their individual definitions for Jewish identity. The Reform rabbinate draws a faint outer line when it suggests that the *presumption* of Jewish descent must be established through concrete and public acts.

A more precise outer limit is drawn by the Israeli Supreme Court's response to another case, that of Brother Daniel. Oswald Rufeisen was born a Jew in Poland in 1927. In his youth he was an active Zionist and during the war he worked in the underground and rescued Jews from Naziism. In 1942 he became a Christian and in 1945 joined the Carmelite religious order, but continued to consider himself a Jew and to declare so publicly. Later, in an attempt to fulfill a long held dream, he settled in Israel and applied for citizenship under the Law of Return, in which Jews are granted automatic citizenship.

From the perspective of Jewish law Brother Daniel is a Jew, howbeit a "lapsed" or apostate Jew. Nevertheless the Israeli Supreme Court refused the petition, establishing a standard of secular, national-historic con-

2. Resolution on Patrilineal Descent, CCAR Conference, March 1983.

sciousness outside the framework of Jewish law. Here is the thrust of the majority opinion, written by Judge Silberg:

> I have reached the conclusion that what Brother Daniel is asking us to do is to erase the historical and sanctified significance of the term "Jew" and to deny all the spiritual values for which our people were killed during various periods in our long dispersion. For us to comply with his request would mean to dim the luster and darken the glory of the martyrs who sanctified the Holy Name in the Middle Ages to the extent of making them quite unrecognizable; it would make our history lose its unbroken continuity and our people begin counting its days from the emancipation which followed the French Revolution. A sacrifice such as this no one is entitled to ask of us, even one so meritorious as the petitionery before this court. [3]

It is important to recognize that the court was not attempting to abrogate the authority or direction of Jewish law. It was, however, recognizing that there is a reality to Jewish communal life and to Jewish identity that transcends the religious definition. The court articulated a principle that echoes in the mainstream of Jewish tradition: By identifying publicly and formally with another religion, one removes oneself from the community of the Jewish people.

Of equal significance, in my opinion, was the court's assertion that certain modern contexts allow or insist upon expanded definitions of the term *Jew;* here, the more inclusive, if vague, notion of nation or people.

Rabbi Arthur Hertzberg reflects the sentiments of many Jews today:

> In the last third of the 20th century there are many Jews, especially that worldwide, intensely Jewish, religiously traditionalist minority, for whom the question of Jewish identity is decided by the *Halakhah.* The overarching institutions of world Jewry, while paying respect to this view, determine their policy by broader and more amorphous considerations of history and situation. So, when the last remaining, completely dejudaized, almost entire intermarried communists of Jewish parentage in Poland were purged in 1968, the Israel government provided them with the necessary exit passports; even though few were going to Israel, the world Jewish social service budget took care of the overwhelming majority who opted to go to other countries. Those who

---

3. *Encyclopedia Judaica* 3:209.

suffer as Jews, regardless of their own perception of that suffering, and those whose Jewish consciousness might one day be rekindled, remain part of world Jewish concern. In the broadest sense, significant elements of world Jewry in the modern era have defined and are defining, Jewish identity as a community of history and destiny of those who still feel their involvement in this community or about whom others feel strongly that these people belong to Jewry.[4]

As a Reform rabbi, living with respect for Jewish law but clearly outside its framework, I similarly answer the question "Who is a Jew?" by extending the most inclusive net possible. A Jew is one who is born of a Jewish parent. Jews-by-choice are those who have formally adopted Judaism and the Jewish people in a religious ceremony; who declare openly and publicly and freely "I am a Jew"; who have no other religious affiliation.

This definition includes Jews by birth who accept their Jewish heritage and identity transmitted via either their maternal or paternal line; all adult non-Jews who make conscious and direct gestures, including a formal ceremony of conversion or adoption, to be Jews and not to follow any other religious way; children whose parent(s) consciously and actively lead them to Jewish identity and Jewish living.

Admittedly this is a very open, inclusive definition that sometimes causes me discomfort. Here is the dilemma: I limit my warrant to perform marriages to those in which both partners are Jewish. I do not officiate at mixed marriages, yet when I am asked to participate in the marriage of two Jews one or both of whom (while born of Jewish parents and having no other religious affiliations) has little or no knowledge of Judaism and little commitment, I question my right to officiate. Frankly, in most instances I do so compelled only by the existential conviction that the energy of the Jewish people is unlimited, that the spirit of Judaism moves in mysterious ways. Beyond my capacity to understand, a spark of Jewish consciousness may be alive, to be refueled in time and circumstances unknown. It may take another generation, but it can happen. (I have seen grandchildren of individuals who formally left the Jewish community pick up the threads of their Jewish heritage.) My obligation as a rabbi is to be as open and as inclusive as possible, while maintaining my authenticity and integrity.

If the task of defining the term *Jew* is complicated for us as Jews, our

4. Ibid., 10:64-65.

Christian correspondents in dialogue must share that burden, eschewing convenient, symmetrical, and simplistic definitions in favor of the ambiguous and complex present realities. In relating to Jews Christians must determine whom we regard as authentic. If you seek to understand Jews, then clearly you must confront a variegated and complicated community. If you want to learn about living Judaism from contemporary Jews, you must be willing to accept the cluster of definitions presented by Jews, in which only the sum total represents the true reality.

II

This appeal brings us to our second task—related and formidable: that of defining *Judaism*. We must consider the complex classical definition in its several elements. Further, we will see that embedded in the traditional understanding are the seeds of ideas that, since the emancipation, have grown into independent references for Jewish identity.

We must define Judaism as a combination of faith, praxis, and corporate entity. Three primary foundations—God, Torah, and Israel—combine to form the integrated whole called Judaism. If we focus for a moment upon each separate part, it is only to heighten our understanding of the unique whole.

God. Judaism begins with the central idea of one God, the Creator of the universe. From this flow the notions of a world unified, ordered, and created with purpose. God demands of humankind, created in the image of the divine, right conduct. God has entered into a covenanted relationship with the people of Israel, elected and electing to live out God's will.

Despite the presence of this critical faith statement at the center, there is an absence of dogma or creedal beliefs by which to define Judaism. In both biblical and rabbinic literature one can find discussions of the basic faith concepts Jews must accept. Creedal statements do exist, the best known of which is that of Maimonides (twelfth century), but even this was challenged in some of its parts and in its use as an authoritative test of membership in the faith community of Israel. Louis Finkelstein reminds us that "traditional Judaism cannot be described as having a universal, accepted creed or formulation of its dogma."[5]

Torah. "If they forsake even me, all would turn out well, provided they

5. Louis Finkelstein, *The Jews: Their History, Culture and Religion* 4:1343.

keep studying Torah." This remarkable, radical statement emerges from rabbinic literature and focuses the Jew's attention away from the discussion of creeds, dogma, and faith statements to the more central concern: the life of Torah. Judaism asserts that the Torah—best understood as divine instruction—provides us with a system of mitzvoth (religious obligations). We demonstrate our belief by fulfilling these commandments—613 mitzvoth governing the yearly calendar, the celebration of significant life moments, our system of worship, our participation in the people of Israel, our personal and collective ethical systems. Halakhah provides the specific guidelines to fulfill the mitzvoth properly. While nontraditional expressions of Judaism (Conservative and Reform) differ with the Orthodox concerning the origin of Torah, the nature of the Halakhah and the Jews' relationship to it, the Torah, and the ways of life derived from it remain central to each of these religious expressions of Judaism.

People. It is within the body of the people of Israel that Torah is brought to life and its total potential is realized. Israel is the covenanted community, "the kingdom of priests and the holy nation" (Exod. 19:6)—individuals joining in the creation of a society made whole and just by fulfilling divine imperatives (Torah). Israel the people becomes the source of blessing for the nations of the world and a light to other peoples. Israel the people occupies the land in which the covenant is realized. It becomes the community where institutions ranging from the house of prayer to the central charity collective provide concrete means of expressing Torah's values. It provides the vessel that holds the stories and the verse, the customs and the habits, the language and the history. It guards and transmits the melodies and memories of God and Torah and covenanted community from one generation to the next.

Within the people of Israel the tension between the secular and the holy is always present. The Jew struggles to actualize the sacred within the world given to humankind and within his/her particular community.

One modern author puts it succinctly, identifying no less than seven strands woven together to form the tapestry that is Judaism:

A doctrine concerning God, the universe, and man; A morality for the individual in society; A regiment of rite, custom and ceremony; A body of law; A sacred literature; Institutions through the foregoing find expression; The people, Israel—central strand out of which and about which the others are spun.[6]

6. Milton Steinberg, *Basic Judaism*, 3-4.

Most Jews today understand that Judaism, even in its classic definition, is a tapestry interwoven of variegated strands. It is important for the Christian correspondent in dialogue to share this understanding, to avoid teasing out single elements and holding them forth as the central or dominant ones in classical Judaism. Jewish faith without people is not Judaism; Jewish law without the values represented by the idea of God and the concept of mitzvah is not Judaism; Jewish people without covenant and commandment is not Judaism.

We must exercise this same caution against reductionism when we approach contemporary definitions and expressions of Judaism, influenced as they are by modern values of autonomy and freedom of choice, unrestrained by the authority of the closed and self-contained community. Nontraditional religionists distinguish themselves by their approach to Torah as something other than God's revealed, immutable word. Both Conservative and Reform Jews see Judaism as a changing and developing religion, although differing in the rate of change and in the standards by which acceptable change is gauged. The Conservative movement, relying on the concept of Catholic Israel—the collective, historic consciousness of the Jewish people, retains the essential framework of Halakhah, adapted to changing needs and circumstances. In outward appearance most of its practices and forms share the sense of classical Judaism. Reform Judaism, based upon individual choice and, in its formative period, much less concerned with the total Jewish community and the historical context of the Jewish people, developed less intense and more westernized forms for worship and practice. While Orthodox Judaism may provide a base for understanding and measuring other religious movements in Judaism, it cannot be understood as the most authentic or as the more authentic expression of contemporary Judaism.

Conservative and Reform movements represent subtle variations in the tapestry of Judaism, particularly when compared with the modern expressions, more clearly labeled "secular." Christians understand Reform movements and "denominations" as legitimate, modern articulations of spiritual search. To admit "secular" categories may be more difficult, but the task must proceed. We must be prepared to broaden our definition to include those expressions which derive from these classical elements, but have assumed a life more independent and different, and sometimes more vital, than the sources from which they flow. Three primary elements must be brought into the equation: community, culture, and Zionism.

A. Community

First we must consider the reality of community—derived from the element of peoplehood—as an expression of Judaism. There is a system of synagogues, centers, philanthropic organizations, community relations agencies, fraternal, recreational, cultural, educational, and service organizations, of newspapers and periodicals that mark out the community. These institutions are held together by a network of family and friendship patterns, neighborhoods and cultural expressions. Together they provide concrete manifestation of the Jewish people at a particular point in time and space. Modern Jews fulfill a primary need of identification with the Jewish people by participating somewhere—or at many points—within this framework.

As an expression of identification with the Jewish people it hardly matters where one belongs. Many still use the synagogue as the primary vehicle for transmitting the Jewish heritage to the next generation (the term *religious education* is something of an anachronism) and many return to the synagogue and rabbi for critical life moments from birth to death. But the synagogue as the religious center of Jewish life takes its place alongside other institutions held equally efficacious, and frequently socially more attractive, as vehicles for demonstrating Jewish identity.

Many of these secular community organizations are modern extensions of earlier Jewish institutions created to provide Jews with the means of bringing to life specific religious values central to Judaism and the Jewish people. There is, for example, a direct line from the biblical imperative to care for the widow, the orphan, the stranger, and the poor through the medieval institutions for dispensing charity to the modern Jewish family and children's service agency. Similarly, Jews today fulfill the command to rescue fellow Jews held captive by enemies (*pidyon shevuim*) and the need to band together to defend self and kin against oppressors—a need made real by history—by participating in the work of the United Jewish Appeal, Jewish Federations (in Boston, the Combined Jewish Philanthropies), and defense or community relations agencies such as the American Jewish Committee. These organizations, dedicated to rescuing and defending Jews in trouble and to advocacy on behalf of Israel and Soviet Jewry, compete successfully with the more narrowly conceived religious organizations in our communities.

I will be the first to bemoan the fact that ties to Torah are weak or absent, knowledge of Jewish history, Hebrew, and Yiddish forgotten, participation in the life of the synagogue tenuous and superficial. But with equal fervor I must admit that the secular community agencies implement elements of the Jewish value system and fulfill a critical role in Jewish life. To understand Judaism and the nature of the Jewish people's modern expressions (and in some ways yesterday's classical experiences), one must examine the contemporary community that is the manifestation of the Jewish people.

B. Culture

Another aspect of Jewish peoplehood we must consider is that which we call "culture" or "ethnicity"—the complex of stories, foods, drama, melodies, language, humor, memories, personalities, even appearance and style. In and of themselves these cultural elements do not represent Judaism. They are the folkways, traditions, forms of communication, and expressions of living that a people develops in its centuries of existence. Some were borrowed long ago from host cultures in which Jews have lived for centuries. Some derive more directly from Jewish religious practices, although the link to their origins has been loosened. Enormous variations in these ethnic expressions exist among different segments of the Jewish people. Whatever their quality, these elements of Jewish culture become yet another way—deeply grounded in the folk experience of the Jewish people—in which this subgroup marks itself off from other groups in society and, thereby, preserves its distinctiveness and its sense of continuity and transmits its substance from one generation to the next.

These concepts of community and culture are critical elements in the modern expression of the Jewish people. They reflect the notion that the Jews are an organically developing, historic community among many in this society. They assume the validity and continuation of the Jewish people within the diaspora.

C. Zionism

Contrasting with this is that aspect of Judaism in the postemancipation period that we call Zionism. It emphasizes the role of *Eretz Yisrael* as the primary or single center of Jewish life, as the guarantor of the continuation of the Jewish people.

The advent of modern political Zionism has radically changed the fabric of Judaism. The twin presses of anti-Semitism and modern nationalism have impelled Jews to see a return to the land of Israel and the creation of a community of Jews protecting themselves as central to modern Judaism. Jews are working the soil in the land of their origin, determining their separate fate and destiny, living out the Jewish ideals of freedom and justice. All of these motifs are cherished as central to the Jewish experience by those who build the land from within its borders and those who support the efforts from their tentative or permanent place in the diaspora.

Allow me to stress my belief that no Jew can allow the Holocaust to become the dominant force in shaping his Judaism, nor can we permit Israel to represent the total or even the primary focus of Jewish energy. But Judaism today cannot be understood without realizing the extraordinary grasp with which modern Israel—the land and the state—holds the heart and the imagination of contemporary Jewry. Israel is central to Judaism today because suffering has been central for centuries; because living as a second-class, oppressed minority has been intolerable; because Hitler attempted to bring a dark road of anti-Semitism to one logical conclusion, genocide; because we have seen that in an atmosphere of freedom in less than a century the spirit of Judaism can bring the soil of *Eretz Yisrael* to life and the oppressed Jewish soul to new levels of spiritual fulfillment.

In the course of short decades we have seen the extraordinarily positive effect of modern Israel on diaspora communities. The cultural creativity of the *Halutzim* (the pioneers of the Zionist movement), the sense of self-pride and strength, the rediscovery and rebuilding of the land of Jewish origins, the rebirth of Hebrew as a living language, the resurrection of dead or dying Jewish communities from Poland to Yemen, from the USSR to Ethiopia on the soil of their homeland, the concentration of Jewish scholarship and of Jews talented in every field from music to physics to agriculture—all of these realities made possible by the new Jewish State—have infused Jewish communities around the world with new purpose and strength, influencing self-image—personal and communal, community organization, cultural variety and creativity.

One cannot understand Judaism or the Jew today—surely we cannot define these terms—without appropriate consideration of the integral relationship between the Jewish people and Zionism, the love of the land of the Jews and the modern state that occupies, preserves, and builds it.

The attempts to define Judaism in the modern age are numerous. Mordecai Kaplan speaks of Judaism "as the total civilization of the Jewish

people . . . [suggesting an] organic unity of the people and its relationship to its land, its language and literature, its mores, laws and folkways,
its folk sanctions, its arts and the social structure in which this living
entity is expressed and practiced."[7]

Abraham Heschel almost ignores the Jewish people as he concentrates
on reawakening the Jew to an understanding of God through nature,
revelation, and the holy deed.[8]

Eugene Borowitz, a theologian identified with the Reform movement,
understands Judaism in terms of covenant, "a way of living . . . [in
which] the individual Jew shares . . . in his people's relationship with
God as a matter of birth . . . [but also] . . . as a matter of will when he
makes the historic covenant, the chief article of his faith."[9]

We could go on. But to explore one contemporary conceptualization of
Judaism or another is to miss the point Jews today must understand. The
many, many elements of the Jewish people, its way of life and its spiritual
underpinnings, come together as an organic whole. One element more
dominant, some eclipsed for the moment, but all present in the unique
phenomenon we call Judaism. The task of the Jew is one of discovery, of
continual self-understanding and renewal of those elements recently or
long ago eclipsed as we live out our lives.

If the task of defining Judaism is difficult for Jews, how much the
more so for Christians. Only one thing is certain: the categories used to
distinguish among Christian denominations or to define Christians and
Christianity will not serve you well. Neither will contemporary categories of nation, race, or ethnic community. All of the above; no one of the
above. Your task—with us—is to understand the organic, multifaceted,
variegated community that continues to define itself in service of humankind and God.

Understanding the Chapter

1. What is Halakhah?
2. How does Halakhah answer the question "Who is a Jew?"
3. Give several examples of situations in contemporary Jewry where
Halakhah appears inadequate in defining "Who is a Jew?"

7. In Eugene Borowitz, ed., *A New Theology in the Making*, 104.
8. In ibid., 150ff.
9. In ibid., 63.

4. How has Reform Judaism recently defined "Who is a Jew?" In what way does the Reform definition established by the CCAR differ from Halakhah of traditional Judaism?

5. Why did the celebrated case of "Brother Daniel" end up before the Israeli Supreme Court? What has been the impact of this decision upon those who profess Christianity today as part of the movement called "Messianic Judaism"?

6. Blumberg states, "In relating to Jews Christians must determine whom we regard as authentic." Discuss what he means by this statement.

7. What three primary foundations combine to form the integrated whole called Judaism?

8. What is the precise point about the nature of Judaism that the rabbis have drawn from the following radical statement attributed to God: "If they forsake even me, all would turn out well, provided they keep studying Torah"?

9. What does Blumberg say is "the primary or single center of Jewish life, as the guarantor of the continuation of the Jewish people"? What twin pressures contributed greatly in bringing this about?

10. Judaism cannot be reduced to a creed alone. What complex of elements—in addition to beliefs—makes up Judaism?

11. Jews place great emphasis on peoplehood and community in their own definitions of the meaning of Judaism. Is this emphasis easy or difficult for evangelical Christians to understand?

12. Blumberg states that "If the task of defining Judaism is difficult for Jews, how much the more so for Christians." Some Christian leaders feel that the church too often settles for a quick, simplistic "easy believism" approach to Christianity. In essence, is Christianity simple or complex to define? Why?

2
A Response to Herman J.
Blumberg by Robert Sternberg

Anyone who has ever studied the Talmud in the original has observed
that its text in the center of the page is flanked by two segments of
commentary in smaller print. These were written by the medieval com-
mentator, Rashi, and a group of later scholars called *Baalei Tosephot,* some
of whom were Rashi's grandsons. Frequently the *Baalei Tosephot* disagree
with Rashi and ask pointed questions about his interpretation of the law.
Later rabbis asked how they could so often question or disagree with their
teacher. The answer given is that because they had Rashi's commentary
before them when they studied, they could "stand on his shoulders" and
gain new insights. I am going to "stand on" Rabbi Blumberg's excellent
and thorough presentation but attempt to open up some fundamental
questions about Jewish self-definition. I hope this will stimulate dialogue and discussion.

George Bernard Shaw once said that "the reasonable man adapts himself to the world but the unreasonable man persists in trying to adapt the
world to himself." By that definition, Jews have been both reasonable
and unreasonable. Jews have always had a problem in trying to come to an
understanding of who they are against the background of a constant
struggle and a sometimes conspicuous inability to adapt themselves to
the world.

Rabbi Blumberg correctly addressed this problem when he said the
task of the Jew is one of discovery and of continual self-understanding and
renewal as he lives out his life. He did not really have to say that
Orthodox Judaism, in today's world, cannot be considered the most
authentic form. True, some Orthodox Jews categorically reject any other
definitions. But very few deny that our community has evolved into
something that is pluralistic and multifaceted. It is a community threatened by a host of problems of far more immediate concern to all of us who
profess the Jewish faith—whatever the specific terms of reference. I
remind you of Rabbi Blumberg's personal confession of ambivalent feelings about officiating at a marriage of two Jews where one of them has no
religious affiliation, little or no knowledge of Judaism, little or no expe-

15

rience of living as a Jew, and little or no feeling for the Jewish people.
This kind of frustration is shared by me and all other rabbis—whatever
their denomination.

Rabbi Blumberg has given an excellent overview of the different ways
modern Jews define themselves. He has also pointed out some of the
problems that arise in taking an approach toward the Jewish faith that is
too monolithic. I wish to build on the structure he created by comment-
ing on some problems that I have with his last three definitions of
Judaism. These are the so-called exclusively secular ones—i.e., community, ethnicity or culture, and Zionism. We must first acknowledge
the fact that exclusively secular definitions of Judaism are fully acceptable
for some Jews. Acknowledging these definitions creates a link between
these Jews and the rest of the community. But, in my judgment, secular
definitions that separate Jews from their religious roots are not really
authentic Jewish definitions. They have come into existence because of
attempts made by members of our community to reconcile a desire to be
Jewish with a desire to live according to the standards of the secular
world. This problem is of far greater concern to me than any debate
among Orthodox, Conservative, and Reform Jews on how best to understand Jewish religious beliefs.

Recently, I got into a rather heated discussion with a rabbinical colleague who told me that when he would listen to potential converts
discuss the Jewish faith he was prepared to accept just about any reason
they would give him as reason enough to bring them into the Jewish fold.
If a person would say that the only commitment that he or she were
prepared to make to the Jewish community was an annual donation to the
Combined Jewish Appeal, this would be good enough. The rabbi would
accept this person as a convert to Judaism. I told him my own policy was
different. The person must take a conversion course, which would include learning the basic prayers and rituals. I would also make the
convert think seriously about thorny issues like the recurrence of anti-
Semitism in different historical periods, the obligation to suffer the fate
of Jews when Jews suffer, and the lack of a real necessity to do that if one is
not a member of the Jewish community. I also pointed out to the rabbi
that in the case of a person converting to Judaism in order to marry, I
always suggest that both partners in the marriage take the conversion
course together. My colleague listened to all this, looked at me as if I had
just stepped off a spaceship, and said in an irritated and defensive tone,
"So don't send me any converts."

Judaism is not a "missionary" faith. Even when it sought converts at the close of the biblical period and during the start of the rabbinic period, it placed considerable demands upon them. The essence of that expectation included both recognizing and being responsible to the basic religious tenets of the faith and understanding the historical experience of Jews as a people. Failure to include both of these in any definition of Judaism, in my judgment, may mean that one day there will be nothing left to define.

The concept of community in Judaism, already pointed out by Rabbi Blumberg, deserves further comment. The present network of Jewish federations, community service agencies, and philanthropic organizations has been part of the Jewish community, in different forms, since ancient times. The Talmud makes mention of several of these. One example was the *Tamchui,* a community fund that provided for the needs of indigent people. In the European shtetls, all of the Jewish welfare and service agencies like the *Bikur Cholim* Society (the members of which visited the sick) and the *Chevra Kadisha* (which handled burials), were operated by the local synagogues. The synagogue coordinated the main institutions of the local Jewish community. By the names given it, one can see that the synagogue was more than a house of prayer. The proper Hebrew words for synagogue are *Bet Knesset* (House of Assembly) and *Bet Hamidrash* (House of Study). In fact, the term *Bet Hatfillah* (House of Prayer) appears only once in the Talmud (tractate Gittin, p. 39B). Our modern variations of these social and charitable institutions were built and maintained by people who, for the most part, were either raised in a religious environment or in a household that, while not observant, had traditional religious values.

Today many of these institutions are experiencing problems in maintaining financial viability and retaining their once burgeoning armies of volunteers. As a more hedonistic and self-centered secular morality replaces one that was oriented toward family, community, and people, the problems multiply and the system erodes further. I believe that these institutions will survive despite their problems, but they are going to be maintained, in the long run, largely by those members of our community who maintain a commitment to their religious faith and to their synagogue in their personal self-definitions.

The same principle holds true of Zionism. Secular Zionism and the secular Zionist movements are presently undergoing a crisis. They have failed to retain large numbers of adherents outside Israel, even among people who were reared on secular Zionist ideals. Yet religious Zionism flourishes, even in the diaspora. The majority of recent North American immigrants to Israel are either religiously observant, or believers in a traditional value system that accepts some form of religious belief. Those who are religious appear to have become increasingly more fervent and zealous—sometimes to excess. We Jews do our community a great disservice when we try to inject "separation of church and state" policies into the organization of our community institutions and structures. In general, fifteen or twenty years ago, the policy of Jewish federations and social service agencies was to leave rabbis to "do their thing" in synagogues and allow the laity to direct the agencies. This is no longer true. Agencies are beginning to realize the lack of wisdom in this and are, once again, seeking the wisdom of the religous perspective.

Ethnicity is another issue worth mentioning. One generation before I was born, it was not chic to be ethnic. My parents and their contemporaries worked very hard to assimilate into the American melting pot and change their "ethnically Jewish" habits. My own generation was raised in a much less ethnocentric environment and, having had much less opportunity to pick up the old ways, was less conscious of being "ethnic" at all. On the other hand, some members of my generation actively seek to be more public about their "Jewishness"—whatever its expression. In Canada, ethnicity is treated somewhat differently than in the United States. Since Canada was a British colony until 1867 and a member of the Commonwealth until 1967, immigrants tended to gravitate toward their own ethnic communities and remain in them longer. The Canadian government maintains a Department of Multiculturalism under the Secretary of State, which promotes cultural pluralism. It also funds educational and cultural projects that promote the languages and cultural heritages of Canada's many immigrant populations. Clearly, the Jewish community, like others, gains from all of this. Nonetheless, I believe that ethnicity, like the other so-called secular categories, has no staying power. The average Canadian or American would much rather fit in with the rest of society than be different from it.

In conclusion, I would suggest that the greatest challenge facing Jews today is the one posed by modern, secular values. They challenge everything our community believes in and everything that we require in order to maintain ourselves in a viable and meaningful way. In order to meet the challenge of secularism, Jews must apply the principle of religious pluralism wholeheartedly to their own household. The pluralistic coexistence of Orthodox, Conservative, Reform, and Reconstructionist Jews may even guarantee our survival, because it provides for a range of religious options, all of which lead to a fulfilled and complete Jewish life. It is true that some Jews can relate to Judaism only by using secular definitions. However, in my judgment, only a self-definition of Judaism that includes religious faith has long-term staying power. Anything less than that may sustain the needs of private individuals but will not ultimately meet the community's collective needs. Rather, it will drive the community it strives to maintain into greater fragmentation.

Understanding the Chapter

1. Who was Rashi and who were the *Baalei Tosephot?* Why are these names important for Talmudic studies?

2. Sternberg raises the question of appropriate motivation and preparation for conversion to Judaism. When both rabbis and ministers confront the question of conversion, what should be the role of personal search, inquiry, and conviction on the part of the would-be convert? In your opinion, what reasons—if any—would you consider to be unacceptable for conversion?

3. Sternberg states that "being Jewish demands a great deal of the Jew." He then states that the essence of that demand includes two main responsibilities that are indispensable to one's personal definition of Judaism. Name both of these.

4. What does Sternberg say is "the greatest challenge facing Jews today"?

5. Why does Sternberg take issue with Blumberg's approval of secularist definitions of Judaism? With which rabbi would most Jews agree? With which rabbi do you agree?

3
"No Offense: I Am an Evangelical"
A Search for Self-Definition

DAVID F. WELLS

The most memorable thing about Jimmy Carter, I regret to say, was his teeth. His smile, like the sun piercing gloomy cloud cover, transformed his humorless countenance and softened his cold, mechanical earnestness. It was a startling transformation.

It was not as startling, however, as the transformation that so many worked hard to accomplish in his religious views. Even before he entered the White House, journalists and pundits were instructing him on ways of minimizing and disguising his barbed outlook. It was not that they entirely disallowed his evangelical convictions, but they did feel that in expressing these ideas Carter should be careful to conform to the standards of "good taste." What "good taste" amounted to, of course, was a kind of etiquette that would hide his essential beliefs. In other words, they embarked him, with or without his consent, on a crash course in civility.[1] Did he allow himself to be browbeaten into finding ways of saying that he was born again without anyone knowing that he had actually said he was born again? I do not know. But I do see in him a poignant symbol of the predicament in which evangelicals now find themselves.

To speak of a predicament may seem odd. What kind of predicament does one encounter at the pinnacle of success? If it is a predicament, it is one that many other religious groups wish they had!

What is not always perceived, however, is that there is a difference between form and substance, appearance and reality. The media can be pardoned, though not excused, for failing to observe this distinction on

1. John Murray Cuddihy, *No Offense: Civil Religion and Protestant Taste* (New York, 1978), 1-10.

the grounds that who is "in" and who is "out" is all they are concerned about. Success is never anything more than an index as to who has power and who does not. And evangelicals right now have power. But what is surprising is that the turmoil within evangelicalism is not understood by those outside of the media who should, almost intuitively, be able to sense its presence.

There can be little quarrel with the proposition that evangelicalism has arrived. By common consent, 1976 was dubbed the "Year of the Evangelical."[2] George Gallup[3] revealed that fifty million American adults claimed to have had a born again experience,[4] and of these, almost half also believe the Bible is literally true and have witnessed to others. This great mass of people is being serviced by a multitude of organizations and institutions that constitute a visible and sprawling "righteous empire."[5] This empire has its own school system, K through Ph.D., its own yellow pages, its own denominations and voluntary associations, and a publishing industry so slick and proficient that it could turn Marabel Morgan's hedonism into a multimillion best-seller in *The Total Woman*.[6] Evangelicals are not only visible but they are also noisy. Their preachers clog the air waves, many of them, I am afraid, in an unseemly scramble for the piles of loose bucks that are simply waiting to be garnered for a good cause.[7] Evangelicals have clout. Ronald Reagan, who can detect political aromas from far greater distances than his peers, feels obliged to carry on a standard ritual with this large bloc of voters. Come election time, like a bird ready to mate, he displays his gaudiest plumage, strutting up and down, talking about prayer in schools, preening himself as an anti-Communist, and muttering about evil empires.

2. Kenneth Woodward et al., "Born Again: The Year of the Evangelicals," *Newsweek* 88 (1976): 68-78.

3. Gallup's statistics on the American religious profile from his newly founded research institute in Princeton are published in an annual summary entitled *Religion in America*.

4. Cf. Martin E. Marty, *Righteous Empire: The Protestant Experience in America* (New York, 1970).

5. See Erling Jorstad, *Evangelicals in the White House: The Cultural Maturation of Born Again Christianity 1960–1981* (New York, 1981), 83-128.

6. See Jeffrey Hadden and Charles Swann, *Prime Time Preachers: The Rising Power of Televangelism* (Reading, 1981).

7. Peter Berger, *A Rumour of Angels: Modern Society and the Rediscovery of the Supernatural* (New York, 1969), 7.

This is the appearance. It is what fascinated the press: the realignment of power blocs in Protestantism, the reappearance in evangelicalism of a part of our national soul that some people imagined had perished along with the first generation of Puritans, and the novelty of spiritual rebirth—a novelty, I may say, that has become irritatingly commonplace as we have read of sports teams reversing losing trends and so being reborn and weather patterns also enjoying rebirth and even Wall Street, which is seldom notable for its spiritual interests, having regular experiences of rebirth! So who are these evangelicals, these odd country cousins who have breezed into town bringing with them an unexpected and worldly *savoir faire?*

The reality in evangelicalism seems to me to be a little different from this appearance of power, success, and dynamic growth. Paradoxically, in the midst of this sense of having arrived I find quite a lot of self-doubt among evangelicals, of uncertainty as to how they relate to and how they should function within a society that is secular and pluralistic. It is this paradox I wish to explore. I will do so first by considering the intended changes wrought in evangelicalism as it outgrew its parent fundamentalism and, second, the internal changes wrought upon it by its function within the modern world.

By approaching this subject in this way I am suggesting that a purely theological definition of evangelicalism will only encompass a part of the reality and that the other part must be viewed from within a sociological perspective. This is a departure from the way in which evangelicalism is often treated. When those who are not evangelical Christians ask about the evangelical movement, they are usually given answers in doctrinal terms. Evangelicals, they are told, believe these doctrines and are opposed to those ideas. This is not illegitimate, for evangelicals have always been *doctrinal* people. The morphology of their belief, however, is undergoing changes because the place of evangelicals in society is changing. It was far easier to preserve pure doctrine when they were strangers in their own country, but now that they are influencing and, at times, becoming the status quo, their doctrine is frequently blended into, if not entangled with, the culture in which they live. It can no longer be considered, then, in its naked purity.

The problem I want to uncover is well known to Jews; Chaim Potok sensitively develops it in both *The Chosen* and *My Name is Asher Lev*. It is this: Where does the psychological boundary lie between the style, norms, expectations, and values of modernity and the nonnegotiable demands of faith? Throughout the Old Testament, the people of Israel struggled with this question and often drew the boundary at the wrong place. Their task was, however, in principle a little easier than ours is today, for national life then was intended to provide for faith an encompassing, comprehensive, and supportive context; secular society never can. Or can it? It is the uncertainty with which this question is being answered that shows how troublesome it actually is. Jews know this because they have a spectrum of answers to it, ranging from the Orthodox and Conservative through to Reform and Reconstructionist. They may not feel entirely at home in America sometimes, but many Jews have felt comfortable with secular modernity. Evangelicals are not at home with secular modernity but they are very comfortable with America. The end result, however, is not all that different, for America is nothing if it is not secular and modern and therefore evangelicals are being brought face to face with a reality as old as the Old Testament itself and as contemporary as contemporary society itself.

THE AFTERMATH OF FUNDAMENTALISM

The most helpful conceptual tool for analyzing fundamentalism is, I believe, Peter Berger's notion of a "cognitive minority."[8] A cognitive minority is made up of a group of people whose view of the world is significantly at odds with that widely held in culture. And by *culture*, I am thinking of the values and meanings assigned to functions of our social life and to the behavior of individuals within that social fabric. Culture is a behavioral language, spoken by a majority in a society. It is no mystery, for example, what values are communicated by the purchase of a Cadillac, or what message is conveyed by an earring in a male's earlobe, or by the appearance of skin burnished under the rays of a far distant sun while the rest of New England suffered in the bleak midwinter! We know instinctively what these things say because we are all attuned to the same cultural language. This is no less true when we enter upon the delicate domain where theology and moral theory do their work

8. The relationship between fundamentalist faith and its cultural context is explored with care and insight by George Marsden, *Fundamentalism and American Culture: The Shaping of Twentieth Century Evangelicalism 1870–1925* (New York, 1980).

and where secular people pursue their interests without reference to the Divine. Paul Tillich was right in arguing that all people have "ultimate concerns." In the Enlightenment world in which we live, however, these concerns are pursued and interpreted strictly horizontally without the process of modernity. This is taken as normative. Those who disagree, whose worldview is at variance with that which our modern, secular world assumes is normal, become a cognitive minority. To be a member of such a minority is to be out of synch. It is to be alienated. It is to be shut out from the action. It is to be lonely. Fundamentalists were a cognitive minority.

In the 1920s, 1930s, and 1940s fundamentalists understood the rules of this cultural game.[9] They knew that to yield their cognitive antagonism was to yield their soul. It would have been an act of cognitive suicide, of spiritual self-immolation. What is of interest, then, is to see not so much what they believed but how that belief defined them as aliens within the culture and sealed off any exits from fundamentalism back into the culture.

It goes without saying that fundamentalists adhered to the formal and material principles in Protestantism. That is, they held that the nature of Scripture as inspired established for it the rightful function of directing and instructing all Christian faith and conduct, regardless of what human tradition might assert or cultural norms might demand. They held, too, that salvation from guilt and deliverance from a way of life under God's condemnation could be found solely through Christ's work of substitution and atonement at the cross. In these two points they were no different from those of evangelical persuasion before and after them.[10]

These convictions, however, were hedged about by supporting beliefs whose function, as I see it, was to establish an indubitable line of demarcation between fundamentalism and culture quite as much as it was to exhibit contours in biblical revelation. Thus the supernatural miracles of Christ, belief in which was central in fundamentalism, not only were a part of the New Testament record but happily also created great offense in a naturalistic age. Likewise, the assertion that the Bible should be read "literally" was not only a protection of its nature as inspired writing but

9. Richard Pierard, "The Quest for Historical Evangelicalism: A Bibliographical Excursus," *Fides et Historia* 2, no. 2 (1979): 60-72.

10. David O. Moberg, *The Great Reversal: Evangelism Versus Social Concern* (Philadelphia, 1972).

was also a convenient way of rejecting the whole drift of modern life, especially in its religious and educational dimensions where theories of literary origins had effectively degutted the Bible of serious religious content. And when fundamentalists insisted on Christ's premillennial return, they were not merely declaring their understanding of Old Testament prophecy read in the light of Revelation 20:1-6, but also declaring that no form of social evolution was ever going to lift society from its woes to some awaited utopia. On the contrary, Christ's return would show that there had been a measure of devolution in the world's progress and that human problems had ever festered unresolved and unhealed outside of God's redemptive grace.

Fundamentalist doctrine, on these and related issues, actually provided a tight perimeter within which fundamentalists lived and beyond which they did not allow themselves to wander. The border was clearly marked. Rules emerged to warn the adventurous as well as the unwary where the enemy territory lay. The headstrong and the unwise who crossed the lines suffered appropriate sanctions. And within each of these countercommunities strong demands of loyalty were made, mutual therapy was provided against the insidious pressures of creeping doubt. Strong, authoritarian preachers emerged who could say—sometimes with unnerving certainty—precisely what God's truth was.

Paradoxically, however, fundamentalists yearned to see the nation saved, not merely spiritually but also socially, despite their own withdrawal into artificially constructed ghettos. This is something that is often misunderstood, and has produced not a few intellectual misdemeanors among those who should have known better. It is true there was a "great reversal"[11] in certain aspects of social involvement during the period of fundamentalism when compared with previous ages. But we need to understand this factor. Fundamentalists had a visceral dislike of any notion that might lead, however remotely, to the proposition that the exercise of social responsibility would produce social redemption. They could not believe that. They therefore discharged their obligation of love in the form of social service in conjunction with missionary work, often in faraway places. In this respect, they notched up many sterling accomplishments.

At home, however, they rested their hopes for a social transformation

---

11. Cf. Richard Pierard, "Social Concern in Christian Missions," *Christianity Today* 20, no. 19 (June 1976): 7-10.

on the outbreak of divinely initiated revival. They were convinced that this tide of renewal would sweep before it both modernism and immorality and, in turn, would lead to the preservation of America. And so, strangely enough, a religious movement that was anticultural to its core and attacked every hope for even small ameliorations in society's woes also developed its own deep patriotism. To be a fundamentalist was to be a true preserver of America. Paradoxically, however, being a fundamentalist also meant being a relentless opponent of America! Only when these competing forces, these inner tensions, are perceived does Jerry Falwell become comprehensible. For he has the capacity to rail at America for its arrogant immorality while, without so much as skipping a beat, he will also argue his passionate belief that the Panama Canal should have been retained forever! Fundamentalism had a social vision but it was sublimated. It expressed itself in odd ways and forms. Few outside of its circles really grasped this until Jerry Falwell made public its social agenda.[12]

It is a curious irony that during the 1930s, 1940s, and 1950s three religious traditions in America lived side by side with one another and none seemed to understand the anguish of the other two. Fundamentalists, deeply wounded by the ecclesiastical upheavals of the '20s and '30s, saw themselves as having been victimized and rejected by a culture that was marching without pause toward the final embrace of Enlightenment humanism. In their literature and sermons they spoke only to themselves and suffered their cultural isolation as a martyr might the flames. But Roman Catholics, too, were essentially outsiders. The waves of Catholic immigrants during the nineteenth century had never been absorbed into the national mainstream. There was never a melting pot; only the pot of sociological theory has been melting. Not until John Kennedy's election in 1960 did many Catholics begin to think of themselves as also being Americans, and only in the 1970s did they began to slice into the American Pie and enter its corporate boardrooms, and only in the 1980s did they first dominate Congress numerically.[13] During this same time, Jews were also outsiders, their sense of aloneness and abandonment heightened by the catastrophe of the Second World War. But these

12. See Jerry Falwell, ed., *The Fundamentalist Phenomenon: The Resurgence of Conservative Christianity* (New York, 1981), 186-223.

13. See Andrew Greeley, *The American Catholic: A Social Portrait* (New York, 1977), 50-68, 112-25.

traditions, whose histories had brought them into a common experience in some ways, seldom even whispered to one another in the coldness of their shared night.

In 1955, Will Herberg published his *Protestant-Catholic-Jew*. In it he noted yet another paradox. While it could not be gainsaid that some kind of religious revival had been underway, so, too, was the cultural drift toward secularism. Secularism, he said, was not so much an overt philosophy, but an "underlying, often unconscious, orientation of life and thought"[14] that plainly made religion a matter of small account. And the reconciliation he saw occurring between these two phenomena, a renewal in faith and a resurgence in secularism, was that authentic religious content, be it Jewish or Christian, was being surrendered. Even when Americans are "thinking, feeling, or acting religiously, their thinking, feeling, and acting do not bear an unequivocal relation to the faiths they profess."[15] He went on to say that it is "this secularism of a religious people, this religiousness in a secularist framework, that constitutes the problem posed by the contemporary religious situation in America."[16] This interpenetration of social and religious realities produced a kind of common religion without hard offensive edges, one in which all could participate because the content to which adherence was asked was so minimal. The devotees of this religion, civil in its dimensions and full of civility and "good taste" in its demeanor, had taken it upon themselves to educate the brash peanut farmer who had made it into the White House. And it is this religion that has all but subdued and domesticated the rampant, ill-mannered evangelicalism that has had the potential, if only through its sheer size, to discomfort the guardians of the civil status quo. The pacification occurred largely in the 1970s.

SHIFTING FORTUNES IN THE 1970S

Those whose task it has been to render a public accounting of what has been happening more or less unanimously decided that the 1960s were a period of turbulence and the 1970s of somnolence. Some even spoke of

14. Will Herberg, *Protestant-Catholic-Jew: An Essay in American Religious Sociology* (New York, 1955), 1.
15. Ibid., 3.
16. Ibid.

conditions being, in the 1970s, reminiscent of the Eisenhower years.
About the only justification I can see for this is that our soldiers returned
home with their mission impossible finally and ignominiously abandoned. But everything else was in turmoil. Daniel Yankelovich has
argued[17] that our entire culture became engulfed in a revolution begun
on the campuses in the 1960s but spread far and wide by the 1970s. Its
real nature had often been obscured. In the 1960s its proponents were the
young who confused its intent by allying it with protest against the
Vietnam War. By the 1970s, however, this revolution had thrown off its
antiwar disguise and now numbered the middle aged as well as the young
among its adherents. At its core was a search for new values, a search so
radical that the very foundations of our culture were overturned. Its
search grew out of the longing for self-fulfillment. The self was understood to be a hierarchy of inner desires that simply had to be identified—
and then little could be satisfied. As it turned out, the psychology of
Abraham Maslow and Carl Rogers had been cohabiting with the ap-
petites of a generation accustomed to affluence—everyone has "higher
order" and "lower order" needs. But then came the interpretation from a
generation thoroughly awash in affluence. Lower-order needs are not
merely those for shelter but rather those for sprawling houses, bright
with new gadgets, and sleek cars parked in the two-car garages. They are
not merely the needs for security but also the needs for Paine and Webber. And the higher order needs are not merely those for freedom but also
those for leisurely indulgence on Bahamian beaches. It was a vision of
plenty, of overindulgence, a vision that was progressively shattered by
the soaring inflation throughout the decade. What inflation destroyed
was not merely the basis of affluent well-being but also the very possibility, for that reason, of meaningful self-fulfillment.

But this sudden shift in fortunes coincided with and perhaps even
abetted a dramatic new alignment in Protestant faith. In 1972, Dean
Kelley published *Why Conservative Churches Are Growing;* it might just as
well have been entitled *Why Liberal Churches Are Declining.* It charted a
dramatic decline in attendance and giving in liberal Protestant churches
and a corresponding growth in more conservative churches. Their appeal,
he argued, was that they had clear answers in a time of great national
uncertainty. Unlike the Liberals, they refused to confuse faith with
passing cultural fads, and they made high demands upon their members.

17. Daniel Yankelovich, *New Rules in American Life: Searching for Self-Fulfillment in
a World Turned Upside Down* (New York, 1982).

Perhaps as significant as this development, however, were the changing roles that followed. Whereas liberal Protestants had always taken it for granted that somewhere there was a divine mandate securing for them their role as custodians of the culture, in the early 1970s this notion was unceremoniously abandoned and the remaining heirs of the liberal tradition became culture's chief critics. The other partner in this neatly choreographed ballet, the fundamentalism that had shed its uncouthness and become evangelicalism, now turned from playing out its role as the vinegary critic of culture to being its guardian and apologete!

William McLoughlin appears to have missed this point. He saw the resurgent evangelicalism of the 1970s as a temporary expedient to deal with a situation of undue stress in the nation.[18] He believed its sudden appeal lay in its seductive vision of retreat from the modern, chaotic world into older values and forms of thought that were invulnerable to the change and decay everywhere else in evidence. Evangelicals, however, were not fundamentalists. They had a different agenda—not one in which the modern world would be dissipated but one in which it would be modestly transformed. The new order would not replace the old but would be inserted into the old. That has happened; but despite the best hopes of evangelical Christians the old has rambled on oblivious to the desires of its earnest new custodians and largely unaffected by their presence. Not only do we have all the structures of a technological society organized centrally around the capitalistic enterprise but we have all the attending norms and values of this order with its moral shallowness, its indifference to the value of human beings, its destructive change, its uncontrolled violence, its political chicanery, its economic lawlessness, its enveloping religiousness resonant with beguiling vagueness and its broken hopes, its broken hearts, its broken homes. Who was transforming whom? we naturally ask. Has the older world in which evangelicals are supposed to live so comfortably been leavening the new, modern world? Or is the new, modern world offering an even more comfortable place in which evangelicals have become ensconced?[19]

This new relationship is casting an entirely different light on evangelicalism. It has been common to think of it as being simply an extension of fundamentalism in the course of which some of the rougher, even

18. William G. McLoughlin, *Revivals, Awakenings, and Reform* (Chicago, 1978), 179-216.

19. Carl F. H. Henry, "Evangelicals: Out of the Closet but Going Nowhere," *Christianity Today* 24, no. 1 (Jan. 4, 1980): 16-22.

cultic, aspects of fundamentalism have been sloughed off. This, however, is misleading. Not only was fundamentalism a deliberately narrowed and overly simplified expression of evangelical faith but there were also deep currents of evangelical faith that never ran into this constricted channel. In that respect, fundamentalism was never fully representative of the evangelical faith that simply flowed around it.

This realization has dawned on the scholarly world with increasing certainty over the last ten years, resulting in a tide of books and articles that have shattered forever any illusions some still might entertain about the intellectual simplicity of evangelicalism. It is true that a rough doctrinal agenda has been consistently maintained from the time of the Protestant Reformation to the present, but in every age that doctrine has been formulated in relation to, and sometimes as a result of a confusion with, the expectations, norms, and events that shaped that age's cognitive horizon. For this reason, it is true to say that evangelicalism has meant something different in every age. Fundamentalism today can still be defined more or less out of relationship with the culture, but evangelicalism cannot.

Leonard Sweet[20] has made this point brilliantly. What he shows is that the entanglements with culture and society in the past have produced a harvest of conundrums as to what evangelicalism actually was. It is not clear to historians, for example, whether the roots of evangelicalism are to be located in the European Reformation, in its development within Puritanism, in the Great Awakening of the eighteenth century, or in the rapid Christian expansion that accompanied the movement of the frontier. Historians are divided as to whether the eighteenth-century Great Awakening was a series of events entirely separate from the American Revolution or whether the Revolution was a product of the Great Awakening. Was the one an inward and spiritual revolution and the other an outward and political expression of it? What about slavery? Northern evangelicals, in the name of their faith, were frequently to the fore in arguing for abolition; Southern evangelicals argued the reverse, pointing out that the institution of slavery had resulted in many Christian conversions among the blacks. They were correct. So what did it mean in the nineteenth century to be evangelical if evangelical faith was capable of generating an ethic that could be pitted both for and against slavery?

20. Leonard J. Sweet, "The Evangelical Tradition in America," in *The Evangelical Tradition in America,* ed. Leonard Sweet (Macon, 1984), 1-86.

Historians have flocked to the problem of millenarianism, too, seeing in it the source for many of the myths about America's origin and destiny and the driving force behind perfectionism, the creation of faith communities, sometimes of religious revival, conservative politics, and some cultural visions. What they have discovered is that the borderland between millenarial conviction and its social outworkings is extremely elusive. Likewise, the relationship between evangelical forms of thought and the forms of rationality in each age has proved to be a question both enticing and frustrating. How can evangelicalism be at the root of some of the most extraordinary outbursts of antirational sentiment and the driving force behind the most powerful expressions given to Christian faith, as in the case of the commanding and profound edifice of thought that we encounter in Jonathan Edwards' works? Is evangelicalism always opposed to all forms of rationality generated by the Enlightenment, or has it been able to co-opt some of those same forms for its own purposes? The answer is that it has done both; and that leaves most observers wondering what it means, then, to be evangelical. Further, should we understand evangelicalism to be a form of faith designed to protect and entrench the interests of the middle class? Evangelicalism has, in fact, so functioned, but it has also worked to undermine middle-class interests. Did revival consolidate class interests or did it act as a broker between classes? It did both. Has the massive missionary enterprise been an extension of essentially American interests and the American outlook or has it been something that has transcended its source, denuding itself of its Americanism? It has been both. Has evangelicalism crushed women's aspirations or has it aided their expression? It has done both. So what does it now mean to be evangelical?

In one respect, it is simple enough to answer this question. An evangelical is someone who has believed that the divinely inspired Bible, consisting of both Old and New Testaments, is God's Word, disclosing his character, will, and ways. In it, the evangelical hears God's promises of salvation and shows his or her gratitude for God's grace by faithfully obeying God's commandments. Salvation is seen to focus upon and climax in the death of Christ who, objectively, in space and time, atoned for the sins of his people, sparing them the wrath of God and delivering them from the full penalty for sins. Christ's substitution is the *sine qua non* of justification whereby sins are remitted and sinners are accepted before God because a righteousness not their own has been imputed to them. Thus evangelicals see obedience to the law by itself as incapable of winning acceptance before God because all such obedience is shot through with imperfection. The radical insufficiency of human merit and moral endeavor underscores the need both for Christ's substitution and for a supernaturally reconstituted nature that will be in continuity, not with fallen human nature but with God's holy character. Conversion (repenting of sin and believing in Christ) must therefore be accompanied by or lead to regeneration (the divinely given new nature). Whatever else evangelicals may have believed, the centrality of these beliefs—the formal principle, the material principle, and the understanding of regeneration that flows from it—has been a constant in all ages subsequent to the sixteenth-century Reformation. This constant has, however, been modified and, at times, obscured by the particular cultural forms in which it has taken expression. Sometimes these core doctrinal beliefs have produced deep and complex rational edifices and, at others, a powerful anti-intellectual animus; at times evangelicalism has had an otherworldly air about it, but at others it has dirtied its hands in political interests and even power-brokering; sometimes it has reinforced the status quo and, in the process, protected its own interests, but at others it has been an unquestionable prophetic voice in society. The result of this is that the simple enumeration of doctrinal points to which evangelicals agree may be a good starting point in defining evangelicalism. But it only deals with part of the reality.

THE SHAPING OF EVANGELICALISM TODAY

When we move from fundamentalism to evangelicalism, we are moving from a countercommunity to a community. Fundamentalism was a walled city; evangelicalism is a city. Fundamentalism always had an air of embattlement about it, of being an island of faith in a sea of unremitting hostility. Evangelicalism has reacted against this sense of psychological isolation and oppression. It has lowered the barricades. It is open to the world. The great sin in fundamentalism was to be a compromiser; the great sin in evangelicalism is to be bigoted, narrow, parochial, or insular. In removing the fundamentalist defenses—principally those of separation from the world spiritually, mentally, and ecclesiastically—evangelicalism has been brought face to face with three of the powerful shaping forces in modernity. There is no question that in the process it has been shaped by these forces infinitely more than it has succeeded in shaping the world from which they arise.

First, this is a technological society with its own built-in rationality as to why things are as they are.[21] A technological society, by its organization of people around great manufacturing centers and the type of relationship it produces between them in their mechanistic environment, creates its own worldview.[22] It is a naturalistic order. Technological societies also produce their own ethic. What is right is what is efficient. It is pragmatism in the search of material well-being. And these societies produce a way of knowing and acting, a cognitive and behavioral style, which resonates with the omnipresent technology.[23] It is a cognitive style interested in quantifying. It is a style that equates knowing largely with knowing statistics. It is, to be sure, a style that is entirely appropriate when engineers are communing privately and intimately with their computers or when governments wish to establish population trends or levels of the national debt, but it is peculiarly inept at understanding broad swatches of human experience that can be transformed into meaningful statistics only by sleight of hand. This, however, seems to be a very small obstacle to us when weighed against the potential rewards that are to be had. For we imagine that we are in possession of the final word on every subject at the very moment when Gallup's statistics are in hand!

This propensity for reducing everything to statistics and all of life's processes to easy, simply followed steps has intruded itself upon evangelicals. The instruction manual for operating a machine is sometimes not unlike the instruction manuals for believing the gospel. Each takes complex matters, reduces the complexity to simplicity, and then formulates that reduction into a series of logical steps. Simplicity and logic are not wrong, but the question one must ask is whether this style should be allowed to take captive the relationship between God and sinner and whether, if it succeeds, it will not establish that relationship on a basis drawn from the culture rather than on one prescribed by God himself. This same question haunts much of the evangelical literature on spirituality. It proceeds, with few exceptions, along a road of schematizing

21. The basis for the material on modernization and its effects on evangelicals in the pages that follow is to be found in James Davison Hunter, *American Evangelicalism: Conservative Religion and the Quandary of Modernity* (New Brunswick, 1983), 11-22, 73-101.

22. The most seminal explorations of this aspect are to be found in Jacques Ellul's books, *The Technological Society,* trans. John Wilkinson (New York, 1965) and *The Technological System,* trans. Joachim Neugroschel (New York, 1980).

23. See Peter Berger, *Facing Up to Modernity: Excursions in Society, Politics and Religion* (New York, 1977), 162-81.

the inner life. It is conducted, all too often, rather shamelessly under a banner of high pragmatism. What is offered are simple, logical steps to achieve a better personality, a larger capacity for handling crises, or a better marriage. These steps are commended not so much because they are true but because they work. Evangelical writing on spirituality is often only a technology of the inner life.

The second driving force in our modern society is pluralism in all of its dimensions: ethnic, cultural, and religious. It is difficult today, given the omniscience our media have bestowed upon us, to remain ignorant of the way other people believe and behave. This factor is, of course, experienced most intensely in cities where contrary life-styles and competing worldviews collide with one another more or less constantly. These collisions produce tensions that are potentially dangerous and disruptive. In America, we are coming to terms with this fact and have recognized that if we are to dwell in peace we must have in force an unwritten social compact that accords to each religious group or tradition its own legitimacy. This legitimacy goes beyond the right secured by the Constitution because it accords to each such group not only the freedom to practice its own particular form of religion but also to have at least a measure of truthfulness. Society declares that for the adherents in each group their style of believing and behaving is to them truth. It has produced a "situational theology."

Evangelicals are, for the most part, also good Americans. They have been weaned on the Constitution, nourishing their perception of national life on its verities, and they see in it a protector if all else fails. Evangelicals share all of the insecurities that typically characterize ethnic minorities. Like any black, or any Jew, they are suspicious of the majority, in this case, a cognitive majority. They rail against it under the symbolic term "secular humanism," which to them is that whole organization of the world that takes its inspiration from the Enlightenment and is intent upon reconstituting life along naturalistic lines. This is deeply threatening to evangelicals, and they see in the Constitution at least some minimal protections of their right of existence. They do not, as a result, attack the Constitution.

The very pluralism the Constitution protects and guarantees, however, is also a pluralism that, from a *religious* perspective, they cannot view as legitimate. Evangelicalism is what it is because it believes that biblical revelation is absolute in its demands. Biblical faith is alone true and all other faiths, be they religious or secular, are simply mythologies.

In this respect, evangelicals seek to see the world in terms that are no different from those of Isaiah, Jeremiah, or Amos.

Or do they? The experience of pluralism, guaranteed under and protected by the Constitution, has to be reconciled with the refusal, on religious grounds, to accord this pluralism legitimacy. How is this achieved? James Hunter contends that the psychological device of privatization produces the reconciliation. Many evangelicals, he contends, maintain their particular kind of absolute faith within a kind of private, inner sanctum while the exterior world, the world of action and of vocation, is more or less ceded to modernity. This produces a demeanor baffling to outsiders, who suspect that evangelicals have not really changed but only outwardly tolerate religious differences, present an unaccustomed civility, and give the appearance of the hitherto unknown virtues of moderation, "good taste," and eirenicism! Have the evangelical leopards really changed their spots? Is this a different kind of evangelical?

The third force within the process of modernization is an organizational pluralism that has sundered private and public life and broken down "natural groupings." Natural groupings are small units within a society, built around personal relations, which become the main means for the transmission of values from generation to generation. The most obvious case in American society has been the conjugal family, but in an earlier generation the extended family often functioned in this way, as did the neighborhood, especially in ethnically differentiated areas. Natural groupings are being destroyed. Spouses often have to travel to their places of work, where a system of values and assumptions are often completely at variance with those held within the home. The working spouse becomes two persons. And when half of the nation's marriages reach the breaking point, the home also becomes two houses. This process of disintegration is accelerated by the mobility of modern society, which has reduced a functioning extended family to little more than a fading memory as it has the older, functioning neighborhoods. The context for values is no longer the natural grouping but is the wider and impersonal culture reinforced by the hours spent in front of the TV.

This bifurcation of private from public life is evident throughout evangelicalism. Evangelical faith is considered something essentially private and interior, rather than public and social. Of all of the religious groups surveyed by Hunter, evangelicals showed the greatest opposition to religious organizations making pronouncements about public morals. This point should not be misinterpreted. Gallup has discovered that evangelicals are more likely to be involved in acts of social service than any other group, and undoubtedly the broader questions relating to public morals are very much on the evangelical mind. These public issues are, however, usually dealt with internally and attitudinally rather than finding their resolution in external debate and action. [24] Evangelical faith wants to include the public domain within its purview and life but, under the pressures of pluralism, it internalizes this desire and usually declares the public domain off limits for evangelical action, where morals and values are concerned. [25]

Technology, pluralism, and the breakdown of natural groupings, the three driving forces of modernity, have affected most religious groups in one way or another, but evangelicals are peculiarly vulnerable. Evangelical faith has always had at its center the conversion experience, an experience that is deeply personal and subjective. The line between personal religious experience and the privatization of faith is so fine that it almost disappears at times. Certainly, in the context of modernity evangelical faith can slip into a religiously debauched privatization almost without noticing. Indeed, much of it has not noticed. It is not uncommon, therefore, to hear TV preachers, among others, peddling Christian faith as *the* authentic expression of the self-movement and seeking to persuade their audience that the only goal in life worth pursuing is self-fulfillment! This undoubtedly resonates with what a generation nurtured on affluence is interested in hearing, but what is being offered is a parody of biblical faith.

The onset of this pall of privatization has also wreaked havoc on the structural cohesion of the evangelical movement. In the 1950s and 1960s, evangelicals enjoyed considerable unity. They united behind the Billy Graham Crusades. They worked together within the aegis of the National Association of Evangelicals, founded in 1942. Carl Henry, first editor of *Christianity Today,* gave intellectual thrust and coherence to the movement, and the educational arm gained in strength and influence most notably at the collegiate level. In the 1970s, however, this unity began to dissipate. Evangelism remained important but was yoked to a host of

24. See James P. Hunter, "Subjectivization and the New Evangelical Theodicy," *Journal of the Scientific Study of Religion* 21 (1982): 39-47.

25. Evangelical practice is quite different from evangelical theorizing on the exercise of social responsibility, but that might be because the theorizers, who are usually academics, are quite different from most lay people. See James A. Hedstrom, "A Bibliography for Evangelical Reform," *Journal of the Evangelical Theological Society* 19, no. 3 (1976): 225-38.

social interests for which a corresponding host of service organizations sprung up. The National Association of Evangelicals failed to realize its potential and began to recede in importance. Henry left *Christianity Today* and the magazine in a short period of time lost its cutting edge. Today, evangelicalism is a sprawling empire, often out of touch with itself, the left hand frequently unaware of what the right hand is doing. The extraordinary growth in evangelicalism in the last two decades has burst the seams of its structures, jeopardized its cohesion and its intellectual coherence. Whether this is just a moment of confusion or whether this signals the breakdown of evangelicalism as a unitary force is not yet clear. But it does not take a prophet to see that the kind of rugged individualism that has always characterized evangelicalism is hard to control once it has broken loose from the kind of minimal organization that evangelicals tried to maintain in the '40s and '50s.

CONCLUSION

The re-entry of evangelical faith into American culture after a partial detour through and brief exile in fundamentalism has coincided with and produced some profound internal changes in the morphology and functioning of that faith. For fundamentalists, doctrinal beliefs were not only a way of keeping the faith but also of keeping out the culture. Fundamentalist doctrine protected both its orthodoxy, in Protestant terms, and its people. It was the means of expressing defiance of cultural norms. In evangelicalism, doctrinal beliefs are now functioning quite differently. At most they are the means of preserving some kind of continuity with the past, but given the extreme privatization operating in evangelicalism they seldom act as a barrier to the culture.

This, in turn, has raised great doubts among evangelicals about the value of cognitive belief at all and certainly of pressing cognitive distinctives among those claiming to be evangelical. Evangelicals by definition affirm the formal and material principles but these are transmuted, in practice, simply into a way of looking at life. What now defines an evangelical is more often than not merely a private, interior quality that he or she has, rather than very specific doctrinal beliefs.[26] Who is and

26. For this reason it is highly questionable to claim, as Donald Bloesch does, that evangelicalism is a "cohesive, growing movement" with "an inner theological unity in the midst of external theological and cultural diversity" (*The Future of Evangelical*

who is not an evangelical therefore becomes a slippery and awkward question. Outsiders, certainly, find it nearly incomprehensible that some evangelicals see their own kind among religious traditions that are so widely diverse theologically as the Roman Catholic, Eastern Orthodox, those Protestant liberals who have been somewhat chastened by reality over the last fifty years and are clustered in the mainline denominations, and even some of the moving spirits of the World Council of Churches.

This raises the question of whether it is possible to be an evangelical at an ontological level, considered especially in its private, experiential aspect, while adhering cognitively to views that are incompatible with evangelical theology. The Second Vatican Council, of course, explored and adopted a similar notion arguing, in the most extreme case, that it was possible for a person to be an atheist cognitively while being a Christian at an unconscious and ontological level. Beneath the level of consciousness, it affirmed, divine grace works in an unseen way, the response to which are good works that are sufficient to secure eternal salvation, even for the atheist. This solution provided a formal basis for the notion prevalent among Catholics, one that derived from Karl Rahner, that there are among people of no religion as well as those of non-Christian faith, "anonymous Christians." Evangelicalism, by a different route, is reaching conclusions that are not dissimilar. It now sees "anonymous evangelicals" sprouting in religious soil that has never before supported evangelical faith. People such as these are being seen as evangelical when judged at an attitudinal level, and the cognitive dissonance created by their conscious theology is tolerated, in some cases even supported, on the grounds of diversity and pluralism.[27]

At the center of this changing topography in evangelicalism is the issue of accommodation. Is accommodation to the mood and cognitive style of modernity synonymous with compromise? Or is this accommodation the necessary concession one must make in a modern world without which biblical faith would remain incomprehensible? Is it

---

Christianity: A Call for Unity Amid Diversity [New York, 1983], vii). The underlying unity, it seems to me, is often only marginally theological and more often predominantly psychological. Cf. Carl F. H. Henry, *Evangelicals in Search of Identity* (Waco, 1976), which is a brief analysis of the opportunities lost and found for evangelicals.

27. Cf. Arthur F. Glasser, "A Paradigm Shift? Evangelicals and Inter-religious Dialogue," *Missiology* 9, no. 4 (1981): 393-408; Gerald Ball, "Important Literature of the Dialogue," *Foundations* 25, no. 1 (1982): 67-80.

adapting faith to modernity or is it losing faith in modernity? The answer to these questions will determine the shape evangelical faith will take in the years that remain in this century and in this millennium.

Understanding the Chapter

1. Wells opens his chapter discussing the surface "appearance" of evangelicalism, which has "fascinated the press." What are some of the aspects of "this appearance of power, success, and dynamic growth" cited by Wells? In your opinion, which of these are commendable virtues and which are questionable or negative? Why?

2. The problem that Wells seeks to address in his essay is the same as that developed by Chaim Potok in his novels. It concerns where the "psychological boundary" lies between two key areas. What are the two areas on either side of the boundary?

3. What is a "cognitive minority?" In what ways did fundamentalists shape their beliefs so as to exclude themselves from the "cognitive majority?"

4. What does Wells mean when he states, "To be a fundamentalist was to be a true preserver of America. Paradoxically, however, being a fundamentalist also meant being a relentless opponent of America"?

5. Wells cites Will Herberg, who defined secularism as an "underlying, often unconscious, orientation of life and thought." This results in authentic religious content being surrendered in favor of a nonoffensive, common religion characterized by civility and good taste. Discuss the threat and impact of secularism in America on both Judaism and Christianity.

6. "It is true to say that evangelicalism has meant something different in every age." Discuss what Wells means by this statement.

7. Discuss Wells' observation that "the simple enumeration of doctrinal points to which evangelicals agree may be a good starting point in defining evangelicalism but it only deals with part of the reality."

8. Compare and contrast fundamentalism and evangelicalism using Wells' metaphor that "fundamentalism was a walled city; evangelicalism is a city."

9. Wells uses the term "anonymous evangelicals." What does he mean by this term?

10. Are evangelicals, as distinct from fundamentalists, a "cognitive

minority"? How have evangelicals been shaped by cultural values such as technology and pluralism, even as they attempted to oppose culture?

11. In your opinion, does Wells approve of or reject evangelicalism's apparent accommodation to culture?

4

A Response to David F. Wells by Thomas A. Askew

In perusing the contemporary religious landscape, Professor Wells has sought to delve beneath *appearances* of evangelical prosperity, power, and prominence. He has opted not to construct a definition of evangelicalism, but to mine for deeper realities by asking probing questions about the cognitive awareness, theological clarity, and cultural propensities reflected in evangelical circles. As a result of his digging, Wells has unearthed not a religious movement independently founded and able to lead a fragmented culture but one marked by self-doubt and uncertainty as to how to grapple with modernity and function in a pluralistic society.

Compounding the problem, according to Wells, is the evangelical break away from the identifiable boundaries of the "cognitive dissonance" erected by the fundamentalists to combat the inroads of modernity. Concurrently, Wells found evangelicals unduly susceptible to the subjectivism, privatization, and narcissism prevalent in the larger society. Thus, "Who is and who is not an evangelical therefore becomes a slippery and awkward question."

At this point, utilizing a metaphor in keeping with both Wells and the weather, I shall venture out on some semantic thin ice. In spite of the slipperiness of the question, I purpose to suggest a useable definition of evangelicalism. It may not stand up to full theological, historical, or sociological scrutiny, but perhaps can help us get on with our task, as evangelicals and Jews, of talking together. Then, after delineating what I consider to be evangelical distinctives, I will offer some comments on Wells' insightful and provocative essay.

Several preliminary comments are in order, however, before I venture a definition.

1. It is well to keep in mind that evangelical Christianity has never been a religious organization, nor primarily a theological system, nor even a containable movement. It is a mood, a perspective, an approach grounded in biblical theology, but reaching into motifs of religious

experience. The evangelical impulse reverberates across the denominational mosaic of American church life.

2. The evangelical faith has historical and spiritual roots that reach
back to European Reformation theology and continental pietism of the
sixteenth, seventeenth, and eighteenth centuries, as well as to the Puritan tradition.

3. Evangelicalism became, in the words of Yale historian Sydney
Ahlstrom, "The Great Tradition," the primary mainstream in American
Protestantism until the 1890s, and, in some regions, far into the twentieth century. Thus, the resurgence of evangelical religion is not something new in American history. The stream has merely become more
surging and visible after being largely shunted out of the center courses of
the mainline denominations in the period following 1920.

Now, without nuance or enumerations of the various denominations
and subgroups that reflect the evangelical heritage, I suggest four primary characteristics or priorities most evangelicals affirm.

1. *The Bible* is the sole authority for belief and practice. Salvation for
   sinful man comes through believing the gospel ("the good news" of
   Christ's atoning death and resurrection to life) rather than through
   sacramental ritual as a means of grace. Since believing the gospel is
   pivotal, the cardinal doctrines taught in the Scriptures and confessed
   by orthodox Christians through the ages are foundational to this
   belief. The above affirms both the formal and material principles of
   the Protestant Reformation.
2. *Conversion* is a necessary experience for beginning a deliberate Christian life. It does not necessarily have to be instantaneous. Individuals,
   one by one, need to repent and believe the gospel to be reborn
   spiritually. Faith is not inherited; one is not born into Christianity.
   Evangelical faith emphasizes an interior, life-transforming religion
   over against exterior, institutionally oriented versions of Christian
   practice.
3. *Nurture* is a desirable ongoing process of self-conscious cultivation of
   spirituality and holiness (at church, at home, and individually). Attention to prayer, Bible reading, attendance at all sorts of instruction-
   al classes, Sunday schools, as well as divine worship, are steps to
   spiritual growth. Conversion and nurture combine to release lay energies for the work of the church over against heavy dependence on a
   professional clergy.

4. *Mission* obliges every Christian to carry out the biblical command to "go into all the world and preach the gospel"—to be a witness. At the same time, mission involves acts of charity and benevolence. In some historical epochs, evangelicals have also been in the forefront of political and social reform, the quest for societal justice.

In bringing my brief commentary to a close, I have several reactions to Professor Wells' essay. First, he brought to the fore one of the larger dilemmas confronting evangelicals, often unperceived by popularizers and lay people: How do evangelicals affirm and preach a divinely revealed biblical message, the unique gospel of Christ, without being written off as obscurantists in a secular, pluralistic society? Wells directly poses the question when he inquires where useful interaction and accommodation end and eviscerating compromise begins as evangelicals grapple with modernity and pluralism. Adherents of Orthodox Judaism and other Jewish communions face similar quandaries.

Second, Wells perceptively exposes the tendency toward religious consumerism in American life, the privatization of faith, and the breakdown of religious communities. This pervasiveness of religiosity and sentiment, ungrounded in theology and cognitive reflection leading to action, helps account for the lack of substantive influence by religious institutions in the larger secular order.

Third, in regard to evangelicalism as an outgrowth of an older fundamentalism, I have more questions than can be raised here. Wells' assertion probably applies only to a particular brand of evangelicals, those primarily associated with Calvinistic Presbyterian and Baptist networks, and especially those found in the North and West. I see the evangelical faith and motif as a much broader tradition or current in American church history, one with a dozen substreams and marked by great diversity. Fundamentalism is merely one exclusivistic subculture within that stream, a mentality whose origins relate to the religious tensions within Protestantism as it faced a secularized American culture earlier in the twentieth century.

Finally, Wells makes a telling observation regarding the evangelical burden now that evangelicals have moved into frontline positions in American religious life. It is one thing to be a religious in-group sitting on the sidelines of the society; it is another to be publicly identified with national political leadership and to assume custodial responsibilities for the nation and culture.

Understanding the Chapter

1. Evaluate and discuss Askew's contention that "evangelical Christianity has never been a religious organization, nor primarily a theological system, nor even a containable movement. It is a mood, a perspective, an approach grounded in biblical theology, but reaching into motifs of religious experience."

2. In seeking to define *evangelicalism,* what four primary characteristics or priorities does Askew point to that most evangelicals affirm? Are you inclined to agree with this list, or do you wish to modify it in some way?

3. Where do Askew and Wells appear to disagree on the relationship of evangelicalism to fundamentalism?

4. Both Askew and Wells call attention to national political leadership, which has involved an increasing number of evangelicals. Does being "evangelical" pose any particular problems for political leaders in our pluralistic society? What do you perceive would be the difference between having an "evangelical president" in the White House rather than a "president who is evangelical?"

5

The Jewish Role in Shaping American Society

HENRY L. FEINGOLD

Jewish historians may experience a certain embarrassment in searching out a specifically Jewish role in shaping American society. It brings them uncomfortably close to the apologetics of the early years of American Jewish historiography when, anxious above all else to justify a Jewish presence in America, they touted Jewish contributions and war heroes. The result was bad history that, when overdone (as it inevitably was), furnished evidence to those who sought it that there was indeed a Jewish conspiracy to shape American society in its own image. The problem of defining such a Jewish role grew no less problematic in the intervening years.

Can one really link a quality or characteristic in the host culture to a specific ethnic group? Even if this were possible, in the case of American Jewry it would describe only one side, the less significant one, of a mutual shaping process. The impact of American culture on the Jewish enterprise has been far greater than the reverse. That is the reason Jewish survivalists are so concerned regarding the Jewish future in America. That reality is in fact a key to the dynamics behind the Jewish projection of influence. It is in their search for accommodation to a benevolently absorbing secular host culture, in the way they reshaped the tenets of their preexisting religious civilization to which they also adhered, that the principal Jewish influence was generated. The rationales and models of behavior Jews found in their accommodation process, the way they thought to make sense of American culture, became the seedbed of Jewish influence in America.

No sooner is the existence of such an influence acknowledged than the historian stumbles upon a new problem. How does one distinguish between the Jewish and the Judaic influence? The two are related but not quite identical. The Jews generate a religious ideology of many facets

called Judaism. But they also produce a distinct folk culture that in the
past has produced its own cuisine, language, music, and theater, and in
the modern period could sometimes be at odds with Judaism. More
important, there exists on the American scene other religious subcultures, spun off from the Protestant Reformation, that also view themselves as Judaic, or at least Hebraic. The Puritans and Pilgrims of the
seventeenth century, and even the later Mormons, anchored their polity
and their life-style firmly in the Old Testament, probably more so than
the Jews. During the colonial period the Congregationalists were certainly the better Hebraists. The seminal influence of the Puritans can be
noted in the fact that eventually American civilization adopted the Judaic
notion of selectness or chosenness. "We are all the children of Abraham,"
declaimed the Puritan thinker Joshua Moody, "and therefore we are
under Abraham's covenant." Centuries later a Vermont descendant,
Calvin Coolidge, observed that it was a "Hebraic mortar which cemented
the foundations of American Democracy." And it was the Harvard phi-
losopher Barret Williams who observed that America was the only society "to whom democracy has been confided not as a philosophical
abstraction, but as an ancestral practice."

The responsibility to carry Judaic scholarship forward, once borne by
the now destroyed communities of eastern Europe, is today accepted by
the American Jewish community. But the required learning is confined
to a comparative few. America's Jews are also its most avid secularists.
The tradition of learning exists in transmuted form. For "the people of
the book," the book today may be a law text or a home computer. The
truth is that in the unlikely case that Jews were anxious to project the
tenets of Judaism, few are learned enough in its texts to do so. Nor does
there any longer exist the kind of group consciousness that might serve as
a launching pad for the projection of influence. The absence of such group
coherence is a major reason for their ineffectiveness during the Holocaust
years.

Only in the anti-Semitic imagination is Jewry still conceived of as a
single cohesive group. Everywhere Jewry has become a riven tribe and
nowhere more so than in postemancipation America. A part of that
disunity is traceable to an adherence to the cultural values of the societies
that had rejected them and from which they had emigrated. Paradoxically, American Jewry acted out the hostility between Latin and Teuton
and between Teuton and Slav, within the Jewish arena. That tragic
phenomenon might serve as evidence that far from being separatist and

disloyal, accusations that everywhere became standard in anti-Semitic rhetoric, the reverse was actually the case. Jews readily imbibed the values of the host culture, even when it despised them, with all the problems of self-esteem that entailed.

Today those passions which divide American Jewry have been partly subsumed beneath a bland secularism. The individuation and freedom everywhere part of modernization have made some inroads on the sense of peoplehood that once bound them. One can no longer be certain whether there exists an American Jewish enterprise willing and able consciously to project a shaping influence or, if there is such a presence in American society, whether its adherents would know what to project. It is far more possible from a historic perspective to conceive of a Gentile society that sought in Judaism a sustaining vision to build and maintain its "new Jerusalem."

Withal America would have been different without its Jews, who were after all "present at the creation" and bore witness to its development ever since. The fragmented character of American Jewry seems to have little effect in diminishing its visibility or energy. It has developed an elaborate organizational substructure through which it can project influence. Every ideology, even every mood, warrants an organizational expression. Jews even have an organization for presidents of major organizations. Within the diversity some unity has also developed, which is apparent in the growth of local and national historical societies that possess no ideological character except to preserve the corporate memory of the community.

Like other subcultures in America, Jews have their own political agenda. Theirs is longer than most because of American Jewry's strategic location within a benevolent and powerful nation. Kinship with Jewish communities abroad compels it to play an advocate role before the American government. This important activity in and of itself could be the answer to our query regarding a Jewish shaping role, focusing entirely on its attempts to project influence in the foreign policy arena. In the nineteenth century it would include the persistent effort to get the American government to intercede diplomatically for oppressed Jewish communities in Russia, Romania, Switzerland, and North Africa. In recent years the Jewish concern with the establishment of Israel and its nurture and development in a hostile world is evidence that the interest is a sustained one. In pressing its case American Jewry spoke in terms of

American self-interest and legal responsibility, not as Jews. In the case of Russia at the turn of the century it insisted that American Jewish citizens doing business there were entitled to the full protection of the American constitution lest the concept of citizenship itself be compromised. Louis Marshall, the second president of the American Jewish Committee, was careful to couch the Jewish interest in American terms. But a focus on Jewish input in the area of foreign policy would not be a very instructive exposition of its shaping role. With the exception of the recognition of the State of Israel in 1948 there are actually few instances where one might say that Jewish influence led to a particular policy. That is so because Jewish interest, when it is palpable, is not couched in Jewish terms and is usually supported by other groups who see it in terms of the broader national interest.

Yet the persistent concern for their brethren does contain a clue, for it has played a role in shaping American Jewish political culture. Jews are hyperactive in the American political process, to be sure not only because they feel themselves linked to Jewish communities abroad by religious, cultural, and family ties. They have an inordinate faith in the democratic process as well, and their energies are not confined to Jewish causes. Yet their interest in foreign affairs goes beyond that of other hyphenates.

Ultimately we may want to dismiss altogether the notion of a Jewish intent to influence American culture, especially in its formative days. In its early days American society was so amenable to change that no great exertion was required to shape it. In the case of Judaism the majority culture actually searched out a shaping influence in order to garner the moral purposefulness it required. It was again Louis Marshall who realized that America required and welcomed such influence. He spoke of the need "to shape the opinion of the people of this country," to "instruct" its conscience. But even here the whole does not seem to equal the sum of its parts. Such influence stemmed from Jewish organizations or individuals who happened to be Jewish and not from American Jewry collectively.

What is left, then? Perhaps Jews helped shape American society in acting out its success ethos so fully. That may have been what the non-Jewish sociologist Robert Parks had in mind when he recommended that courses in Jewish ethics be incorporated into the high school curriculum in 1923. Parks thought that the remarkable economic performance of American Jewry could serve as a model for other subcultures and native Americans. He was not alone in believing that a special affinity between Judaic and American values was behind the Jewish achievement.

Here too there are special problems, for Parks covers only the temporal Jewish sphere and neglects the Judaic. He was interested in what Jews contributed to American culture, scientific technology, and the general economy, but that is hardly the same as the impression of the Judaic value system on the consciousness of America. The achievements of a Jonas Salk or a Woody Allen are made by individuals who happen to be Jewish. And clearly Jews did not have to be present in America to project the Judaic ethos. The founding fathers were well versed in Scriptures without ever having seen a Jew.

There is no need to enumerate the astoundingly long list of purveyors of American high and low culture of Jewish origin. It is probably claiming too much to observe that Jews are the merchandizers and packagers of American culture. While this is a conspicuous influence, it is far from a majority one. Yet even a strong minority voice in the area of culture can have a special importance since it is through art, literature, and theater that a society identifies itself. But is it a Jewish voice that Jewish writers, comedians, and actors project? More precisely, do Jewish culture carriers achieve popularity because of the projection of a Jewish sensibility or because what they say has a universal meaning? "Fiddler on the Roof" was as popular in Tokyo as it was in New York because the problems it presented have universal application just as does the Salk vaccine or the Jarvik mechanical heart.

In the economic sphere, where it may be possible to conceive a collective Jewish ethos and transmuted Jewish values at work, the problem seems much easier. The success of a Jewish innovator in engineering or in genetic engineering or in the reproduction of microchips is individual. It is a contribution by someone who happens to be Jewish rather than a Jewish contribution. The American reward system is individual rather than group oriented. Yet the prominence of Jews in these new areas of development is so remarkably sustained that it warrants a search beneath the surface to account for it. What we need to determine is whether the Judaic religious belief system contains values, thinking modes, affinity for abstraction, and general assumptions regarding progress and mastery that enhance the process of modernization.

There is some evidence in the American Jewish experience that this may be the case. In the three and a half centuries since they settled in America three distinct Jewish communities stemming from radically different national cultures and active at different stages in the economic development of the nation have produced commercial and professional elites. Even the immigration codas, the German Jews who settled here in the thirties from which stem Einstein and Kissinger, have produced such elites. The only thing the Sephardic Jews of the colonial period, the German Jews of the nineteenth century, and the eastern European Jews of the twentieth held in common was their religious tradition. Otherwise they were radically different from each other in all respects. There is nothing quite like the "Grandees," the "Crowd," and the "egghead millionaires," descendants of the eastern migration, in other immigrant subcultures.

Yet it almost seems that by merely mentioning these elites their importance in the economy has been overstated. This is so because American Jewry is such a small minority that even when it plays a disproportionately important role it remains perforce a minority one. Yet considering that America is the first society to have solved the problem of pervasive scarcity that shaped the thinking of all prior societies, even a minority contribution assumes a special importance. One suspects that centuries hence historians will conclude that the most significant contribution of American civilization is in its sufficient production of goods and services for all.

Even so the problem of stamping an ethnic or religious identity on achievement remains unresolved. In our society the discovery of the vaccine, the building of a business, the skill in reading the law is achieved by individuals with courage, vision, and talent. Yet in the case of the Jews the ethnic or religious background may be more than coincidental. The more we learn about who achieves in America the more we observe that achievement is not totally random. Some individuals and entire groups are better situated than others to achieve. Yet Jews do not fit into the picture cliometricians draw of the successful American entrepreneur. In the nineteenth century he was usually a native-born Protestant from New England whose parents already had some money. The American success odyssey was not "from rags to riches" but from comfort to wealth. The one distinct exception was the Jews, who went from poverty to riches in less than one generation. Measured by job status and income, the most successful single group in America are the sons of Protestant ministers. We have no figures for the children of rabbis, but one suspects that they would rate high too.

Of course one could as easily postulate that rather than seeing subcultural values at work, what we are witnessing is the impact of secular American values on Protestants and Jews. When Leonard Goldenson, the founder of the ABC network, was asked whether his success and that of Mr. Sarnoff, who built NBC, and Mr. Paley, who established CBS, had some link to their common Jewish background, he denied it without equivocation. He pointed out that all three had virtually no Jewish education and were in other respects only marginally Jewish. But are the disproportionate number of Goldensons among the Jews merely coincidence, or is there something at work here that has an impact even on marginal Jews?

We are compelled to return once again to the Judaic value system that Jews and Protestants to some extent share. There are differences of opinion among Jews and Christians about the precise properties of that ethos and who has the rightful historical claim to it. But for our purpose it makes little difference whether we view it, as some Christians do, as a patrimony gone awry in the hands of its original Jewish recipients and then given to the Christian community, or, as the Jewish thinker Franz Rozenzweig describes it in *Conditions of Belief*, we see Christianity simply as the Judaism of the Gentiles. In the case of the Christian community these values originated in their perception of the Old Testament; in the case of the Jews they are based on rationales, philosophies, and strategies of accommodation conceived to make ancient values fit into the thrust of modernization stemming from the Enlightenment. This thrust was felt especially in America where it was invested with transmuted Hebraic properties by both groups.

In both cases it released new energies and talents. Both groups believed that what had been created was a better and more just order of human organization. In the eighteenth and nineteenth centuries this image took firm hold of the underclasses of Europe, of which Jews were part. It motivated the massive waves of immigration that peopled America, especially by the Jews. Heinrich Heine, a German poet of Jewish origin, penned the famous lines, "Amerika Du hast es Besser." It resonated a belief especially strong among European Jews emerging from the ghetto. The hope they held out for America was behind their choice of uprooting themselves and immigrating to the New World in proportionately larger numbers. To some extent the American dream, which still prevails in much of the world, was incubated in the Jewish imagination.

In the nineteenth century the "chosen people" chose America and discovered that America, too, felt itself chosen. The Pilgrims spoke of it in biblical terms as the "land of milk and honey" and thought of themselves as the select of God and a "light unto the nations" (Isa. 42:1-7). The notion of covenant was embodied in the Mayflower Compact and the founding charters of the new nation. It fed into the early foreign policy of the young republic. The quest for isolation from Europe embodied in Washington's Farewell Address (1796) and the Monroe Doctrine (1823) counseled apartness inherent in the sense of the sacred. The new social experiment ran the risk of contagion if it came too close to a Europe in the throes of dynastic corruption.

Similarly, the early perception of the Indian has something distinctly Hebraic about it. At first the Indians were considered to be the ten lost tribes of Israel and therefore fit subjects to be brought back into the fold. But when they resisted they were metamorphosed into pagans, Moabites, and Canaanites, who had to be destroyed "root and branch." The westward movement also had distinct Judaic properties. Its divine rationale was provided by the concept of manifest destiny. God's intention was for America to expand, and nothing, not even the existence of whole peoples already in possession of the land, could interfere with that sacred mission.

As we look back at two centuries of foreign affairs we find it difficult to avoid the conclusion that the sense of mission and righteousness that informs this policy is remarkably similar to that of the ancient children of Israel. It comes to the fore in the "Cuba Libre" movement that preceded the war against Spanish "tyranny" in 1898. We entered World War I, if Wilsonian rhetoric is taken at face value, not to enhance the security of a threatened North Atlantic community, but to "make the world safe for democracy." In 1928 two Jewish lawyers proposed outlawing war altogether. War, they reasoned, should at least have the stigma of illegality. Twenty-six nations signed the resultant "parchment peace," the Pact of Paris (1928). Europeans laughed at such naivete, but for Americans who had similarly legislated moral behavior by outlawing liquor, it did not seem strange at all. Subsequently we proposed "free elections" almost everywhere: in Poland, Yugoslavia, Korea, Vietnam, and El Salvador. We did so not so much because it was considered a magical cure but because it was "right." When President Reagan speaks of "evil" empires Americans know almost instinctively what he means. There is after all evil in the world. But unarmed with such a Judaic sensibility that views the world in terms of a simple morality tale, a struggle between good and evil, our European allies find such classifications dangerously simple. They are more sophisticated regarding morality. Perhaps the Canaanites were not evil after all, they argue. They might even suspect that the children of Israel, the chosen of God, were not righteous. Where Americans strain for morality they note that we are merely moralistic. They are not alone in this perception. George Kennan, America's most eloquent foreign policy specialist, observed in the 1950s that American foreign policy was pervaded by moralism and legalism, which tended to conceal baser motives for what was done in the international arena. These same characteristics mark the quintessential Judaic spirit. There is no duplicity involved here. American foreign policy, when it is interested in the world at all, is often marked by an Isaiahlike fervor to improve the world. It often entails extraordinary generosity. We discover only later that we really want to make the world over in our own image. As with the children of Israel, ideal principles are compelled to confront the demands of national interest that require the exercise of power not for some transcendent purpose but in its own right. From historical hindsight actions taken for moral purpose look far different. The ancient Hebrews had their moral imperatives for invading Canaan—it was the land their God had promised them. Surely they were aware that it was a land also claimed by other nations. But how could that be allowed to stand in the way of doing the Lord's work? Morality here depended on the superiority of their God as well as whose ox was being gored. When the temple was destroyed it was also the Lord's work. Once armed with such righteous fervor they never had to see the world as it is.

Contemporary American Jewish political culture continues to be freighted with a heavy ideological cargo. It assigns mission to governance and politics. It rejects the Hobbesian assumption that government is merely an instrument to stave off the ravages of man living in a state where each is at war with the other. In the Judaic tradition civil peace is important, but it is not a sufficient rationale for man to hold power over his fellowman. We must also pursue justice, without which we cannot achieve domestic tranquility. Jews are enjoined to seek justice actively in the affairs of men. Historically that has been a difficult commandment to obey because, not possessing a sovereignty of their own, they are compelled to seek it in the society where they dwell, whose governing principle may have different priorities. The Jews, Jefferson observed, did not appear to be noticeably different in their political behavior than other denominations that crowded the religious landscape of the republic. As a deist he placed his religious passions on a low-flame backburner. The Jews did not. He saw in their religious fervor only clannishness and superstition. If they did not abuse power it was not, he thought, because they heeded their prophets but because they had none to abuse. They were powerless. Things would be different if they had power. That is what he told Mordecai Noah, the best-known Jewish politico in early American history: "Your sect by its suffering has furnished a remarkable proof of the universal spirit of religious intolerance inherent in every sect, disclaimed by all when feeble, and practiced by all when in power."

Jefferson did not understand the wellsprings of Jewish political culture nor the fact that his own fears of power had, in some measure, Hebraic roots. Like Jefferson, the prophets believed that unchecked power in the hands of governors was bound to be abused, that is, it would inevitably be deflected from its true mission to do justice. There is in the political culture of American Jewry a continuing search for transcendence through politics. They have been attracted most to those leaders and movements in American history whom they perceive to be similarly inclined. The "constellation of values" that draws Jews is not, however, based on the Christian notion of *Caritas,* which relates to love and concern, but on the Judaic concept of seeking justice and righteousness that must be expressed through deeds. It must be fulfilled even when one does not love. That is one reason why they are today the most active political constituency in the American electorate. It is also the reason why Jews are easily the most generous givers in America and possess a philanthropic apparatus that is the envy of other subcultures.

The major Jewish contribution to the shaping of American society is made in the process of accommodating their religious values to a relentlessly modernizing secular society. They have sought out those values in the host culture that facilitate the retention of these values in transmuted form. It is no accident that such American Jewish thinkers as Horace Kallen emphasized the notion of cultural pluralism. American Jews, like most Jews in the West, fully accepted the transaction embodied in emancipation. They would purge their religious culture of its separatist and particularist aspects in turn for a full measure of civil and political rights. But they soon discovered not only that most Christian societies were reluctant to fulfill the bargain but that the accommodation entailed an abandonment of the communalism and sense of chosenness at the heart of Judaic religious culture. Moreover, living Judaism prescribed an entire way of life and could not easily be converted into a "going to church on Sunday" type of faith. Nevertheless, the Reform branch of Judaism undertook the extirpation of the corporate communal aspects of Judaism in favor of a protestantized, individuated, privatized religious sensibility, leaving a triangulated religious community in its wake. When the accommodation was completed, a consonance between what modern Jews now professed to believe and the values of American society was perceptible and proudly proclaimed by Rabbi Kaufman Kohler, a principal exponent of classical Reform:

> American Judaism! What power of inspiration lies in these two words! The spell of triumph of the world's two greatest principles and ideals, the consumation of mankind's choicest possessions, the one offered by the oldest, the other by the youngest of the great nations of history, the highest moral and spiritual and the highest political and social aim of humanity, the God of righteousness and holiness to unite and uplift all men and nations, and the Magna Carta of liberty and human equality to endow each individual with God like sovereignty. . . .

By vacating millennia of rabbinic interpretation of Jewish law, by reshaping its esthetics and by concentrating on the prophets, Judaism could be made to fit into American society and the ethos of the enlightenment which it upheld. It would become part of an interchangeable civil religion to which all would adhere. There was no conspiracy to become a part of what Will Herberg would later see as a Protestant, Catholic, Jew triad. Tradition-minded Jews fought the idea of substituting religiosity for religion, and still do. But Jews, despite the obvious differences in their religious culture, especially the concept of chosenness, were willy-nilly included in the formula for religious blending. Few realized what a radical departure that was. For an ethnically, racially, and regionally divided America the prospect of a further division on religious grounds was too threatening. The division of the polity into "ins" and "outs" during the colonial period and the creation of states like Rhode Island and Utah served as sufficient evidence of what could happen should religious passions win the day.

Even so the Reformist strategy of full accommodation did not hold sway. The Jewish immigrants from eastern Europe who began to arrive in large numbers after 1881 were more traditionalist and far more aware of a separate Jewish peoplehood. Rather than accept such a radical reshaping they sought to broaden the tolerance threshold of the host society so that sufficient space might be attained for a distinctive Judaic as well as secular Jewish culture to flourish. The rationale to do so, cultural pluralism, was not conceived by Jews. It too was embedded in the Protestant culture and was advocated by thinkers like Barrett Wendell, who taught it to his students—Jews and non-Jews—at Harvard University. But thinkers like Horace Kallen pushed it to its logical conclusion. They challenged the "melting pot" model that paradoxically was coined by the Jewish playwright Israel Zangwill. Rather than speak of making one out of many, *E Pluribus Unum,* Kallen spoke of the importance of diversity in a free society. The analogy he preferred was that of the symphonic orchestra, where every instrument played a different part for the purpose of rendering a superior harmony. The music of democracy was similarly polyphonic. This more complex model of American identity permitted ethnic particularism.

Louis D. Brandeis, whom Franklin Roosevelt called "Old Isaiah," observed after his rediscovery of his Jewish heritage that the ideals of twentieth-century America were the same as those cherished by Jews for twenty centuries. Being a good Jew, one could not help but be a good American. It is true, as we have shown here, that America needed no Jews to cherish Judaic values. But it did receive something from the living physical presence of Jews in its midst. Their contribution emanated from a desperate search to accommodate to a benevolently absorbent society while trying to retain something of their ancient culture. Jews did retain some of the values inherent in that culture and transmuted other values so that it became possible to release fully their energies and talents. But their success entailed a price. The philosophy of cultural pluralism that became an integral part of American ideology provided the space required for Jewish particularism but did not assure that the powerful solvent released by the host culture, which corrodes the bindings of all subcultures, would stop flowing. There is some doubt today that Jews retain the cultural energy to renew their culture indefinitely. They no longer know instinctively what to plant in the space provided by a pluralistic society. They are as perplexed as others on how to move from the fraternal brotherhood of their tribal culture to the universal otherhood of a modern secular one. They have lost their sense of the sacred that went hand in hand with apartness. They have accepted democracy to the extent that the laity often assumes greater importance than the deity. Everything in their religious culture required a search for transcendent purpose, but in modern society its meaning is in constant flux and is lately imagined to have something to do with quantities of data pouring forth from a computer. They are losing their way.

That sense of lostness they hold in common with all Americans. They have in addition the optimism that stems from the injunction to "choose life" (Deuteronomy 30:19). It has been a prime factor behind their remarkable contribution to the development of American society. Perhaps it is that injunction which America will most require from its Jews in future years.

Understanding the Chapter

1. Discuss Feingold's observation that "the impact of American culture on the Jewish enterprise has been greater than the reverse."

2. What distinction does Feingold draw between the "Jewish" and the "Judaic"? What factor has had the greater influence in shaping American culture?

3. Feingold says, "Only in the anti-Semitic imagination is Jewry still conceived of as a single cohesive group. Everywhere Jewry has become a riven tribe. . . ." Discuss the factors that have contributed to what Feingold calls "fragmentation," "disunity," and lack of "group consciousness" in modern Jewry.

4. According to Feingold, what is the one notable instance in the area of American foreign policy where Jewish influence actually led to a particular policy supported by the American government?

5. Feingold points out that "Jews did not have to be present in America to project the Judaic ethos. The founding fathers were well versed in Scriptures without ever having seen a Jew." Discuss the various ways Judaic (Hebrew) influence was exerted by non-Jews upon early America.

6. What does Feingold mean when he states, "the early perception of the [American] Indian has something distinctly Hebraic about it"?

7. What one major reason does Feingold give to substantiate why Jews are today "the most active political constituency in the American electorate" as well as "easily the most generous givers in America." Why is this same reason *not* the motivating factor in most Christian circles?

8. What contributions have American Jews made to the ideal of cultural pluralism? Why?

9. What biblical injunction producing optimism does Feingold suggest America may "most require from its Jews in future years"?

6
Evangelical Christianity and American Culture

TIMOTHY L. SMITH

The dissolution of religious consensus in twentieth-century America, not only within the major religious traditions but in the external relations of each to the others, tends to distort our vision of the nation's religious history. The more extreme parties of Protestant modernists, whom secular scholars feel most comfortable with, and the most combative party of evangelicals, the fundamentalists, flourish by persuading academia and the news media that theirs is the only game in town. Middle-class black evangelicals stand aloof from black Pentecostals, and both groups reject the radicalism of Christian black nationalists. The vast majority of Roman Catholics, like the majority of white Protestants, stand midway between extremist camps, yet both insiders and outsiders are coming to see Catholics as divided into parties of modernists, social activists, charismatics, and reactionaries. Meanwhile, the world honors an activist and deeply spiritual pope who seems to fit into none of these parties and who embraces some of the most starkly competing ideals of each one. Jewish religious differences, of course, have been muted in this century by the strength of their united opposition to anti-Semitism, by their substitution of the language of ethnicity for that of religious faith, and by support of the State of Israel and its ethic of national survival. The result is to obscure the religious history both of the Jews who settled in this country before 1881 and of the vast company whose migration from central and eastern Europe began that year. Likewise, Eastern Orthodox Christians, whose numerous ethnic segments were able in the late nineteenth century to think of themselves as adjusting to life in the United States and Canada on the same religious terms, have in this century faced repeated challenges to their ancient commitment to ecumenical ideals. The flight after World War I of anti-Bolshevik White Russians and after World War II of Orthodox refugees from central and eastern Europe included many who had been in business or the professions and a few who had owned large estates. Unlike the peasant migrants of earlier decades, the new exiles were inclined to embrace reactionary political and social policies as the only proper Christian response to the threat of communism, whether in Europe or America.

The consequences of this widespread breakdown of consensus has been the growing public and scholarly illusion that American society has been secularized—this despite the verifiable fact of an extensive revival of personal commitment in every North American religious tradition, including those that originated in Islamic or in Oriental Hindu and Buddhist cultures. That illusion is, I think, socially and politically unproductive. The prompting it gives to both political and religious obscurantism and the dissension it breeds over what Americans once thought were shared values seem to me too great a price for either the United States or Canada to pay.

In the hope, therefore, of lighting up pathways that could lead us to a renewed though perhaps more modest consensus, I wish to lay out here a straightforward history of the relationship of evangelical Christianity to the shaping of American culture, and to underline those aspects of the story that contributed to the moral and political consensus that my colleague John Higham has called "pluralistic unity" or "integrative pluralism." The conviction of our diverse oneness held this nation together in the nineteenth century, despite a bitter sectional conflict, and it helped to make our experiment in government of, by, and for the people a beacon of hope to almost the entire world.

Let me begin by stating what I imagine to be a rigorously historical definition of Protestant evangelicalism that seems generally acceptable to all these competing religious groups, yet one that admits of no easy compromises among them. I and my younger colleagues have employed it with increasing satisfaction in the analyses of twelve North American evangelical "movements" that we have made for the essays in our forthcoming book, *The American Evangelical Mosaic.*

The term *evangelical* and its historical definition first became widely popular in England and America during the religious revivals of the eighteenth century associated with John Wesley's Methodist Arminianism, with George Whitefield's and William Tennant's Puritan Calvinism, and with the worldwide mission movement stemming from German Reformed and Lutheran Pietism. Though in Germany and elsewhere on the Continent the term *evangelical* was unsatisfactory because of the older use of it to denote Lutheran as distinct from Reformed Protestants, contemporaries understood Pietism, particularly in its more aggressive Moravian expression, to be part and parcel of the developments that Britons and Americans called "evangelical."

In all of these movements, thoroughgoing commitment to the authority of the Old and New Testaments, and hence to careful study of them, was both the basis of moral and spiritual revival and a chief means of spreading it. This had been true of Protestantism from the beginning, especially of the radical Mennonites, Brethren, and Quakers. These "peace churches" slowly identified themselves as a fourth evangelical movement. For they shared with the others the conviction that the Hebrew and Christian Scriptures were permeated with the promise of a personal experience of salvation from sin, received in a moment of living faith, which Jesus called being "born again." Finally, all four of these inwardly diverse movements found that both the Scriptures and this inward experience of love for God and one's neighbor impelled them to missionary evangelism. These three characteristics—commitment to scriptural authority, the experience of regeneration or "new life in Christ," and the passion for evangelism—have marked evangelicals ever since. They were distinguishing marks not only in the four parent movements, but in the parties of evangelicals that emerged in the older state churches and in new movements that sprang up along their edges through the course of the nineteenth and early twentieth centuries.

RELIGIOUS PLURALISM

The larger impact of evangelicalism on American culture will be clearer, I think, if we begin by stressing its original pluralistic character. In our day, the notion prevails that pluralism in societies that were or are predominantly Protestant has been forced on a recalcitrant and usually Anglo-Saxon majority by mass Catholic and Jewish immigration, especially in the growing cities that were the centers of rapid cultural change. And modern students generally assume that pluralism led directly to a secularization of the culture. I do not wish to challenge such truth as may lie in either of those assumptions, but want simply to stress how the evangelical situation itself generated and circumscribed the force of pluralism. Understanding that fact might help contending parties in our present conflicted situation to search more hopefully for a consensus about moral and religious values rooted honestly in today's interfaith diversity.

Where, then, should we begin the study of North America's religious history, in order to lay bare the roots of our twentieth-century situation? Certainly not, I think, either with the landing of William Bradford's tiny company of separatists at Plymouth in 1620 or of John Winthrop's great migration of Puritans to Charlestown and Boston in 1629. No colonial city was more unlike modern American ones than seventeenth-century Boston, where Cottons and Mathers dominated the religious scene. And claims that the less religious Chesapeake Society of Virginia and Maryland was modern America in embryo are even less persuasive. Save for their English and Protestant character, neither of these points much more clearly to the modern situation than the establishment of New France. We should begin rather with the middle colonies, from Long Island Sound southward, paying attention to Maryland only at the end of the colonial period when Baltimore's ties to an increasingly diverse back-country made it over into the religiously plural and ethnically diverse community that Dutch-English New York and English-German Philadelphia had been for a hundred years. These three cities remain to this day classic models of North America's religious pluralism.

Colonial Philadelphia displayed with special clarity evangelical Protestant pluralism. William Penn not only welcomed to his new commonwealth his fellow Quakers—English, Welsh, Irish, and Dutch—but Rhineland German pacifists from both Mennonite-Anabaptist and radical Pietist circles. Poor Englishmen of Anglican or Puritan backgrounds soon began following the Quakers, as did Scottish and Scotch-Irish Presbyterians, in whose homelands evangelical beliefs and attitudes were spreading rapidly. Presbyterians in the Delaware and Susquehanna valleys soon were experiencing the religious awakenings that William Tennant and his sons first led and George Whitefield brought to white heat. Calvinists, however, were not Christian pacifists. Neither were the poor Germans of varying Lutheran and Reformed backgrounds who arrived in Philadelphia a generation behind the peace people. The missionary pastors that these poor settlers were able to secure, after a number of years during which congregations of lay persons operated without benefit of clergy, were the Pietists Henry M. Muhlenberg and Michael Schlatter. These two were soon to be revered as founders of the Pennsylvania German Lutheran and Reformed communions, chiefly because they were able to persuade other young Pietist ministers to come over to America to help shepherd their "lost" countrymen. The result, of course, was the transformation of their congregations into evangelical communities.

Baptists came to the Delaware Valley a bit later in the century. Sufficient numbers of English Baptists settled in and around Philadelphia to make the area the first heartland of the American Baptist movement. The city itself was the home of the Baptist Missionary Convention until the slavery controversy disrupted the denomination's unity. John Wesley did not send over Methodist preachers until the decade preceding the Revolutionary War. They found that the poorer families of English people who had filtered into New York City, Philadelphia, Wilmington, and Baltimore were a ripe field for the Wesleyan harvest, whether or not they had been faithful Anglicans in Great Britain. And so were the Anglican yeomen of Maryland, Delaware, and Virginia.

The adoption of the Quaker-Anabaptist idea of the separation of church and state by New York Presbyterian William R. Livingston and a growing number of the city's Anglicans and Dutch Reformed stemmed directly from not only the fact of religious pluralism but its evangelical character. The conservative parties of Anglicans and Dutch Reformed who opposed it were both antidemocratic and suspicious of evangelical fervor.

The myth of a steep decline of religious commitment in revolutionary New York turns out to rest on the writings of conservatives who wished to perpetuate the remains of a religious and social establishment as a counterweight to the republican tendencies of evangelical culture. The New York missionary society, founded in 1795 on the model of one organized shortly before by diverse dissenters in London, anticipated the formation of the Connecticut missionary society by several years. The multiplication of local revivals throughout the United States and English Canada that are sometimes called (I think incorrectly) the Second Great Awakening did not begin either at Yale College or at Cain Ridge, Kentucky, as variously argued in the past. They originated rather in the concerted effort and the growing sense of unity among evangelical pastors and congregations in New York City, Long Island, and northeastern New Jersey. Evangelicals in that region, as in the Delaware and Susquehanna valleys and the Maryland and Virginia back-country, had become used to the idea that Christians could secure the order and sustain the idealism of a religiously plural republic by bringing the unchurched into a biblical experience of moral transformation. Whatever modern social scientists have made of the emergence thereafter of what they are pleased to call "civil religion," the ruling religious and moral ideas that pervaded the intellectual, economic, and political culture of the United States and Canada in the nineteenth century were grounded in biblical faith, defined evangelically, and experienced personally.

It is not surprising, therefore, that new evangelical movements added during that century to the American Protestant kaleidoscope fit readily both into the evangelical religious consensus and into the social and political order the consensus sustained. Consider, for example, the movement in which one might expect to find an exception to this rule, the increasingly segregated black Methodists and Baptists. Separate congregations emerged first in the mid-Atlantic cities and then, while troubled slaveholders were developing more stringent codes of both legal and social oppression, in the urban South. Black Christians demanded, first within the white churches and then in their own separate ones, a full measure of both the liberties and the moral and political responsibilities that other evangelicals enjoyed in a pluralistic nation. They read the Bible from the point of view of the oppressed, to be sure, and doing so nurtured a different sensibility. But in historical perspective, black Methodist and Baptist culture was simply more intensely evangelical than its white counterparts, whether in respect for Scripture, spiritual experience, or evangelism. This is evident both in the fervent music, prayer, and preaching of their worship and in the moral insight of their lay and ministerial leaders. Negro preachers dreamed more powerfully than white ones did of a kingdom of God in which unrighteousness (meaning, biblically, injustice) would be banished from the nation by the spread of saving grace.

The evangelical character of other new Protestant movements of the nineteenth century seems also obvious. Alexander Campbell's Disciples of Christ sought from 1809 onward to unite all true Christians on a platform that renounced "human" creeds in favor of Scripture alone. They saw in the Bible, of course, the same call to repentance and saving faith that others had seen, and the same obligation to soul-winning. Despite his irenic evangelism, however, Campbell became instead the founder of a New Testament sect. Its adherents, now numbering in three great aggregations possibly as many as six million persons, affirmed both Jacksonian democratic ideals and the separation of church and state, because they believed that the conversion of individuals is the only way to bring on the millennial dawn. The Adventist movement, which took shape a bit later among those who were shattered when the Second Coming of Christ did not take place in 1843/44, fits the same pattern. So do other more radical millenarian movements such as the Mormons and the Jehovah's Witnesses, whose evolving self-definition moved them away from not only a Protestant but a Christian identity. The unique early teachings of Joseph Smith stem from his reaction not so much against the evangelical style of religious belief and ethical behavior as against what the young prophet believed were the contradictions in doctrine, ethics, and expectations of the future the Bible had allowed diverse Protestant movements to embrace. *The Book of Mormon,* and a large portion of Smith's subsequent revelations that now constitute the *Doctrine and Covenants* of the Church of Jesus Christ of the Latter-day Saints, proclaimed a Christian faith that became complete and coherent only when a new volume of sacred writings had reconciled old theological conflicts and charted the history and the future of that faith in the New World.

I must cut short here this account of evangelical diversity in the United States and Canada. It moves on to the emergence during the last half of the nineteenth century of ethnic Protestant evangelical denominations (such as the Missouri Synod of Lutherans, mostly German, and the Christian Reformed Church, mostly Dutch) and of the Wesleyan holiness movement. Three new movements of the twentieth century stand in the same religious lineage, the fundamentalists and the two communities of Pentecostals, one white and the other black.

But I must underline the self-conscious character of the evangelical embrace of the cultural and political implications of Protestant pluralism. By the middle of the nineteenth century, leaders of all these movements affirmed that biblical religion would flourish best under the separation of church and state, and that only such a religion could generate both the moral sensibility and the social idealism that were necessary to sustain a modern republic. Viewed against the broad sweep of Christian history since the Reformation, this was an immense achievement, though not one we would expect to find Jewish and Catholic leaders of that era applauding. Nevertheless, I think both the formal structure and the social tendencies of that pluralism were parents to the interfaith idealism that Americans in the United States and Canada have struggled throughout the twentieth century to incorporate into law and custom.

A BIBLICAL CULTURE

The extent to which explicit reference to biblical teachings characterized every aspect of American culture was sometimes a surprise to Europeans who traveled here during the middle decades of the nineteenth century. Nowadays, however, scholars specializing in many aspects of our nation's history have found it commonplace. Why did respect for the Hebrew and Christian Scriptures become so important to nineteenth-century Americans? Certainly the task of forming a nation among people of diverse ethnic, political, and religious backgrounds required an authority that transcended tradition. The founding generation made a sharp break with old customs of aristocracy, royal authority, and class prerogative, appealing not only to reason and common sense but to scriptural teaching. Moreover, they regarded a democratic republic boasting freedom of religion as a perilous experiment. The selfish passions of competing groups and classes would tear it apart unless all could willingly submit to ethical principles that transcended particular religious traditions. The Bible set forth those principles, as even deists like Thomas Jefferson and Benjamin Franklin affirmed and rationalists like Thomas Paine could not deny. But what could secure the willing submission of self-interested citizens to it?

The principal evangelical contribution to making the Hebrew and Christian Scriptures the living constitution undergirding the document forged at Philadelphia and adopted by popular vote was the religious experience of saving faith, empowering human beings, as the Epistle to the Romans put it, to fulfill the righteousness of the law. In the formation and structure of their congregations, in the exposition of Christian ethics and theology, and in their successive revolts from both ecclesiastical and political authority, Puritans, Presbyterians and Pietists, Methodists, Baptists, and Mennonites had appealed to Moses and the prophets, to Christ and the apostles. Now, in the shaping of what they prayed would be a Christian republic, they relied on the moral authority the Scriptures exerted over the consciences of persons who believed they had found through their teachings the experience of salvation.

By the eve of the Civil War, the influence of biblical ideas in American culture was evident on every hand. As popular literature expanded beyond the explicitly religious forms of sermons, devotional manuals, and Sunday school lessons, American authors drew upon a common store of biblical narratives, poetry, ethical teachings, and apocalyptic visions— what Northrop Frye has called *The Great Code*. Popular writers embraced ancient Hebrew and Christian assumptions about human sin and its punishment in this life and the next and the promise and rewards of righteousness. Numerous studies of school textbooks, travel guides, children's literature, newspaper editorials, and political oratory make this point clear, as do analyses of such things as self-help books, women's magazines, and Catholic novels. Intellectual historians have found biblical ideals pervasive also in the learned worlds of law, literature, science, and moral philosophy. Ralph Waldo Emerson, Louis Agassiz, and Herman Melville were as notable examples of biblicism as Nathaniel Hawthorne, Frances Wayland, and Mark Hopkins. The rhetoric and the moral substance of court decisions and the speeches of such statesmen as John C. Calhoun, Daniel Webster, and Abraham Lincoln employed biblical teachings as vehicles of persuasion, certainly, if not always as sources of thought. Both defenders of the new industrialist class and champions of the workers whom they oppressed appealed to Moses and Jesus, as did the college men who lectured on political economy. And Americans who dreamed of the steady progress of their society toward the goals of justice and mutual love stated their ideology in millennial rhetoric drawn from the prophecy of Isaiah and the preaching of John the Baptist. The first generation of professional engineers, as Raymond Merritt has shown, built bridges, railway tunnels, water systems, and ocean docks in the conviction that commerce, science, education, democracy, and evangelical religion were engines of human progress set in motion by divine providence.

The "civil religion" of nineteenth-century America, displayed most profoundly in the later speeches of Abraham Lincoln, was cast in biblical terms. It found ready acceptance on all sides because it seemed in accord with the evangelical consensus about faith and ethics. True, Romanticism, flowing into the new nation from German and English sources but also generated in North American situations, drew deeply upon the spiritualizing tendencies of Platonic thought. But the Bible's Hebraic realism about social injustice and individual sin, about the human need for health, a good conscience, reward for toil, and the faithfulness of love, I think, was a far more powerful source of liberal political convictions.

In retrospect, this towering preeminence of the Bible over past traditions, whether social, cultural, or religious, also opened the way for Jews and Roman Catholics to embrace the nation's ideals. Leaders of the German Jewish communities saw this earliest, I believe. During and just after the Civil War, Isaac Mayer Wise was able to draw together the majority of American rabbis in a movement called Reform Judaism. Wise's profound engagement with Scripture, his emphasis upon the Mosaic sources of law (rather outweighing, I think, his appreciation of the ethical idealism of the prophets), and his conviction that the mission of the Jews was to share both the ethics and the spirituality of Judaism with the non-Jewish world, were the life and breath of Reform. He did not perceive his movement to represent either Americanization or secularization, but a restoration of the essence of the law of Moses (to love God with all your heart and soul and strength, and to love your neighbor as yourself) and a recovery of the prophets' vision of a new age of the spirit in which justice would pour down the mountainsides like a river. When, toward the end of the century, Conservative rabbis reacted against the accelerating pace of accommodations to modern culture, they also appealed to Scripture, and in a manner that Protestant evangelicals understood. In 1902, Cyrus Adler persuaded young Solomon Schechter, a native of Romania and a lecturer in Jewish studies at Cambridge University, to come to New York City to head the Jewish Theological Seminary of America, and Conservative Jews found a leader. Schechter understood very well that the immense scholarship invested in studies of the Hebrew Bible during the previous hundred years opened the door to full Jewish participation in America's biblical culture. At the dedication of the new seminary building in 1903, Schechter declared that the United States was "a creation of the Bible, particularly of the Old Testament." Jews could not only feel at home here, they could teach the nation about God's covenant with them and his promise for all humankind.

A parallel but less fully developed tendency appeared in Roman Catholic circles. Here, also, such early leaders as Bishop John England, of Charleston, South Carolina, had affirmed American liberty, appealing to its biblical foundations. At mid-century, former Methodist Isaac Hecker and one of Charles G. Finney's converts, Clarence Walworth, were converted to Catholicism. They studied in Rome, then returned to New York to found the Paulist Fathers, devoted to preaching an intensely ethical and spiritual version of Catholic faith to Protestant Americans. I think some recent students of Hecker have overemphasized the Methodistic character of his spirituality, particularly his preoccupation with sanctification. There seems little doubt, however, that the "Americanist" party among the Roman Catholic bishops recognized that a common scriptural foundation promised a growing rapprochement with Protestant America, despite the bitter history of anti-Catholic attitudes in the young nation.

Perhaps pointing out a small moral is now in order. Those who still believe that America offers something valuable to the future of the world should nurture here a pluralism that encourages each religious group to affirm its own faith and declare it to all humankind. All of us should rejoice in whatever good we can find in the others. And all of us need all the help we can get in moving our race off its present suicidal course toward the righteousness and *shalom* that is the work of the Spirit of God.

RELIGIOUS EXPERIENCE AND MORAL COMMITMENT

The experience of the new birth, which became an important theme in most denominations, endowed American idealism with the expectation of individual moral transformation. By the middle of the nineteenth century, the notion that young adults would pass through a period of heightened guilt over their moral inadequacies and find that guilt resolved in a crucial experience of faith or moral commitment was pervasive. Nonreligious sources of such an expectation, of course, are easy to identify, as a glance at Benjamin Franklin's *Autobiography* brings to mind. But can we imagine that Franklin did not bring to his self-examination and commitment to self-discipline memories of the Puritan expectation of regenerating grace? Moralism in America has never been far removed from piety; and among the vast company of diverse evangelicals, it seemed organically connected to it, as fruit to a vine.

The ethical significance of the experience of the new birth in nineteenth-century Christianity needs reemphasis. For in the twentieth century popular preaching in many denominations minimized the notion of transforming grace and thus made room for a relaxation of moral discipline. Calvinistic evangelists from George Whitefield to Dwight Moody and pastors from Timothy Dwight to R. E. Torrey proclaimed that to be born again was to be freed not only form the guilt of sin but from bondage to its power, very much as Wesleyans did. The Holy Spirit who gave believers "new life in Christ" would lead them in the paths of righteousness. Young William Ellery Channing passed through just such an experience shortly after his graduation from Harvard in 1803. At an opposite pole, in Church of the Brethren circles, young people were not expected to seek to be born again until their early twenties. At the end of a period of repentance and reflection that might last as much as six months, they found themselves able to trust in the redeeming power of Christ, confessed their faith, and committed themselves to the standards of behavior that this German Baptist denomination had practiced since the seventeenth century.

The experience of regeneration thus served as a moral "rite of passage" into the assumption of adult ethical responsibility. Nineteenth-century preachers, from Horace Bushnell to the priests who conducted preaching missions in Roman Catholic parishes, rarely failed to insist, as Moses and Jesus had, that loving God is inseparable from loving one's neighbor. The disengagement of these two summary commandments began only when the moral crusade against slavery produced among its defenders a "spiritual" definition of salvation. Thereafter, Southern evangelicals— Presbyterians, Baptists, Lutherans, and, after a time, Methodists—gradually confined their moral concerns to abstinence from alcoholic beverages, gambling, illicit sex, theatergoing, and the like.

Seen thus in its actual nineteenth-century understanding, the experience of the new birth was a spiritual catalyst of major social movements, as I and many other historians have long argued was the case. Gordon S. Wood, in his powerful reinterpretation of the movement for American independence, stressed the moral seriousness of the quest of virtue in republican ideology, and rooted it not only in evangelical but in Enlightenment thought. My colleague John Pocock described and gently derided the emergence of the idea of public virtue with the phrase "a Machiavellian moment." I think, however, that the widespread devotion to the Hebrew Scriptures among colonial evangelicals of nearly all traditions, and their embrace of the idea of the new birth on the moral terms that John Wesley and George Whitefield laid out, suggests a better phrase: "the Mosaic moment." The alliance between evangelicals and deists in the early stages of the revolutionary movement rested, as I see it, on a more solid foundation than some have believed, namely, the commitment of both parties to an ethic that was thoroughly biblical, even when defended on rational grounds. Thomas Jefferson's famous truncation of the ethical teachings of the New Testament in his "Bible" illustrates this fact.

In this light, I think, we can understand better the spiritual sources of the moral crusades of the nineteenth century, whether for common schools, against slavery, or for justice to the poor. Charles G. Finney and those who followed in his train insisted that their first ministry must be the conversion of sinners. For such conversion promised both the moral renewal of individuals and the presence and power of God to sustain Christians in a crusade for justice. Charles Howard Hopkins wrote in his *Rise of the Social Gospel* that despite the emergence in that movement of a corporate ideology, its fundamental method remained throughout the consecration of individuals and their resources to the will of God.

Such a view of conversion was accessible to both Roman Catholics and

Jews; for it was rooted in the stories of decisive moral change that permeate the Hebrew as well as the Christian Scriptures. Jay Dolan's recent volume, *Catholic Revivalism,* shows that such an experience was what the Redemptorist priests aimed at in preaching missions in German Catholic parishes, using sermons and appeals developed for such missioners during preceding decades in Germany. Isaac Hecker's Paulist fathers sought the conversion of Protestants by stressing the intensely moral character of the life that was rooted in the sacraments and the spirituality of the Roman Catholic Church. Meanwhile, Reform rabbis who preached the spiritual and ethical mission of Judaism to Gentile culture often found the men of their congregations preoccupied with material success and the social advancement of their families. Especially in the solemn occasions of the Day of Atonement, but at other times as well, they called them back to the supreme dedication to the kingdom of God that the prophets had demanded. In Jewish understanding, that kingdom sought both justice in society and the moral perfection of individuals. At the end of the century, the leaders of the National Council of Jewish Women thought that teaching children, as one of them put it, "loving dependence upon the Creator, begotten of that sense of intimate relationship with him which constitutes the essence of spirituality," was the highest goal of religious education. The persistence of notions of dramatic moral transformation into our own times is apparent among such Jewish novelists as Bernard Malamud, whose novel, *A New Life,* records the frustration of one man's hope for a new beginning.

THE IDEOLOGY OF THE KINGDOM OF GOD ON EARTH

During the past thirty years, the discovery and widespread study of the significance of millennialism in nineteenth-century America have yielded both affirmative and negative interpretations. But no one has questioned the close link of millennial ideology with mid-century evangelism or with the social vision that permeated Protestant Christianity in the decades after 1880. I have learned recently, with the help of two of my students, that millennial hopes also sparked the missionary and evangelistic movements that after 1795 spread from New York and Connecticut into the western frontier and throughout the nation. The notion of perfecting society, like the idea of the spiritual and moral perfection of individuals, was integral to these hopes, though more their result, I now believe, than their cause.

Two points remain unstressed, however. The first is the Hebraic character of the millennial vision, both during the early years of the nineteenth century as well as in the later social gospel movement. Only recently have scholars begun to grasp the broadly Hebraic character of the New Testament. The Hebrew sensibility, as contrasted with that of Hellenic Platonism, stressed the wholeness of human beings, the unity of their psychic and physical existence, and the bonds that link social experience to inward spirituality. The salvation promised in Torah, in the prophets, and in the Christian gospel reflects these outlooks: it offers to redeem both the bodies and the souls of individuals and the societies and cultures that nurture them. Biblical ethics, therefore, both Jewish and Christian, never divorce spirituality from acting justly (the literal meaning of the Hebrew word translated into English as "charity") on behalf of the poor or oppressed. The biblical idea of the millennium that such evangelicals as Samuel Hopkins and Methodist Gilbert Haven proclaimed, therefore, was a social and political as well as a spiritual one.

Methodists, in particular, found this view sustained whenever they read John Wesley, which was most of the time. Wesley's salvation theology was grounded in the prophetic promise of the renewal of all creation that is to climax the age of the Spirit. In that day, all of created nature, like all human beings who in faith have embraced God's covenant of holiness, are to be made new in the perfection of the first creation, and heaven is to begin on earth. Edward Hopper's famous folk painting "The Peaceable Kingdom" caught the imagination of Americans precisely because it pictured so simply the least believable biblical symbol of that hope: lambs lying down with lions, and sleeping very well at night. The conviction that millennial theology was realistic social ideology was not in the eyes of nineteenth-century evangelicals a distortion or diffusion of the biblical sources, but a straightforward exposition of them. God's kingdom must prevail, cried Catherine Booth, cofounder with her husband of the Salvation Army, until divine grace has conquered not only all evil in human hearts but all injustice in human societies.

The other neglected point is the ecumenical character of millennial ideology: its proponents believed it to be a promise to the entire inhabited world. To be sure, from the time of the earliest settlement of America, Christians thought a special divine providence was at work in the opening of these new and unspoiled lands, and some of them saw a special mission for the United States in bringing forward the kingdom of God. Historians have made a great deal of a few scattered statements by Jonathan Edwards and others suggesting that America, the "new Canaan," was to be the center of the coming kingdom, and that the new Jerusalem would be located somewhere here. But the literature of early nineteenth-century millennialism, read systematically, constantly affirmed that the promises of the kingdom were for the entire human race. All parties insisted that God's redeeming purposes included not simply the "new Israel" of the Christian church, but the Jews as a people. Even such a theological maverick as Joseph Smith, founder of the Church of Jesus Christ of the Latter-day Saints, taught that the New Jerusalem was to be built on the ruins of the Old.

This inclusive millennial vision inspired and sustained the foreign mission movement of the nineteenth century, not only in the United States, but in England, Scandinavia, and Germany as well. Its consequences are evident everywhere today—in Africa, Southeast Asia, and, as the Hebrew prophets had foreseen, "the islands of the sea." Demographers and futurists predict that sub-Saharan Africa will soon be the most Christianized of all the great populated regions of the world; and recent developments in South Korea and Indonesia sustain predictions of a similar outcome in much of the Orient as well.

Moreover, it is clear that the millennial ideal of theocracy permeated evangelism in this country as well as overseas. God would rule as the revelation of his steadfast love and the power of his sanctifying Spirit brought sinful persons into submission to his will. Christian missionaries, at home and abroad, did not think military or political power could be used to further the kingdom of God. Most of them believed, however, that the growth of democracy in America and its spread to other nations would enable the future Christian majority to act in love and justice to produce a righteous society. Government of, by, and for the people, as Lincoln put it, was the hope of the earth. Evangelicals also believed that God was using other developments to move humanity toward the millennium: universal public education, advancements in science and invention, the liberation of women, and the prosperity stemming from international trade. Robert Frykenberg's account of how Christian missionaries to India in the eighteenth century resisted the conspiracy between the British East India Company and the Brahmin masters of that land to suppress the aspirations of the untouchables joins other recent studies to demonstrate the consistency between biblical, evangelical, and missionary ideology.

Millennial ideology was one source of interfaith pluralism. The notion of the transformation of society into a kingdom of justice and love was never far from the center of Jewish religious thought, whether in the universalist idealism of Reform, in the messianism that flowed out of medieval mysticism and spirituality, or in what Judah L. Magnes called spiritual Zionism. Magnes, who was from 1904 to 1909 associate rabbi of the nation's most eminent Reform congregation, Temple Emmanu-El, in New York City, discovered this fact during three previous years of study and spiritual reflection in Germany and central Europe. He became at once both an uncompromising religious Zionist and the champion of what Christians might call a Hebrew social gospel. Rabbi Magnes spent the years after 1909 as head and guiding spirit of a communal movement that sought to unite all of New York City's Jews. He then moved by stages toward settling in the Holy Land, where he wound up as the long-time chancellor of the Hebrew University of Jerusalem. In 1907, Magnes was convinced that he stood biblically, morally, and spiritually on the same ground Isaac Mayer Wise had occupied fifty years before. Unlike Wise, however, he believed the mission of Jews to humankind must begin with a revitalization of their own faith and hope. He thought the Kehillah movement in New York and the establishment of a homeland in Palestine would help bring the Jews of the world, from Hasidic and Orthodox to the most radical party of Reform, to renew the covenant of righteous love. That covenant would bring holiness not only to their inner life but to all their relationships with non-Jewish peoples, including the Palestinian Arabs.

Ought we not to compare Magnes, whose eventual commitment to pacifism matched his love for Zion, with his great evangelical Protestant contemporary, John R. Mott? Mott became a leader in the Student Volunteer Movement and organized the World Christian Student Federation. He helped to shape the moral vision of God's rule on earth that revitalized the ecumenical movement and eventually brought Protestant and Eastern Orthodox Christians together in the World Council of Churches. Although popes John XXIII and John Paul II arrived late on this ecumenical scene—so late as to discover Protestant and Orthodox Christianity and Judaism as well in general retreat from the idea of a kingdom of God on earth—ought we not to regard them as in fact standing in the same tradition as Mott and Magnes and such beloved Eastern Orthodox ecumenists as Alexander Florovsky and Alexander Schmemann? If all this seems far-fetched to you, I submit that one accomplishment of evangelical Protestants in nineteenth-century Canadian and American culture was to lay the foundations for what they hoped would become in the twentieth a steady march toward peace and justice on earth. That hope called for shared commitment to biblical ethics and a shared confidence in the faithfulness of the Holy One of Israel. It made no place at all for the balancing of nuclear armaments and the manipulation of national economic interests that pass for peacemaking in our tragic times.

If this chapter, or sermon, or rabbinical discourse is to close, as all such declarations should, with an exhortation, mine is this: your first duty is to be truly what you are, to drink again from the wells dug by your father Abraham, to let the Holy Scriptures speak their persisting message of *shalom* to your own mind and heart. If you will, the evangelical Christians and Jews you represent or can influence may learn how to stand together on biblical principles of righteousness. And if that happens, the leaders of not only North America and Israel but of the nations we fear may find a way out of our present social, moral, and political darkness into the dawning light of a new age.

Understanding the Chapter

1. What three characteristics of evangelicalism does Smith consider to be the "distinguishing marks" of the evangelical movement from its origin?

2. Smith singles out three eastern American cities that remain to this day "classic models of North America's religious pluralism." What are these cities? Can you suggest any other significant examples?

3. What ideas in evangelical theology led nineteenth-century evangelical leaders to endorse the principle of church-state separation?

4. How did biblical ideas, in Smith's view, provide an intellectual setting in which religious diversity and cultural pluralism could be affirmed?

5. How did America as a "biblical culture" enable Jews and Catholics to participate in society?

6. Smith gives some practical application for the future direction of pluralism in America by stating that Americans "should nurture here a pluralism that encourages each religious group to affirm its own faith and declare it to all humankind. All of us should rejoice in whatever good we can find in the others." Discuss the implications of these statements from both evangelical and Jewish points of view.

7. In nineteenth-century Christianity, what experience cited by Smith served both as a moral "rite of passage" for the assuming of ethical responsibility of adulthood and as a spiritual catalyst of major social movements?

8. Describe what Smith means by "the Hebraic character of the millennial vision." What factors have tended to cause Christians to separate social and political concerns from the world of the spiritual?

9. How did the vision of Rabbi Judah Magnes and his move for "spiritual Zionism" contribute to interfaith pluralism and the millennial ideology found in Protestant evangelicalism?

10. Do you agree with Smith's thesis that evangelical Christianity has contributed to democratic pluralism?

11. In his closing exhortation, what does Smith say is the first duty of both evangelicals and Jews so that they may "learn how to stand together" with the hope of influencing others so that the nations of the world may be brought from darkness to the light of a new age?

7

What and How Evangelicals Teach about Jews and Judaism

DAVID A. RAUSCH

It seems a bit presumptuous to be tackling a topic such as this, in light of the breadth of the movement referred to as evangelicalism. The plethora of theological and social stances haphazardly woven into this patchwork quilt are often competitors and, sometimes, combatants. From Pietist pacifists to Reformed militants, from Arminians to Calvinists, the turbulent sea of evangelicalism reminds the scholar of Judaica of the great differences within Judaism itself. That is why a topic such as this one *must* be assigned and not chosen.

Because of the nature of my research interests, a good deal of evangelical literature crosses my desk, much of it pertaining to attitudes toward the Jewish community. Over the years, I have tried to catch a glimpse of this "perception of the other," and what I relate to you today is one scholar's view of this phenomenon.

I should state at the outset that a large portion of the evangelical movement historically has had a special regard for the Jewish people and holds them in high esteem to this very day. Believing that the Jewish Bible is the very Word of God, these evangelicals feel a kinship and identification with the Jewish community that I suppose would surprise (and perhaps petrify) many Jews. Often they will defend and revere Jewish people without having had the remotest personal contact with them. To these evangelicals, the Jewish people are a People of the Book and the People of their Saviour. I have watched a number of these groups entering a synagogue for the first time, listening reverently to the rabbi, and delighting in the prayers. I have seen them travel fifty miles to the nearest "temple" with a Sunday school class or a confirmation class, cherishing the hospitality of the congregation and grasping each moment as if to squeeze every drop of the experience into their being. I have observed students who traveled one hundred miles to share in a Sukkot celebration with a Jewish congregation and with exuberance question when they could attend again. This sympathetic grass roots movement of admiration and appreciation is spread throughout evangelicalism in every state. Its fervency usually transcends that of the professors, writers, and scholars of evangelicalism.

For the evangelical, Sunday school is an important influence from the earliest years of life through adulthood and into the golden years. Considering the scope of this particular study, I chose at the outset to read the materials (from two-year-olds to adult) published by the three major evangelical distributors of Sunday school literature: David C. Cook Publishing Company, Gospel Light Publications, and Scripture Press Publications.[1] As I waded through the student guides and workbooks, the looseleaf handouts, the teacher's manuals, and other curriculum aids, I specifically concentrated on what perceptions they sought to instill in evangelicals about Jews and Judaism. The project proved quite revealing, for it solidified some previous conceptions I held about such literature and enlightened me concerning changes that have occurred in the past decade.

On the positive side, a child can hardly go through this curriculum without cultivating a high regard for the heroes and heroines of the Jewish faith. The Hebrew men and women of faith become the child's examples of faithfulness to God. The errors that the Hebrews made are correlated to the errors that the child makes. The mercy and love of God toward those who make mistakes in the Jewish Scriptures are used as representative of God's mercy and love toward the child. The enemies of the Hebrews are the enemies of God and they, in turn, become the child's enemies. Thus, Primaries (grades 1-2) will discover this spring how the Israelites worked together to rebuild the Temple and Jerusalem, and the teacher will emphasize the importance of working together and worshiping together to celebrate God's goodness (Gospel Light). They will approach this study after exploring the life of King Solomon to ascertain how he used his time and resources wisely and unwisely, the teacher

1. I would like to thank each of these publishing companies for sending me their March-May 1984 materials as soon as they left the press in December (I had access to their earlier publications). Each of the companies seems to be as interested in my findings as I am.

discussing the ways children may wisely use their time, abilities, and possessions. Primary-Juniors (grades 3-4) learn of the life and exploits of Moses, Caleb, and Joshua, finding through the lives of these heroes that God always guides his people if they trust and obey him (David C. Cook). Through lessons on the Israelites' wanderings in the wilderness, students learn how God meets different kinds of needs in their own journey through life. Pre-primaries (four- and five-year-olds) preface a study on the life of Jesus with several weeks on the life of Daniel, David, and Abraham as heroes of the faith (Scripture Press).[2]

There has also been a concentrated effort to eradicate any semblance of the "Christ-killer" theme in these materials. Especially with the younger children, there is not even a hint of Jewish responsibility for the death of Jesus. In fact, Jews are Jesus' friends. Nevertheless, in separate adult study packets where an outside book is used the theme does creep in. Gospel Light, for example, uses Paul E. Pierson's *Themes From Acts*. Pierson is a Presbyterian minister who served as a missionary in Brazil and Portugal for seventeen years. Receiving his M.Div. and Ph.D. from Princeton Theological Seminary, he was pastor of the First Presbyterian Church of Fresno, California, for seven years and is currently dean of the School of World Mission at Fuller Theological Seminary. Dealing with Peter's message in Acts 2, Pierson writes: "Yet the Jews, led by their priests, had engineered His condemnation and handed Jesus over to pagan rulers to be crucified. But even though they were guilty of His death, they had unconsciously fulfilled the purpose of God. He had revealed through His prophets that the Messiah should suffer and die for the sins of many."[3] One has to wonder what images of Jews and Judaism such statements engender in the mind of the average adult.

Pierson continues:

> Martin Luther often said we must hear the bad news before we can hear the Good News. Peter's message, if true, must have appeared to be the worst possible news to the crowd. They and their leaders had not only rejected the long-awaited Messiah; they had put themselves clearly in opposition to God by crucifying Him! Was it any wonder they were cut to the heart and cried for help!

2. Surveys of Hebrew men and women of faith as well as the Jewish biblical books abound in both elective and regular curriculum during the Fall and Winter quarters. Each publishing company puts a high priority on these studies for all ages.

3. Paul E. Pierson, *Themes From Acts* (Ventura, Calif.: Gospel Light Regal Books, 1982), 29-30.

Peter's message is a marvelous example of the preaching of the cross. His hearers realized as never before the depth of sin and its effects. It was both collective and individual, national and personal. Not only had their leaders rejected the Messiah and been responsible for His murder; they too had been personally involved and were responsible. Some who were there had no doubt been part of the mob which had shouted, "Crucify Him!" Now they felt desperate.

Peter answered their cry with the amazing Good News. They were not lost; they were not irrevocably rejected by God. Through repentance and faith in this crucified Messiah they would receive two gifts greater than any they had ever hoped for.[4]

For Pierson, the first gift was "the forgiveness of their sins" (the "greatest" of which was "complicity in the death of Jesus"). "It was an indication of the greatness of God's power and love," he informs us, "that He could take that seemingly tragic event and make it the means of redemption even for murderers of His Son."[5] The second gift was the Holy Spirit.

While one could make a strong case that Dr. Pierson is not anti-Semitic, his book (as so many others) lacks sensitivity to the historic problems such statements have caused the Jewish people, and he shirks his responsibility as an educator to correct such impressions.[6] Irresponsible statements that foster negative images about Jews and Judaism are an ever-present danger to the electives offered by evangelical publishers of Sunday school materials. The great number of writers from varied back-

---

4. Ibid., 32-33.

5. Ibid., 33.

6. Cf. W. Robert Cook, *The Theology of John* (Chicago: Moody Press, 1979), 191-92 n.20, for his lengthy explanation of how "it is seen that even though the legal act of execution was performed by a representative of the Roman government the Jews are viewed as those who pierced Christ. Thus the historical fact is given its theological significance and the Jews are thereby seen to have a special accountability for Christ's death." Cook recognized the fact that anti-Semitism has arisen throughout church history, perpetrated by those who have taken the unbiblical charge to punish the Jew, and he emphasizes that "some readers will immediately cry 'anti-Semitism.'" Nevertheless, he avers: "That Israel is accountable in some national sense for Christ's death is a matter of New Testament *and* Old Testament theology. Such is God's evaluation, and He is not anti-Semitic." Cook's rationale, which ends with Jesus' statement, "Father forgive them; for they do not know what they are doing" (Luke 23:34), will be of interest to the reader.

grounds, the demand for the particular subject matter, and, frankly, a
lack of sensitivity to the total problem, combine to form a problem area
likely to remain a long time. I take offense at such inane statements
arising from time to time in this literature, such as Bill Myers' explanation in *Dr. Luke Examines Jesus* (Scripture Press high school elective):
"Since only Jewish money can be used in the temple, the money-changers
are making outrageous profits by changing foreign currency into Jewish
money at sky-high exchange rates."[7] What kind of images does this
produce in the impressionable mind of a teenager?

Evangelical publishers of Sunday school literature have provided
teaching guides of nearly every conceivable kind to facilitate their teachers in accurately portraying the topics of the Bible and to improve teaching techniques. With regard to dangers involved in fostering negative
images of Jews and Judaism, however, these frequent aids are silent.
Positive pointers on engendering proper views toward Jews and eliminat-
ing stereotypes (including the "Christ-killer" theme) from one's class-
room are totally neglected. Because the same Scriptures and proof-texts
are used that have suffered misinterpretation for centuries, the unin-
formed teacher can easily contribute to the propagation of negative images of Jews and Judaism (even unintentionally). Changes in the curriculum in this regard are never brought to the attention of the teacher, and I
have personally viewed the disastrous results. This is unfortunate in light
of some of the fine evangelical scholarship that has sought to enlighten
and enhance proper perceptions of the Jewish community. And lest one
attribute this phenomenon to "narrow biblical bigots," a recent writer for
the National Council of Churches has reported *his* concern over *their*
denominational literature—a concern that parallels mine.[8]

The Sunday school curriculum used by evangelicals is indicative of the
general trends in evangelical literature published today, both positive
and negative. For example, Christians of all generations have used the
word "Pharisee" in the worst connotation possible. Jesus' harsh words to
some religious leaders have been taken out of context and misrepresented. Evangelical literature has fallen into the same trap. Books, articles, pamphlets, and lectures are currently using the word "Pharisee" in

7. Bill Myers, *Dr. Luke Examines Jesus: Want Your Life Changed?* (Wheaton, Ill.:
Scripture Press Victor Books, 1981), 126.

8. Note the statement by David Simpson, director of the NCCC Office for
Christian-Jewish Relations, in *NCCC Chronicles* (Winter 1983): 5.

this misguided fashion, never attempting to understand the ancient movement (and, unfortunately, alluding to modern Judaism as well). Realizing the dearth of accurate and balanced material, I was pleased to see a chart in the David C. Cook materials that sought to explain the Pharisees and their beliefs. My joy was sustained for only a fleeting moment, however, as I realized that the traditional negative connotations permeated the description.[9]

Ironically, many of the Pharisees were the best people of their day, trying to live the life millions of evangelicals want to emulate. They were tenacious defenders of the worship of the one true God and firmly opposed to pagan practices, idolatry, and polytheism. They defended the doctrine of the resurrection of the dead and earnestly asserted that there was recompense for this life in an afterlife. They attempted to imbue the masses with a spirit of holiness; the Gospels and Acts make mention of the virtuous character of such Pharisees as Nicodemus, Gamaliel, Joseph of Arimathea, and the young man Saul (who became the apostle Paul). Knowing and appreciative of the Pharisaic tradition, Jesus warned religious people of all generations about the pitfalls of pride and hypocrisy. By scapegoating the Pharisees of the first century (and, indeed, the entire Jewish population), Christian publications for centuries have missed the very important lessons directed straight at their lives and ministries. There is ample reason to believe that Jesus would use the very same words to segments of evangelical leadership today if he had entered the twentieth century rather than the first. Unfortunately, this lesson has been lost to most evangelicals today, including the seminary graduate who illustrated on a blackboard the difference between Judaism and Christianity to his Sunday school class in this fashion:

JUDAISM	CHRISTIANITY
LAW	GRACE
DEATH	LIFE
PHARISEES	SAINTS
O.T.	N.T.

It is important to note, however, that evangelicals of all ages seem to be very receptive to a proper perspective when taught that perspective

9. The chart, "Pharisees and Sadducees," is found in the Adult Creative Teaching Aids packet, and was to be used with Lesson 2 on March 11, 1984.

(much more so than many other religious groups). They need only to be told (and often ask: "Why didn't someone tell me this before?"). [10]

Christianity has historically insisted that it is the fulfillment of Judaism; that following Jesus the Messiah is better than Judaism. In like manner, Jesus becomes for most evangelicals the full revelation of God, a revelation superseding the "partial" revelation of Judaism. As the Scripture Press Adult Series on the Epistle to the Hebrews states: "Much that was taught in Judaism was basic. These principles are enlarged, filled out, and built on in the fuller revelation of Christianity." [11] A good friend of the Jewish community, Vernon C. Grounds, emphasized this basic message to the readers of *Christianity Today* when he wrote:

> Following the New Testament argument, therefore, as elaborated especially in the Letter to the Hebrews, evangelicals maintain that by the whole Christ event, Judaism *qua* religion has been superseded, its propaedeutic purpose accomplished. Since Messiah has come and offered his culminating sacrifice, there is no temple, no priesthood, no altar, no atonement, no forgiveness, no salvation and no eternal hope in Judaism as a religion. Harsh and grating expressions as to its salvific discontinuity are called for—abrogation, displacement, and negation. Those expressions are set down here, I assure you, with some realization of how harsh and grating they must sound to Jewish ears. [12]

"In short," he concluded, "as James Parkes, the distinguished Anglican scholar who was an authority on Jewish-Christian beliefs and a devoted friend of the Old Covenant people, summarized the relationship between these two biblical faiths, Judaism is 'not an alternative scheme of salvation to Christianity, but a different kind of religion.'" This is a basic teaching among evangelicals that, among other things, guides their appeal for the right to evangelize all groups (including Jews). [13]

10. I have found that these errors are made in liberal as well as conservative congregations in many locations in the United States. It is not just an evangelical problem. However, within the evangelical milieu, I have found a desire to take a positive perspective when given the rationale. This is my experience, and may be disputed in the experience of another.

11. Roy Irving, ed., *Studies in Hebrews,* commentary by Irving L. Jensen, Bible Knowledge Series (Wheaton, Ill.: Scripture Press, 1984), 51.

12. Vernon C. Grounds, "The Delicate Diplomacy of Jewish Christian Dialogue," *Christianity Today* 26 (April 24, 1981): 27.

13. Dr. Grounds' topic in our 1980 conference was "The Problem of Proselytizing: An Evangelical Perspective." This article appears to be based on his paper. Cf.

Although evangelicals are generally more pro-Semitic than those Christians who dispense with the Bible and its Jewish root, they nevertheless have been bombarded continually with and influenced by the same propaganda against the Jewish community that historically has plagued Christendom. Those evangelicals espousing a form of covenantal theology, which argues for a continuity between the Christian and Israelite covenants, face the same danger as the early church fathers, that is, a triumphalism that so thoroughly "Christianizes" the Jewish Scriptures that all sense of Jewish identity is lost and Jewish tradition becomes an object of disdain. Amillennial and postmillennial eschatologies have insisted that the Christian church is the "spiritual Israel" and have often attributed the curses of the Bible to the Jew while assigning the promises to the Christian. Evangelicals of these persuasions constantly must be on guard against repeating the horrors of the past. Premillennial eschatology, a strong belief within fundamentalist evangelicalism, theologically has allowed for a Jewish peoplehood and heritage apart from the Christian church and has maintained an aversion to other eschatologies that would strip the Jewish community of their national rights and their biblical promises. Often influenced by various forms of dispensationalism, this view historically has overcome covenantal problems by stressing that God's covenants are still applicable to the Jewish people and that the Jewish people remain God's chosen people. While greatly supporting the Jewish people and their peoplehood, it has frequently disdained any Christian participation in Jewish practices (except for demonstration purposes) as "Judaizing."[14]

Sadly, when it comes to anti-Semitism or triumphalism, no evangelical (regardless of his or her theological perspective) is immune. The heretical notion that Christians make better doctors, lawyers, or politicians is infesting contemporary Christianity, including evangelicalism.

---

my article, "Paranoia About Fundamentalists?" *Judaism* 28 (Summer 1979): 304-8, where I point out that evangelism should not be blown out of proportion or hinder Jewish relationships with fundamentalist evangelicals.

14. Note David A. Rausch, "A Break with the Past," *United Evangelical Action* 42 (July-Aug. 1983): 8-9 for a short discussion of these theological perspectives and their historical results in Christian-Jewish relationships. On the premillennial movement, see my book, *Zionism Within Early American Fundamentalism, 1878–1918: A Convergence of Two Traditions* (New York: Edwin Mellen Press, 1979). Vol. 4 in the Text and Studies in Religion Series, this book includes chapters on the modern period as well.

This reached the epitome of asininity for me personally when an evangelical seminary professor at a conference suggested that I use Hebrew Christian Holocaust survivors in my Holocaust classes instead of unconverted Jewish Holocaust survivors. He stated that he found their testimonies "much more uplifting" than the "Jewish" testimonies, and he was absolutely positive that I would find this to be true as well. I must confess that I hit the ceiling with regard to his triumphalism and his anti-Semitism. His attitude was not just a momentary lapse, but a way of life. This man is a disgrace to the name "evangelical" (which, by the way, he wears with pride). And it is partially because of individuals such as this that today a growing number of evangelicals are refusing to be labeled as such. By the way, this triumphalistic seminary professor never taught the Holocaust, knew little about it, and did not care to learn any of the lessons it taught.

Evangelical magazines and journals give relatively little information to pastors and lay persons to combat these misconceptions. Since our last meeting together in 1980, a few seminal issues have been dedicated (or partially dedicated) to Jewish-Christian relationships and related themes.[15] For the most part, sporadic articles devote themselves to fostering an understanding of the Jewish community, but are scattered and rare among the voluminous pages of evangelical publications.

Historically, the Hebrew Christian movement has assumed the role of explaining the Jewish community to evangelicals, often in a sympathetic fashion. While imposters and hucksters have appeared in this history, Hebrew Christians were some of the first individuals to point out the deception. Today, however, the Hebrew Christian movement is facing some of its greatest challenges within its own ranks, and because of its historic role of interpretation to the evangelical community, the evangelical community faces danger as well. A few leaders of Hebrew Chris-

---

15. Included in these seminal issues would be the April 24, 1981 issue of *Christianity Today* (which unfortunately featured a three-page article on Christian Retirement Homes on the cover, masking the wealth of material on Jewish-Christian relationships inside), and the July-August 1983 issue of *United Evangelical Action* (which unfortunately featured an inaccurate assessment by a religion writer of the *Chicago Tribune* stating that evangelical-Jewish relations had been "derailed"). Rabbi Marc H. Tanenbaum wrote for the *Christianity Today* issue, and Rabbi Joshua O. Haberman for the *United Evangelical Action* issue. Both of these are popular periodicals. The June 1982 issue of the *Journal of the Evangelical Theological Society* should be considered seminal among scholarly journals.

tian missionary organizations appear to be suffering from "battle fatigue." As incredible as it may seem, their deep "love for the souls" of the Jewish community has turned to contempt and even apparent hatred of Jews and Judaism. One leader began stereotyping the Jews during his evangelistic seminars in the latter 1970s, stating that "many of the key media people are Jewish," and adding that "anything that displeases the Jewish people is very likely to have an effect in the media, television, and newsprint." He was bitter. Some evangelicals picked up the message and were alarmed by his attitude. Later, on a rare occasion when Hebrew Christians happened to be left out of a publication effort featuring Jewish-Christian relationships, he emphasized that *Christian* Jews should be more important to evangelicals than *unconverted* Jews (a message that spelled the death knell for the German Evangelical Church during the early Hitler years). And now, joined by a few other evangelicals, he is attempting to sabotage evangelical-Jewish dialogue by insisting that one *must* compromise the gospel message to dialogue with Jews. He claims that the Jewish community has promoted dialogue with evangelicals to stem the flow of Jewish converts to Christianity—a spurious diatribe at best. How does one help such a man? How does one repair the damage he is doing? Other Hebrew Christians have tried to talk to him, to rationalize with him, but to no avail. Will the evangelical movement capitulate to his message? I don't know. I hope not.[16]

In addition to this superficiality and ignorance, which can infect the teaching of evangelicals, there are dangerous fringe movements on the periphery of evangelicalism that are gaining adherents. In the past few years, many pastors have shared with me their concerns over parishioners who have succumbed to the literature of conspiracy theory and survivalism, much of it maliciously attacking the Jewish people and Israel. British Israelite groups ("Identity" movements) are fostering racism across the United States. Ranging from hard core to soft core, they teach that the ten lost tribes of Israel are the white Anglo-Saxon western peoples who, in turn, are destined to rebuild God's kingdom. Some of the more radical groups claim that Adam and Eve were the parents of only

16. On the historic role of the Hebrew Christian movement in explaining the Jewish community to evangelicals, note Louis Meyer's *Eminent Hebrew Christians of the Nineteenth Century: Brief Biographical Sketches,* ed. with an introduction by David A. Rausch (New York: Edwin Mellen Press, 1983), and David A. Rausch, *Messianic Judaism: Its History, Theology and Polity* (New York: Edwin Mellen Press, 1982).

the white races. These "Two-Seeders" believe the other races to be demonic or subhuman in origin (and this includes Jews). Soft-core groups peddle the slander that the Jews control Communism, the world monetary system, etc., and that the Holocaust did not occur. More and more, they are encouraging evangelicals to read conspiracy tabloids such as *The Spotlight,* published by Liberty Lobby in Washington, D.C. Their success has been so alarming that Pat Robertson told viewers of "The 700 Club" on April 14, 1983 that they should not buy or read the publication, and Jerry Falwell as well has taken *The Spotlight* to task.[17]

Nevertheless, as its Letters to the Editor section suggests, *The Spotlight* has some evangelical readers among its subscribers. These individuals are zealously evangelistic in disseminating their new-found "truth" from the paper that claims to be "The Paper You Can Trust." For example, two avid readers from Pennsylvania are pastors, one of whom leads the largest church of his denomination in that state. The other recently published a glowing article in his denominational magazine, announcing that his was the *only* evangelical church in town. As I read the article, I noted the marked contrast between his words about the "Lord's accomplishment" and the desire to "do God's bidding" in his community, and his personal conversations and sermons against the Jewish people (e.g., that God was through with them, that the Holocaust did not occur, that there were Jewish plots) and his rabid attitudes toward Israel. In an endeavor to show him the dangers of *The Spotlight,* an article from the publication was sent to him that featured the former grand wizard of the Knights of the Ku Klux Klan (Metarie, Louisiana), David Duke. *The Spotlight* had neglected to tell its readers (including this preacher) of Duke's notorious background. To prove to the preacher that indeed Duke was a Klansman, an identical picture from a newspaper article about the KKK was included for his inspection and response. He refused to respond.

It is incredible how naive members caught up in various movements can be, and I am very concerned about the gullible, face-value acceptance of statements published by these tabloids. A member of the Christian Reconstructionist movement (sometimes referred to as Theonomists) was asked by another evangelical why he read *The Spotlight.* When questioned whether or not it was racist, he answered: "I never noticed. I read it for the economics."(!) He has since "noticed" that it is "racist." I would be

---

17. I discuss these modern racist movements and their effects in my book *A Legacy of Hatred: Why Christians Must Not Forget the Holocaust* (Chicago: Moody Press, 1984).

amiss if I did not mention that I have grave reservations about this very same Christian Reconstructionist movement that is a fringe movement of Reformed theology (and yet claims to be the true adherents of the evangelical Reformed faith). It may be the only faint hope for a resurgence of postmillennial eschatology on the evangelical scene today, and I consider it a very dangerous movement. Unlike Jerry Falwell and the Moral Majority who insist they are not attempting to institute a "Christian" society, leaders and members of the Christian Reconstruction movement unabashedly campaign to "reinstitute God's Law" and to turn the United States into a "Christian Nation." They believe that in relation to God's Law and Christian society, the Byzantines had some positive ideas, Calvin's Geneva progressed the idea further, and the Puritans had a "better idea." Their goal is "dominion" by Christians of their mentality, and they insist that the "case laws of the Old Testament" should be enforced (as limited in scope by their Christian interpretation of the Bible). Unfortunately, their particular covenant theology is deceiving people in the area of morality. I will never forget a leader's response to a question from the audience to which he was lecturing. "If you obtain your Christian society run by your Christian lawyers," it was asked, "what happens to unbelievers?" "They will be allowed to live in our society," he responded, "*if* they quietly keep their beliefs to themselves." Ironically, while despising communism and socialism, these men and women exhibit a Social Darwinism, a survival-of-the-fittest ethic, which is preposterous. One can readily conjecture the danger the Jewish community would face under such a "system" and, as history teaches, the danger many Christians would also face.

In light of the positive *and* negative perceptions concerning Jews and Judaism related in this brief analysis of the broad and complex evangelical movement, what concrete suggestions might a researcher propose to aid in fostering more positive perceptions in the future? First, if Jewish people are important to evangelicals and if it is realized that the historic danger of anti-Semitism is not only on the horizon but also present in the body of evangelicalism, there must be a forthright attempt to communicate and educate the teachings of contemporary Judaism as well as historic Judaism. I believe that this is the responsibility of evangelical publishing houses, whether they be committed to books, periodicals, or Sunday school materials. Evangelicals know little about Jews and Judaism, and they must become familiar with the terrain if proper perceptions are to be cultivated. It is indeed depressing that while evangelicals and Jews on the leadership level are just "coming of age," books and articles are beginning to appear fearful that each group will get to know the other too well. The surface is just being scratched on understanding and friendship, and these educators (who know even less about Jews) are decrying the endeavor before viable learning takes place. With regard to Sunday school materials, the possibility of anti-Semitic perceptions must be faced and teachers given some guidelines written by sensitive and knowledgeable evangelical leaders. For example, illustrations of how modern forms of Jewish worship convey the historic traditions (such as Passover, Shavuot, etc.) in an introduction to a lesson would not only be helpful in this regard but also enlightening to the student. Evangelicals across the United States are interested in Jewish tradition, yet many of their respected publishers have failed at this point. I believe a Sunday school elective devoted to understanding your Jewish neighbor is not at all out of line. However, the publisher must be careful to get someone who understands the Jewish milieu; and in our day that someone is not necessarily a Hebrew Christian.[18]

Second, evangelicals must be alert to the dangerous groups that abound. It is the responsibility of a vigilant evangelical leadership not only to protect their constituency but to protect the Jewish community (and other communities) as well. Only in this way will religious freedom be protected in our country. This responsibility includes putting ideas that sound "reasonable," "biblical," and "logical" to the evangelical mind into a proper perspective. The evangelical press has to spend more time in this endeavor.

Third, in this same vein, I believe that the study of the Holocaust should be instituted into the curriculum of evangelical institutions, including liberal arts colleges and seminaries. The Holocaust is a case study that provides a springboard for understanding the ramifications of all religious and racial prejudice, honing the student's perceptions in an amazing fashion. Its careful study is absolutely essential for the furtherance of evangelical-Jewish relationships. Usually until it is tried in an evangelical institution, neither the administration nor the faculty has any comprehension of the valuable asset of such a course. Lives are

---

18. As I point out in *Messianic Judaism,* the large majority of Hebrew Christians and Messianic Jews do not understand the Jewish milieu at present. A few within both groups are currently making great strides, but it is a definite mistake to believe that a modern Jewish convert to Christianity knows a great deal about Judaism.

changed for the better; students develop moral perceptions and critical skills that will continue with them throughout life. In addition, they then minister their learning to a thirsty and vulnerable Christian public.

Fourth, I strongly recommend that dialogue be maintained and that evangelicals and Jews continue to get to know one another personally. This should occur not only at the leadership level but also on the grass roots level (and it is occurring!). Friendship does dispel caricature, stereotype, and distorted views. Such interaction should be nurtured and misperceptions as to its efficacy should be laid to rest by a more knowledgeable evangelical leadership. I believe that it is also the obligation of an informed leadership to provide the materials and opportunities to enhance and engender such interaction.

Relationships between evangelicals and Jews are stronger today than at any other time in history. This is due in large part to the concentrated efforts of segments of both communities, and the tensions that I have related should not detract from this endeavor. Perceptions should be honestly discussed (the repulsive as well as the attractive) in the hope of strengthening mutual understanding and respect. The dangers facing the evangelical community today are really no different from those found within more liberal churches and organizations,[19] and evangelicals may have stronger resources than other groups in combating them. At this critical juncture, the prospects look promising; the perceptions portent.

Understanding the Chapter

1. Rausch raises the "Christ-killer" theme found in Sunday school literature. Discuss the following: (a) What do the Gospels teach as to who was responsible? (b) What difference, if any, do you feel this should make today? (c) What is implied by the charge of "corporate guilt"? (d) What potential impact on the problem of anti-Semitism today does the handling of the crucifixion narrative by Christian teachers have?

2. How does Rausch say the word "Pharisee" has been misrepresented in evangelical literature?

---

19. Liberal Christianity is plagued by radical movements of the right *and* the left. As Walter Rauschenbusch found in his propagation of the social gospel, theological liberals are not necessarily *social* liberals. I have found the plague of racism and proponents of hate literature within the most liberal of congregations.

3. Christians have sought to scapegoat all Pharisees—and hence Jews as a people—as hypocritical and proud, based on certain texts in the Gospels. Accordingly, comment on Rausch's statement, "There is ample reason to believe that Jesus would use the very same words to segments of evangelical leadership today if he had entered the twentieth century rather than the first."

4. Rausch cites the seminary graduate who illustrated on a blackboard the difference between Judaism and Christianity to his Sunday school class. He did this by using the terms *law* and *grace, death* and *life, Pharisees* and *saints, Old Testament* and *New Testament.* Take each set of alleged "opposites" above and point out the dangers or errors inherent in this approach.

5. What are the positive aspects of evangelical curricula dealing with Jews and Judaism? What are the negative?

6. Are evangelicals any more prone to anti-Semitism than liberal Christians? Are they less prone? Why?

7. Rausch notes that "historically, the Hebrew Christian movement has assumed the role of explaining the Jewish community to evangelicals." What questions does Rausch raise about this approach?

8. What is the thrust of the present-day movement called Christian Reconstructionism (Theonomy)? What impact is this movement bound to have upon the Jewish community and the concept of religious pluralism?

9. Rausch concludes his chapter by pointing out *four* concrete suggestions to aid in fostering more positive perceptions in the future. What are they?

10. What is the main reason Rausch recommends that Jewish-evangelical dialogue be strengthened? Do you agree?

8

What and How Jews Teach about Evangelicals and Christianity

JUDITH H. BANKI

The American Jewish Committee's—and my own—interest in the subject assigned me emerged from a larger concern about the problem of prejudice in religious education that initially focused on Christian teaching about Jews and Judaism. I cannot even begin to address my topic without providing some of the historical background that prompted a series of research projects related to this concern.

It should come as no surprise that Jews long suspected that certain traditions of Christian teaching and preaching about Jews and Judaism constituted a deep and enduring source of anti-Semitism. Such teachings, summarized most succinctly by the French scholar Jules Isaac as "the teaching of comtempt," emphasized certain basic themes, among them: Judaism as a degenerate religion, already ossified at the time of Jesus (echoes of that theme still predominate in the use of the term *late Judaism* to describe what was actually fairly early Judaism); the theme of a carnal people, incapable of understanding their own Scriptures—or anything else—except in a grossly sensual way; the theme of a reprobate people, who rejected Jesus out of willful self-blindness; and perhaps most destructive of all, the theme of a deicide people, the Jews as accursed Christ-killers. Were such things actually being taught to young students in Christian Sunday schools or parochial schools?

AJC's approach to these questions was to stimulate a series of textbook self-studies, which began as early as the 1930s but became more systematic and concentrated in the late '50s and '60s after World War II, when the consequences of unbridled anti-Semitism were laid bare and the need to trace and confront its roots became inescapable.

The Protestant self-study was undertaken at Yale University Divinity

School by Dr. Bernhard Olson, published in book form as the classic *Faith and Prejudice*. A follow-up study, *Portrait of the Elder Brother*, by Gerald Strober, was jointly published by the American Jewish Committee and the National Conference of Christians and Jews. The Catholic self-studies were undertaken at St. Louis University under the direction of Fr. Trafford Maher, and were eventually summarized in Fr. John Pawlikowski's book, *Catechetics and Prejudice*. Dr. Eugene Fisher's follow-up study is felicitously entitled *Faith Without Prejudice*. Additional studies of religious textbooks used in Italy, Spain, France, and Germany have been undertaken at several European universities.

Noblesse oblige! The third branch of our early self-study research was a Jewish textbook project undertaken at Dropsie College under the supervision of Dr. Bernard Weinryb. It explored how Jewish textbooks viewed "outside" racial, ethnic, and religious groups—as well as other Jewish groups. (The Yale and St. Louis studies also investigated racial and ethnic references and inter-Christian attitudes.)

The statistical findings of all the early (late '50s to early '60s) studies are quite out of date; most of the textbooks are no longer used in the schools. But I suspect some of the underlying problems are the same, and I will focus on these.

First, however, we will look at some similarities and differences between Christian and Jewish education that emerge from the textbook studies.

A. SIMILARITIES

1. Whether the religious school is seen as the transmitter of a body of faith, of a set of moral and ethical attitudes, or of group identification and loyalty, the textbooks inevitably stress the *distinctiveness* of the particular faith, perhaps even more so in a pluralistic society like the United States, where diverse religious and cultural groups must assume for themselves the responsibility of transmitting their own heritage. Emphasis on the unique history, values, and beliefs of the "in group" is necessary in order to help separate it from the surrounding community, but it may encourage a defensive or polemical attitude toward the "others."

In addition to stressing its unique tradition, each group will tend to see the larger patterns of history in the light of how they have affected the destiny of the group. Obviously, Roman Catholics and Anglicans have different views of Henry VIII, just as Protestants and Catholics do of Luther. Thus, what Jews may view as positive or negative developments or personalities may not jibe with majority viewpoints. Roman Catholics, for example, view the Islamic conquest of Spain in a negative light, but Jews will tend to view it more affirmatively, because they found more tolerance and acceptance under Moslem rule.

Moreover, each religious community has at some point in history suffered at the hands of others. Recounting these episodes of martyrdom may fulfill important psychological needs. But themes of victimization and persecution also call for the image of an oppressor. This is a problem for all religious groups, but particularly for Jews, who have lived as a minority in Christendom for the past two thousand years, much of the time under duress from Christian ecclesiastical legislation or the policies of Christian rulers.

2. Materials are invariably more positive when they have been explicitly or consciously prepared to describe the faith of others, such as comparative religion textbooks or lessons on intergroup relations, or to point to the common roots for pursuing social justice. Negative images are found where textbook writers may not be aware that their references to others may affect attitudes toward contemporary groups. For Christians, negative content toward Judaism comes when they are expounding their own faith, particularly in lessons dealing with certain New Testament passages and themes, such as the crucifixion, or the early conflict between church and synagogue, or in lessons touching on the Pharisees, to name a few. For Jews, the negative content (toward Christendom, rather than Christianity) comes through telling the history of the Jewish people.

B. DIFFERENCES

1. Perhaps the greatest difference between Jewish and Christian education is that Christianity cannot avoid coming to grips with Judaism on a theological level.

Christianity was originally a Jewish sect. The earliest ideological conflicts between Christians and Jews occurred within the matrix of Judaism. The disavowal of normative Judaism that Jesus was the promised Messiah, and the continuity of Jewry as a corporate community side by side with its daughter (or younger sibling) faith, creates a theological problem—or if not a problem, a challenge—for Christianity. It is impossible to expound Christianity without reference to and comparison with Judaism.

Thus, Christian education requires an encounter with Judaism on doctrinal grounds as well as from the standpoint of history and contemporary relations. Judaism, however, *can* be expounded without theological reference to, or comparison with, Christianity. The Jewish-Christian encounter, as described in Jewish textbooks, is largely social and historical rather than doctrinal and theological. There are some newer comparative religion textbooks, but they represent a very small proportion of the school curriculum, and are descriptive rather than doctrinal.

2. A secondary difference is that much of normative Jewish education requires the teaching of what is a foreign language for all but Israeli Jews—Hebrew. This consumes a great deal of time—60-80 percent at the time of the Dropsie study; probably less now that there are better teaching methods for Hebrew, but still a large chunk of religious school time.

3. A third distinction is that in Christian textbooks, Jews are generally referred to as Jews (with some occasional variations such as Hebrews), whereas in Jewish textbooks, Christians are more often described in terms of their national or ethnic background rather than of their religious identity, such as Poles, Ukrainians, French, or Spanish—unless, of course, the Christian identity is paramount to the event being described.

Some additional information on Jewish education may be of general interest here, and will provide a context for our textbook findings.

Jewish schooling in the United States today is what it has been since the earliest days of Jewish settlement in this country—a voluntary effort of autonomous institutions related to one another more by common aspiration than by ties of formal structure. The vast majority of Jewish schools continue to be linked to synagogues; they are sponsored, maintained, and ultimately controlled by individual congregations. Jewish education is largely supplementary schooling that takes place in midweek afternoon and one-a-day week schools.[1]

Just one decade ago two-thirds of all school-age Jewish children were enrolled in some type of Jewish school. Today—although exact figures

1. Walter I. Ackerman, "Jewish Education Today," in the *American Jewish Yearbook, 1980,* published by the American Jewish Committee and the Jewish Publication Society of America.

are hard to come by—the figure is closer to 40 percent. Moreover, Jewish education is overwhelmingly elementary school level. Eighty-five percent of all Jewish students enrolled in Jewish schools of all types are pre-bar or bat mitzvah. Only 10 to 15 percent of Jewish children continue their Jewish schooling into their high school years. Of those who do elect to continue, most stay on only one to two years. Current estimates of Jewish children who never receive any formal Jewish schooling range from 40 to 60 percent. On the other hand, the all-day school movement has grown remarkably over the last decades. Only 78 such schools existed in 1945. Today, approximately 110,000 Jewish students attend over 540 Jewish all-day schools. The overwhelming majority of these schools are under Orthodox auspices. Eighty-six percent of day schools are Orthodox, only 8 percent are Conservative-sponsored, 5 percent are independent or communally controlled, and 1 percent designate themselves as Reform. Most of the all-day schools provide both a first-rate general education and intensive Jewish instruction. However, only 20 percent of day school students continue to enroll on the post-bar or bat mitzvah level. Congregational supplementary schools, where 70 percent of Jewish students receive their Jewish education, are also declining in enrollment, but it is uncertain how much of this is due to demographic changes, to the extremely low Jewish birth rate, and to the higher median age of the American Jewish community. [2]

With all of this as background, how is Christianity written about in Jewish textbooks? On the primary school level, very little. On the high school level, more explicitly. On the seminary level, Christianity and the Jewish-Christian encounter are taken seriously, and there are some excellent courses, but they tend to focus on specific periods or specific aspects of Jewish-Christian relations; major developments may be omitted by default.

At the outset, it is important to distinguish between textbook treatment of Jesus, Christianity as religion(s), and the church as institution.

On the basis of various studies and my own cursory reading, I would emphasize that Jesus is either neutrally or, more likely, sympathetically depicted; I did not find one hostile reference to Jesus in any Jewish textbook. But they treat Jesus as Jew, that is, not as Messiah nor as the son of God. He is most frequently portrayed as "one of ours," like so many

2. "Jewish Education: Who, What, How," Background Papers in Jewish Education (American Jewish Committee, 1983).

of his countrymen and fellow Jews, a victim of Roman cruelty and political oppression. A few examples will give the flavor:

> Jesus was a Jew and taught the best and the noblest that was in the Jewish tradition. He proclaimed the Shema, and asked the people to love the Lord their God with all their heart and soul and might, and to love their neighbors as themselves. He cured the sick and crowds gathered whenever he appeared in a village or town to hear him speak about God's love. [3]

> There is a great difference between the Jewish Jesus and the Christian Christ. According to Judaism, Jesus was a man, a teacher who taught the ideals of his Jewish faith. He was not the Messiah, because he did not fulfill the messianic expectations. He did not bring an end to Roman tyranny. He did not bring an end to poverty and hatred and ignorance. He was a rabbi, a Jew, touched by the messianic fervor of his time. He lived as a Jew. He died a Jew.

> According to Christianity, Jesus was and is the Messiah, the anointed one, the Christ, the savior who took upon himself the sins of mankind and died so that humanity would be saved. Years after his reported death, there crept into Christianity another belief that was completely un-Jewish. That belief is that Jesus was the only begotten Son of God, that Jesus was God incarnate, made flesh, God come to earth as a man. In time he was made part of the Trinity, which means God in three parts: the Father, the Son and the Holy Spirit or Ghost. [4]

When Christianity in its various forms is described in terms of beliefs, festivals, ceremonies, liturgies, and values, such treatments appear not only sympathetic but empathetic. However, such full-blown treatments are found only in comparative religion textbooks or occasional periodicals. As previously noted, however, there are few such materials, and these have been prepared in full consciousness of the task and with information as a deliberate goal. Since the aim of such materials is to help the Jewish student better to understand his or her own faith in relation to others, the contrasts between Christian and Jewish beliefs are clearly emphasized—as well as the similarities—but not in a polemical sense. Since the authors wish Jewish students to value their own tradition, they

---

3. William Silverman, *Judaism and Christianity* (New York: Behrman House), 93.

4. Ibid., 86.

may occasionally resort to oversimplifications or superficialities in describing Christianity; for the most part, though, these materials strive to be fair. Moreover, they are activity-oriented, suggesting that students read basic Christian documents themselves, visit Catholic and Protestant churches in their communities, and interview priests and ministers. For example:

Prepare a report on Protestantism in your own community. How many different denominations are there and what is the membership of each? What are the distinctive teachings of each, and what beliefs and practices do they share in common?[5]

It is when Christianity is discussed in the context of the temporal power of the church and the anti-Jewish policies that brought so much suffering to Jews across the ages that Jewish textbooks turn heavily critical and negative. The image of the institutional church as oppressor is a formidable one in Jewish history textbooks. Since major patterns of anti-Jewish church legislation, calumnies such as the Blood Libel, massacres in connection with the First Crusade and the Black Death, and enforced disputations took place or had their genesis in pre-Reformation Europe, it is the Roman Catholic Church that bears the brunt of the heaviest criticism, but neither is Luther spared.

We should note that the negative image of the church as *institution* is somewhat balanced by a conscientious effort to acknowledge righteous Christians, both clergy and lay persons, who defended and protected Jews. This is found even in lessons dealing with the medieval period, but is particularly evident in lessons dealing with the Holocaust. Also—a critical point in my judgment—the distinction between Christian, and Nazi, or racist, anti-Semitism is carefully maintained.

In the United States, an important factor in fostering affirmative attitudes toward Christianity is the very strong commitment to religious liberty and to religious and cultural pluralism in Jewish textbooks. One might say that the call for Christian-Jewish understanding and cooperation is in the Jewish self-interest; perhaps so, but it is nevertheless a source of very positive thinking:

It is essential for the survival of our civilization that Judaism and Christianity join hands and hearts together for a great and sacred pur-

5. Miller and Schwartzman, *Our Religion and Our Neighbors* (rev. ed.; New York: Union of American Hebrew Congregations, 1971), 124.

pose. It is a vital necessity for Jews and Christians to recognize and
understand the differences that separate them, but it is even more vital
and more crucial for Jews and Christians to concentrate on the great
ideals and the sacred objectives that unite them. . . . "We are God's
people." Jews will say "that refers to us." Christians will say "that refers
to us," and both will be right.[6]

As noted above, Jewish history textbooks distinguish between Roman
Catholicism, Eastern Orthodoxy, and Protestantism, not so much on the
level of beliefs or doctrines but in descriptions of historical encounters
between these religious groups and the Jewish community. The comparative religion textbooks give a much more detailed treatment of beliefs and practices of Roman Catholicism and of various Protestant
groups. In one such book, this information is incorporated under such
headings as Baptism, Communion, The Protestant Reformation (including mention of Luther, Calvin, Knox and Presbyterianism, Episcopa-
lians, Congregationalists, John Wesley and Methodism, and the Church
of Jesus Christ of the Latter-day Saints), and comparisons of festivals and
holy days. A second commonly used volume provides substantial information about the history and development of various churches and a
digest of "Key American Protestant Denominations," listing, in chart
form, world and U.S. membership, church organization, chief practices,
and major beliefs for some twelve denominations and, also in chart form,
a comparison between key beliefs of Protestants and Jews. (Similar information is provided on Islam, Hinduism, Buddhism, and Confucianism.)

Where are evangelicals in all of this? They are not mentioned as a
separate category. Both *evangelical* and *evangelist* are defined objectively in
a glossary of terms, but information about Protestant groups is by
denomination. Nevertheless, the *theme* of Christian evangelism and the
Jewish response to it is not absent from Jewish education. First of all, it is
there in our history. Efforts to convert Jews to Christianity—frequently
by coercion—and the persecutions and expulsions that followed Jewish
resistance to these efforts run like a thread through much of Jewish
history in Christendom. Given that history, the approach to contemporary Christian conversionary efforts in Jewish educational materials is, in
my judgment, remarkably sensitive and free of bitterness. Christian
missionary approaches to Jews are not denounced or frontally attacked;

6. Silverman, *Judaism and Christianity*, 240-41.

rather, Christian and Jewish views of conversion, mission, salvation, resurrection, and afterlife are compared (the Christian views come from Christian sources) and students are asked to write essays, draw charts, interview ministers, or to role-play in order to clarify the differences. Obviously, there is a defensive purpose here—to reinforce Jewish commitment and Jewish identity—but I found no malice. Describing for teachers the goals of a lesson series on Judaism and Christianity, one Jewish after-school curriculum put it this way:

> The purpose is *not* to denigrate Christianity but to differentiate between Judaism and Christianity. The goal is not resentment, disdain or hatred for either Christianity or Christians but differentiation, disassociation and *internalization* of the conviction that Jewishness cannot be blended with Christianity (i.e. there cannot be a "Jew for Jesus" or a Hebrew Christian for example, because this represents a contradiction in terms). . . . The student, without rancor, should emerge . . . with the conviction that conversion is actually disassociation from Jewishness.[7]

Most of the above excerpts relate to secondary level Jewish education, which, as previously noted, reaches only a small proportion of Jewish students. On the primary level, there is even less reference to Christianity, because of the nature of the curriculum. A Jewish educator told me: "We have the children only three or four hours a week; we have to teach them Hebrew, the holiday cycle, some Bible, some prayers, and a smattering of history in quick outline. You want me to teach them about Christianity? I'm lucky if they learn anything about Judaism!"

Ironically, the same *kind* of argument—albeit on a more scholarly level—militates against expanding teaching about Christianity on the seminary level. Rabbinical school curricula are highly structured, with demanding requirements in rabbinic texts, Bible, Jewish history, philosophy, and literature, as well as proficiency in Hebrew, various courses in professional skills (homiletics, the congregational school, pastoral psychology), and some form of community service. Not surprisingly, it is difficult to elicit support for additions to the current curricula. Jewish seminary education is characterized by an "introversion" that stresses traditional subjects (Talmud, codes, Bible, philosophy, etc.). These

---

7. *A Curriculum for the Afternoon Jewish School,* experimental ed. (New York: United Synagogue Commission on Jewish Education, 1978), 557.

subjects are deemed crucial to maintaining religious Jewish culture, but do not normally involve significant consideration of other religions.

Nevertheless, a survey of the teaching of Christianity and Jewish-Christian relations at major American rabbinical schools, undertaken for AJC by Samuel Weintraub, a rabbinical student at the Jewish Theological Seminary and an intern in our Interreligious Affairs Department, reveals that four seminaries offered at least one course (in all cases elective) with primary emphasis on Jewish-Christian relations or on Christianity per se:

1. At Hebrew Union College—Cincinnati, Michael J. Cook, professor of Intertestamental and Early Christian Literature, regularly offers three courses about Christian origins, history, literature, and beliefs, and their encounter with Judaism. "The Gospels and Book of Acts as Sources for Understanding First-Century Judaism and Christianity" considers the interrelations of Jewish, Christian, and Roman history, as well as the scientific study of the New Testament and selected problems in the Gospels. "The Evolving Jewish and Christian Perspectives on the Historical Jesus" emphasizes modern Jewish and Christian scholarship. "The Citation of Jewish Scripture in Christian Apologetics and Missionizing" investigates Christocentric interpretations of the *Tanach* and historical Jewish responses. History professor Ellis Rivkin teaches "Reconstructing the Intertestamental Period," which develops the Jewish background of early Christianity and examines Hellenistic and Christian texts.

2. At Hebrew Union College—Jewish Institute of Religion (New York), philosophy professor Eugene Borowitz teaches "The Jewish-Christian Encounter," whose selected themes include New Testament attitudes, medieval disputations, contemporary American Jewish-Christian issues, and contemporary Christologies. History professor Martin Cohen offers "Judaism and Christian Beginnings," a course in the Jewish origins and early development of Christianity, and the eventual parting of the ways.

3. At the Bernard Revel Graduate School (Yeshiva University), history professor David Berger teaches "Jewish and Christian Polemics through the Thirteenth Century." Major foci include the classical themes of Jewish-Christian disputations, the relevance of polemic to philosophy and biblical exegesis, and its role in shaping the social and legal relationships of Jews and Christians. History professor Leo Landman offers "Sectarians in the Talmudic Era," a study of the relationship of rabbinic Judaism and the Jewish Christian sectarians of Judea and Babylonia.

4. At the Jewish Theological Seminary, philosophy professor Seymour Siegel and professor Roger Shinn of the neighboring Union Theological Seminary (Protestant, nondenominational) team-teach a course in contemporary issues. Its students, a mixture of JTS and UTS seminarians, utilize writings by Jewish and Christian philosophers and social activists to examine a variety of social concerns.

5. The Reconstructionist Rabbinical College in suburban Philadelphia now offers a course in religion and society by professor John Raines, a Christian ethicist. The faculty also projects a course in the history of Christian thought, also taught by a Christian scholar. To the best of my knowledge, these will be the first such courses in rabbinical schools to be taught entirely by Christians.

Interreligious dimensions are also brought into other courses, for various reasons and in several fashions. In Bible and philosophy, Christian scholarship is occasionally introduced to illuminate a subject. For example, HUC-JIR Bible students study the highly developed Christian scholarship about New Testament canonization in order to understand the roughly parallel process of the Jewish canonization of the *Tanach*. Some professors employ Christian readings to prepare rabbinical students for Christian questions or interpretations of the subject matter. As mentioned above, Christian sources are used in courses regarding social and ethical issues as well.

At four of the seven seminaries, extracurricular programs include a variety of activities with Christian seminaries, such as academic colloquia, informal dialogue groups, social gatherings, and weekend retreats.

In five of the seven seminaries, rabbinical schools share some curricular arrangement with Christian seminaries or with the religion departments of nonsectarian universities. These programs may involve student cross-registration, guest lectureships, or formal arrangements for Christian seminarians to study rabbinic Judaism.

Most of the courses focus on the encounter between Judaism and early Christianity. Here again, there seems little opportunity to teach about contemporary evangelical Christians as a separate category. But the very emphasis on the "parting of the ways," as it were, relates to issues that remain central to the dialogue between evangelical Christians and Jews today.

In sum: formal Jewish education teaches relatively little about contemporary evangelicals as a distinct group. About the *claims* of evangelical Christianity, Jewish education says a bit more. These claims are

Lincoln Christian College

firmly rejected, but they are rejected without malice or invective, and in the context of a powerful affirmation of religious pluralism and the kinship of all humankind.

Understanding the Chapter

1. The "teaching of contempt" identified by Jules Isaac saw Judaism as a degenerate and ossified religion; the Jews as a carnal, reprobate, and deicide people, and Jewish suffering across the ages as divine retribution. Discuss the possible origin of this terminology and where it still may be expressed today.

2. Banki points out that "each religious community has at some point in history suffered at the hands of others." How many historical illustrations of this victimization and persecution can you cite? How many of these same religious communities at some time in history served in the opposite role as oppressor? Why does Banki point to the Jews, who have lived as a minority for two thousand years, as a particular problem in the study of oppression?

3. Banki states that Christianity cannot avoid coming to grips with Judaism on a theological level, but Judaism *can* be expounded without theological reference to, or comparison with, Christianity. In this connection, Banki points out that Jewish textbooks describe the Jewish-Christian encounter in largely social and historical rather than doctrinal and theological terms. Discuss why there is this difference of approach and perception on the part of each group.

4. Much of normative Jewish education requires the teaching of Hebrew, which consumes considerable time. Discuss the pros and cons of Christian education requiring the teaching of Hebrew and/or Greek on the precollege level.

5. Banki notes that Christians are more often described in Jewish textbooks in terms of their national or ethnic identity, i.e., Poles or French, rather than their religious identity. Do you feel this fact promotes, in any way, the widespread confusion that "Gentile" is just another way of referring to "Christian"? Discuss.

6. What do Jewish and Christian textbooks have in common with respect to their treatment of other religious groups?

7. How do Jewish textbooks portray Jesus? Christianity?

8. According to Banki, are the terms *evangelical* or *Christian evangelism*

absent from Jewish education? Discuss Christian and Jewish views of witness, mission, and conversion.

9. What accounts for the manner and degree to which Christianity is taught in Jewish schools?

10. In Jewish seminaries, how much course work in Christianity and Jewish-Christian relations is offered prospective rabbis? What do evangelical seminaries offer students in the understanding of Jews and Judaism? What *is* being done and *ought* to be done to bridge the gaps in this area?

9
The Place of Faith and Grace in Judaism

DAVID R. BLUMENTHAL

In the years after the Holocaust, many people have wondered: How is it possible for a person to be subjected to such an experience and still have faith in God and in his grace? This question was posed to one of the survivors, a Hasidic rabbi, who answered, "Had it not been for the fire of the Divine Presence and faith, I should never have survived the flames of the Holocaust or liberation." As I think about this story, I ask: How can I, who did not know Hitler, speak of faith and grace? Who am I, who have known none of the suffering of my people, to speak on these matters? What right have I, whose faith has never been tested, to represent sainted ancestors, pious brethren, learned rabbis, one million innocent children, and, yes, even God as Jews understand him? I ask their forgiveness and the reader's indulgence.

Furthermore, there is no single understanding of what Judaism teaches on any topic. The tradition is four thousand years old, and many powerful minds and hearts have differed on matters of faith and action. On this occasion and on this topic, it is I who have set forth the teaching, and I ask you who read this to be aware of this limitation.

GRACE

The Jewish concept of grace is bound up with the Hebrew word *ḥesed,* often translated as "grace," "mercy," or "lovingkindness." It has been used of God in three ways and of humankind in one.

Creation is God's first act of grace. We see this clearly at the very beginning of our tradition, in the Bible, in the great psalm of praise, 136: "Give thanks to the Lord, for He is good; His grace *{ḥesed}* endures forever." Following this introductory verse are eight verses praising

God's creative power, each of which ends with the refrain "for His grace endures forever."

The motif of creation as grace recurs in the daily liturgy of rabbinic Judaism before the recitation of the profession of faith (the Shema): "for He alone does mighty acts, performs acts of genesis. . . . He renews in His goodness, each day, the work of creation, as it says, 'to Him Who makes the great lights, for His grace endures forever' (Ps. 136:7)."

This motif occurs again in medieval Jewish philosophy. Maimonides, in his *Guide for the Perplexed* (III:53), wrote: "*Ḥesed* is . . . the exercise of beneficence toward one who has no right at all to claim something from you [or] the exercise of beneficence toward one who deserves it but [who receives] in greater measure than he deserves. . . . Hence, this universe as a whole—I mean, His having brought it into being—is [an act of] *ḥesed*."

Finally, the motif of creation as grace recurs in the Jewish mystical tradition. Levi Yitzhak of Berditchev, a Hasidic rabbi of note, wrote (*Kedushat Levi, Toldot*): "Grace {*ḥesed*} alludes to the spreading outward of the radiance of the Creator, may He be blessed. But, when grace reached to this world, God had to contract it and dim the radiance so that the world would be able to bear it." In all levels of Jewish tradition, then, God's creative act was experienced as an act of grace and given literary and conceptual form as such.

Covenant is God's second act of grace. His covenant has three elements: the Jewish people, the Holy Land, and the Torah. All three are indissolubly linked with his grace, both by the texts and by the logic of his divinity.

Again, the root of this understanding can be found millennia ago, in the Bible. We begin once again in the great psalm of praise, 136. After the eight verses of creation as grace come fifteen verses extolling God's redemption of the Jewish people, each of which ends with the refrain "for His grace endures forever." Note especially verses 21 and 22: "He gave them their land as an inheritance, for His grace endures forever; An inheritance for His people, Israel, for His grace endures forever."

Another very telling biblical source for covenant as grace is the phrase that occurs in Deuteronomy 7:9, 12 and elsewhere: Moses reminds the people that God did not choose the Jews because of their numbers. Rather, because of his love for them and the oath he swore to their forefathers, he took them out of Egypt. Moses continues: "You shall know that the Lord your God is the God, the faithful God, Who watches over the covenant and the grace {*shomer ha-brit veha-ḥesed*}." By linking these two terms with the word "and," Moses clearly means to teach that God is faithful to the covenant that is rooted in grace and/or that God is faithful to the covenant and to the grace that covenant promises. In either case, covenant and grace are inextricably linked.

The motif of covenant as grace also occurs in the later rabbinic, philosophic, and mystical traditions.

A rather straightforward, almost naive, logic underlies this theology: Before the beginning, there was only God. He did not have to do anything; as a result, every act of his was motivated by grace, by the simple desire to reach out from himself. And so, he created—in grace. Having seen creation become corrupt, he again acted, out of no selfish motive but only in order to extend his goodness. And so, he chose a people and a land, and he revealed his will—in grace. These acts are not in response to the needs of humankind. Nor are they in response to a teleology inherent in being. They are one-way acts, by God, toward us, motivated by his own being, independent of our ability to recognize or to respond.

Forgiveness is God's third act of grace. God has not one but two types of forgiveness. One is that which he grants in response to what we have done. This forgiveness flows from his justness and his fairness, and is linked to the covenant. Based on this, the Jew, facing God each day, prays, "Grant us justice in judgment." The other type of forgiveness is that which he grants us even when we do not deserve it. It flows from his grace, and is a one-sided extension of his love. Based on this, the Jew, standing in judgment before God each year on Yom Kippur, prays, "Our Father, our King, have mercy on us and answer us, for we have no good deeds. Act toward us in justness and in grace, and redeem us."

This motif of forgiveness as grace is deeply rooted in the Bible, as in Psalm 33:22: "Let Your grace be upon us, O Lord, in proportion to our longing for You." It is also found in rabbinic Judaism, as in the following commentary to Psalm 119:124 *(Midrash on Psalms):* "'Deal with your servant according to Your grace'—You really do have pleasure in our good works! But, if we have no merit or good works, act towards us in Your *ḥesed.* As you redeemed those of old, not through their works but through Your grace, so may You act toward us."

Perhaps the most beautiful expression of this motif is found in another work by Levi Yitzhak *(Kedushat Levi, Rosh ha-Shana):* When Moses ascended Mt. Sinai to pray for the children of Israel after the sin of the golden calf, God himself came down, wrapped himself in a prayer shawl, and taught Moses a prayer. It reads: "Lord, Lord—God Who loves compassionately and cherishes, Who is patient and overflows with grace and truth. He stores up grace for thousands of generations. He forgives rebellious sin, purposeful sin, and inadvertent sin. He cleanses" (Exod. 34:5-7). Because God taught it to Moses and it was used at the moment of greatest sin in Jewish history, this prayer became central to Jewish liturgy. Significantly, in the penitential prayers of the High Holiday season, composed of a confession of sins preceded by verses from Scripture and liturgical poems, this ultimate invocation of God's grace, as taught to Moses, is set between each group of verses and between the poems; it is the refrain of the penitential liturgy. What, however, do the various terms in this prayer mean? Are they synonymous or do they teach us different things about God?

Levi Yitzhak addresses these questions as follows: To say that God *overflows with grace* is to say that God loves us, irrespective of our merits. This love comes from him because he is God. It is a one-way flow from him to us. It sustains us in our existence. It is a powerful, unconditional love that he has for us. Levi Yitzhak points out, however, that nothing in grace compels God. Nothing in grace is a product of anguish, pain, and suffering.

To say that God is *compassionately loving,* however, is to say nonethelesss that God feels for us, that he is internally affected, that he cannot stand to see us suffer, and that he has a deep desire to do good to us. Love implies empathy, and empathy compels. God, then, is not only "overflowing with grace" but also, and perhaps more importantly, "compassionately loving."

To say that God *cherishes* also implies a degree of relatedness. It implies that we have "found favor" in God's eyes, that he likes us and is attached to us—as a child "finds favor" in the eyes of its parent. We see the face, the body, the person—and we just like it, as a whole. This is not compassionate loving, nor is it grace; it is cherishing, and God cherishes us.

Finally, to say that God is *patient* is to say that he knows us, that he studies our ways and our patterns of behavior and thought. He does not choose to judge us only on the basis of our manifest being. On the contrary, he chooses to blind himself and to see and accept us for what we are, in spite of ourselves.

Thus, according to Levi Yitzhak, there are four kinds of divine love: unconditional one-way love (grace), compassionate empathetic compelling love, love that cherishes being for its own sake, and love that purposely blinds itself to the faults of the other.

If grace can be used of God in three ways—in creation, in covenant, and in forgiveness—it can be used of humans in one way: *For us,* ḥesed *is an act of exceptional kindness and goodness.* We have our social and moral responsibilities, but there is also room in our lives to do acts of grace. These acts of human grace serve to build a protective barrier around sinners. Thus, we speak in the daily liturgy of "the acts of grace of the forefathers." We invoke this "merit of the fathers," these acts of grace by our ancestors, in our plea at the judgment of Yom Kippur. (Note: The rabbis recognized that not all acts of grace are good for us. Some blessings are "mixed." Hence, the same daily liturgy that speaks of "the acts of grace of the forefathers" also reads, "Blessed are You . . . Who grants *good* acts of grace.")

The ultimate act of human grace according to our tradition, the ḥesed shel ʾemet, is burying someone, for the dead can no longer do us favors. To bury a dead person is to act without expectation of any tangible reward.

FAITH

During the Middle Ages, under the influence of Islam and Christianity, Judaism came to understand "faith" as a matter of belief. Quickly, the sage-rabbis distinguished between faith based in reason and faith based on authority. Arabic, the language of early Jewish philosophy, even has two separate roots to denote these two forms of faith. This, however, is not the deepest Jewish understanding of faith.

The deepest Jewish understanding of faith is bound up with the Hebrew word ʾemunah. It begins with our reading of the story of Joshua's fight against Amalek. The Bible tells us that Moses did not participate in the battle directly. He sat on a hill overlooking the battle. When he raised his hands, Israel triumphed, but when he lowered them, Amalek triumphed. Aaron and Hur supported his hands and, the Bible tells us, "his hands were ʾemunah until the setting of the sun" (Exod. 17:12). ʾEmunah, in this context, means "firmness"; this meaning set the tone for the subsequent use of the word. *"Faith" is "faithfulness,"* as our teacher Abraham Joshua Heschel used to say.[1] The biblical verses that support this understanding abound. One of the clearest is the play on words in 2 Chronicles 20:20 (paralleled in Isa. 7:9), *"haʾaminu ba-ʾAdonai . . . veteʾamnu*—Be faithful to God and you will be firmly established."

The word ʾemunah received a special connotation very early in scriptural

1. Abraham Joshua Heschel, *God in Search of Man* (Philadelphia, 1956), 132.

history. In Genesis God comes to Abraham, who is already quite old and childless, and tells him that his seed will be as numerous as the stars in the sky. Abraham does not question this, even though it does not seem very likely. Rather, we are told, "And Abraham had faith in God" (Gen. 15:6). Abraham remained faithful to God in spite of the earthly evidence. This nuance in the meaning of 'emunah, in the understanding of faith as faithfulness, was to remain and prove enduring.

This motif of faith as faithfulness, especially with its contrary-to-fact nuance, recurs in rabbinic thinking. It is well illustrated in the beautiful exegesis of Psalm 31:24 *(Midrash on Psalms):* "'Love the Lord, all His pious ones; God guards faithful ones {'emunim}. [The term "faithful ones"] refers to Israel, who say, 'Blessed is He Who resurrects the dead,' and in faith they answer 'Amen' [a pun with 'emunim], for with all their strength they have faith that He will resurrect the dead, even though it has not yet happened; and they say, 'Blessed is He Who redeems Israel' and answer 'Amen,' even though they are not yet redeemed; and they say, 'Blessed is He Who rebuilds Jerusalem,' and they answer, 'Amen,' even though it is not yet rebuilt." In rabbinic thought, every "Amen" is an affirmation of faithfulness to God and his covenant with the Jewish people.

Faithfulness of God

Faith as faithfulness is not only an attribute of humankind; it is as much a part of God's being as it is of ours. Thus the Bible speaks of God as "faithful" (Deut. 7:9; Jer. 42:5). It is in this context that one must understand those verses that link grace *(ḥesed)* with faithfulness *('emunah):* "to speak at morning of Your grace and at night of Your faithfulness" (Ps. 92:3; cf. Pss. 89:2, 25; 98:3; 100:5). If we push this insight just a bit further and look again to the differentiation Levi Yitzhak makes between "grace" and "compassionate love," we will understand his interpretation of this verse: "at morning"—when we are in daylight and secure—we appreciate "Your grace"; but it is only "at night"—when we are in trouble and oppressed—that we appreciate "Your faithfulness." It is deeper than "Your grace," for it is rooted in covenant, in involvement, and in moral bonding. I should note that, for God, faith as faithfulness also has the nuance of faithfulness despite the evidence. God is faithful to the human race in spite of the clear evidence of its sinfulness, and he is faithful to his people even though the evidence of their waywardness is undeniable.

Faithfulness of Humankind

For God, then, "to be faithful" means to be constantly *engagé*, attached to those acts of grace by which he formed the destiny of the universe: creation, covenant, and forgiveness. What shall we say of humankind? To what are we supposed to be faithful? Or, to put it differently: What does it mean to have faith in God? There are four ways in which we have faith in God.

To have faith in God is first and foremost to hold oneself open to the presence of God, to become aware of him.

> "Faith itself is an event . . . a moment in which the soul of the human being communes with the glory of God. . . . For God is not always silent, and humankind is not always blind. His glory fills the world; His spirit hovers over the waters. There are moments in which, to use a Talmudic phrase, heaven and earth kiss each other; in which there is a lifting of the veil at the horizon of the known, opening a vision of what is eternal in time. . . . 'These words the Lord spoke unto all your assembly on the mountain, out of the midst of the fire, of the cloud, and of the thick darkness, with a great voice that goes on forever'" (Deut. 5:19, with the Targum and rabbinic commentaries).[2]

Second, "faith is sensivity, understanding, engagement, and attachment."[3] Faith is being embarrassed at the vulgarity and the cruelty of the world, being ashamed of humankind's stupidity. Faith is feeling guilty that sin pervades our lives. "In faith, we do not seek to decipher, to articulate in our own terms, but to rise above our wisdom, to think of the world in terms of God, to live in accord with what is relevant to God."[4]

Third, deeds give concreteness to faith. "By enacting the holy on the stage of concrete living, we perceive our kinship with the divine, the presence of the divine. What cannot be grasped in reflection, we comprehend in deeds."[5] *To have faith, then, means to live a life of concrete holiness—in deeds of kindness, in deeds of social conscience, and in deeds of ritual.* This is the true meaning of Law: the em-bodiment of faithfulness, the way to faith. "To a Jew, [to have faith] is to be attached to God, Torah, and Israel." For a Jew, the redemption from Egypt was dependent upon

2. Ibid., 138.
3. Ibid., 154.
4. Ibid., 118.
5. Ibid., 296.

faith; likewise, the future redemption is dependent upon faithfulness to God, Torah, and Israel.

Fourth, life has a strange way of causing us to doubt and to question everything we do. As soon as one takes a stand on any issue, whether intellectual, personal, or social, something in the mind and the heart rebels. *To have faith means to take a position and then to resist those kinds of questions that would bring all one's efforts back to nothing.* To have faith is to affirm and reaffirm one's commitments. It is to draw the baseline of one's personality and say, "This is how it is. This is who I am."

I should like to add here that faith, in the sense of faithfulness, is not at all easy to achieve, for we are not dealing with a single transforming experience that, having happened to us, shapes our lives. Nor are we dealing with an act of intellect or an act of will. *To have faith is to be open, vulnerable.* It is also to wince and to withdraw. For this reason, faithfulness has a plodding quality. It is more stick-to-itiveness than it is power and glory. The key to faith is persistence. In the face of sin—be it outright evil or simple distraction—it is very difficult to persevere in faith. In the presence of temptation—be it desire or disaster—it is difficult to remain faithful. Yet, for the religious Jew, there is only *teshuvah,* repentance or re-turning, as the compass needle always returns toward the north.

CONCLUSIONS

Doubly Reciprocal

Three things strike me about this analysis of grace and faith. First, faith and grace are doubly reciprocal concepts. By this I mean that grace evokes faith and faith evokes grace; that acts of unmerited love call forth acts of faithfulness, while acts of faithfulness call forth acts of unmerited love— in all dimensions of existence. Thus, God loves us in grace and we are faithful to him and, vice versa, we are faithful to him and he loves us in covenantal grace. However, we might also say that, in the realm of internal personal dynamics, we act graciously toward ourselves and in doing so evoke faithfulness from ourselves; vice versa, we act in faithfulness toward ourselves and in doing so evoke acts of grace from ourselves. We might even say of God that he too acts in grace toward himself, evoking his own faithfulness; vice versa, he acts in faithfulness toward himself, evoking his own grace. The depth of the reciprocity of faith and grace becomes more and more astounding when we begin to meditate upon it.

Concreteness

Second, both faith and grace, in Jewish tradition, are steeped in concreteness. These are not feelings, not even momentous experiences of consciousness. Faith and grace are rooted in law and deeds. Faithfulness and unmerited love are located in real contexts of history and human living—in peoplehood, in land, in Torah, in study, in ethics, in ritual, in prayer. Faith and grace are of this world, in its mundaneness and in its crises. Faithfulness and unmerited love are incarnate in life, in its ordinariness and in its vicissitudes. Both have their origin in transcendence, but they have their real existence in immanence—in the here and now.

It is this concrete aspect of faith as faithfulness that is most central to my own religious life. For me, to live faithfully in the world means to be sensitive to many things. It means being pained by the plight of the homeless or feeling one's insides turn at the specter of the starving. When I see photographs of refugees and of people ravaged by famine, I see at the same time the images of my fellow Jews who starved in the concentration camps and were homeless afterwards. My blessings are so great; what do I owe my brothers and sisters, who are also children of my Father? What must I do? I have never been hungry.

For me, being faithful to God also means involving myself in the cause of nuclear arms control. We are God's partners in creation. He can destroy it, but so can we. I am not a communist. In fact, because of the way the communists treat Jews—imprisoning and persecuting them for the simple fact of their being the chosen people—I am an anticommunist. And, as a Jew, I appreciate more than most the freedoms of the western world and its need to remain strong. But do we, West and East, have to have so many arms? Do we have to live in a pool of gasoline with two lighted matches? Must we force our children to live in fear of utter annihilation or nuclear winter? To be faithful, for me, is to be sensitive, concerned, and active.

And I always read the news from the Middle East. For me, to be faithful is to live a life of alertness to the dangers that beset God's people in his land. We are but stewards of the land and shall be judged by our righteousness. Therefore we must be alert to any danger—there are many formally sworn to destroy us—and we must be conscious of the justice of our own actions at all times. Yes, I follow these matters with greater faithfulness than those of Asia or Africa. Faithfulness exists within the bond of God's love and his covenant, of our loyalty to him and to his will.

Faithfulness is lived; concern is the measure. Grace is embodied; action is the standard. When I stand before God in judgment, I want to be able to say, "I *acted* faithfully." And if, God forbid, some great evil were to occur, I want to be able to look my children and my students in the face and say, "I *acted* in faithfulness."

Openness to Transcendence

Third, no matter how concrete my faithfulness, I need faith as openness to transcendence. I marvel at the faith of others. I know a man who is a survivor of the concentration camps, who saw his mother taken away and lost his father and most of his family. He came here, reestablished himself, and then lost his son; and recently he lost his wife in a violent death. When I sit next to him in synagogue on the Day of Atonement, I marvel at his faith and I am embarrassed. Who am I to pray next to him? What is my faith compared to his?

I know of a man who is a nonbeliever who sits in Russian prisons, hospitals, and Siberian labor camps, and whose sentence has been prolonged for no reason. He is about my age, and they have incarcerated him only for the crime of being Jewish. What faith sustains him? Could I hold out under those conditions if the Lord called me to endure them? It is too easy for me to have faith.

Similarly, I know Christian men and women who have worked with me for years, hand in hand, to bring about deeper understanding between our peoples. They do not wish to see me become a Christian, and I do not wish to see them become Jews. We are both rewarded if each responds to the call of God in his or her own way. Yet we struggle together. I marvel at the strength and beauty of their faith, at the transforming presence of Jesus in their lives—as Torah and God transform my life.

Finally, there are moments of doubt and times when the burdens of family and professional life almost block out the presence of God. There are moments, too, of sin and sinfulness. In those times, I remember God's compassionate love, his covenant, and his faithfulness to Israel. In those moments, I recall my own feeble faithfulness to him and to his concrete way. And I open myself to his grace, to his unmerited love. As the liturgy says: "Our Father, our King, be gracious unto us and answer

us, for we have no deeds." Then I try to re-turn to the ideal state described
in the Song of Songs (5:2): "I sleep but my heart waketh; the voice of my
Beloved knocks." For faith is also faithfulness to living in that loving
Presence.

Understanding the Chapter

1. What three acts of God exemplify grace (*ḥesed*) in the Bible and
subsequent Jewish tradition?

2. How does Maimonides define grace (*ḥesed*)?

3. What three elements of covenant are indissolubly linked with
God's grace?

4. Blumenthal says the acts of God's grace in Scripture are "one-way
acts, by God, toward us, motivated by his own being, independent of our
ability to recognize or to respond." How does this theological definition
of grace differ from popular understandings of the term?

5. What, according to rabbinic tradition, was the moment of greatest
sin in Jewish history—a time also when God's forgiveness as grace was
manifest to the people of Israel?

6. *Ḥesed* may be used of God in more than one way; but it can be used
of humans in only one way. What is that way?

7. According to Jewish tradition, what is the ultimate act of human
grace? Why is this so?

8. Describe the use of *'emunah* (faith) in the biblical account of Exodus, which sets the tone for the subsequent uses of this word in Scripture. What is the basic root meaning of *'emunah* in this context?

9. What does Blumenthal mean when he says that, for the Bible,
"faith" is "faithfulness"? What nuances are associated with "faithfulness"?

10. There are four ways in which Jews are said to "have faith in God."
What are these four ways of expressing faith?

11. How are grace and faith related in Jewish tradition? Contrast this
relationship with the Protestant understanding of grace and faith.

10

A Response to Professor David R. Blumenthal by Alan F. Johnson

First, let me stand back in amazement and appreciation for this clear and yet profound explication of grace and faith in Judaism. I was certainly intellectually illumined but as importantly I was also spiritually blessed, uplifted, and enriched by the insights presented. Furthermore, it is obvious that we must lay to rest the illicit stereotype that makes Judaism a legalistic religion of law and good works in contrast to Christianity as a religion of grace and faith. At this many Christians will be surprised and perplexed. Somehow Professor Blumenthal's exposition does not fit the image of Judaism often held by evangelicals.

Professor Blumenthal's method is quite interesting. While rabbinic, philosophical, and mystical traditions are woven together, the principle root source of the concepts is from the biblical notions of *ḥesed* (grace) and *'emunah* (faithfulness). My response is difficult because I find so much that could be dittoed and easily endorsed by Christians. But rather than simply dwell upon these commonalities, it may be more profitable to comment on certain aspects of the chapter where there may be tensions or even disagreements.

Rabbi Blumenthal demonstrates convincingly that *ḥesed* is evidenced in creation, in covenant, and in forgiveness. Further, that there is not only an inseparable link between *ḥesed* and *'emunah* but that they have a "doubly reciprocal" relationship is both illuminating and edifying. Finally, that faith and grace are "steeped in concreteness" and "located in real contexts of history and human living" is a thesis with which I as a Christian am in wholehearted agreement. So is there really any fundamental disagreement between Jews and Christians in this traditional theological battleground? In the splendid elucidation of Rabbi Blumenthal there seems to be little with which to disagree. Nevertheless, let me explore a few tensions that upon further dialogue may or may not turn out to be disagreements.

First, in regard to the discussion on *ḥesed* (grace), I very much appreciate the clear emphasis on the covenant being rooted in God's grace. What is not so clear is the individual Jew's relationship to the covenant. Does an individual recognize that his or her inclusion in the covenant is only on the basis of God's one-way act of grace, a forgiveness that he grants us "even when we do not deserve it"? I suppose this gets us theologically into an area that unfortunately was not part of the original assignment: the relationship of grace and faith to "righteousness." Is righteousness before God likewise rooted in God's grace *(ḥesed)?* Such a connection appears to be present in Psalm 85:10: "Steadfast love *{ḥesed}* and faithfulness *{ʾemeth}* will meet; righteousness and peace will kiss each other." Earlier in the same psalm salvation and grace are linked together: "Show us thy steadfast love *{ḥesed}*, O Lord, and grant us thy salvation" (v. 7). If Jews affirm this connection, then I would see a quite strong similarity between this and the New Testament teaching on the relationship between grace, covenant, and righteousness before God.

Also it is not clear to me what the relationship is between "merited" forgiveness, which is linked to covenant and arises from God's justness and fairness and is expressed daily by "grant us justice in judgment," and "unmerited" forgiveness that flows from God's grace and is expressed each year in the words, "Our Father, our King, have mercy on us and answer us, for we have no good deeds. Act toward us in justness and in grace, and redeem us." How are we to reconcile these seemingly opposite concepts of God's dealings with us?

Finally, along the same line: How does an act of human grace "serve to build a protective barrier around sinners" such that "merit of the fathers" may be invoked in "our plea at the judgment"? Does this mean that the acts of kindness of the patriarch Abraham, for example, can accrue to those of succeeding generations so that these later are somehow insulated from God's judgment or are more acceptable to God because they have the righteous deeds of their forefather Abraham to help make up their own deficiency? If this is the meaning, then does not this introduce the idea of meritorious human works into the area of righteousness before God and thus contradict the thesis that covenant and forgiveness are rooted in God's unmerited grace—"for we have no good deeds"? Curiously, neither this idea nor the previously mentioned "merit of the father" is rooted in the Bible in the author's exposition. Does this represent an indication of a dual contradictory thread that runs through rabbinic Judaism—a strand that emphasizes that acceptance before God rests solely on God's unmerited love and forgiveness (grace), and another thread that emphasizes that meritorious deeds (our own and those of our fathers) do in fact help us at judgment? If this is so—and I hope it is not—then the old stereotype referred to in my introduction would seem to be reinforced at least in part. Perhaps further dialogue can clarify the tension at this point.[1]

Incidentally, the reference to the "ultimate act of human grace, the ḥesed shel ʾemet," made me wonder for the first time whether this fact relates to the words of Jesus to one of his would-be Jewish followers who said, "Lord, let me first go and bury my father," to which Jesus replied, "Follow me, and leave the dead to bury their own dead" (Matt. 8:21-22). This would seem at least to intensify the importance of following Jesus if discipleship to him took priority over even the "ultimate act of human grace, the ḥesed shel ʾemet."

Finally, as to Professor Blumenthal's clear and edifying exposition of faith (ʾemunah) as "faithfulness" I have mostly words of great appreciation for this fine and inspiring analysis. I was especially helped by his discussion on the four ways we have faith in God. I can affirm each of these ways and would want to stress them to my Christian students. However, I would want to emphasize in addition to these existential ways another way. I would stress that this way is an *essential* ingredient in the biblical view of faith, namely, faith as "trust" in the content of divine revelation. God reveals himself in both words and deeds. The "word of God" (*davar Adonai*) is the basis of our faith. This "word" is disclosed by

---

1. Perhaps Rabbi Michael Wyschogrod has spoken to this point when he says,

In Judaism, God has two attributes—justice and mercy. At times he acts as the judge dispensing justice to his creatures. At other times he acts mercifully by forgiving man's transgressions and withholding deserved punishment. There is no discernible rule that determines when mercy displaces justice. If there were such a rule, the application of mercy itself would be ruled by law and it would then cease to be mercy. The point, however, is that in Judaism it is the same God who is sometimes just and sometimes merciful. In Christianity, these two aspects of God are personified by two persons—the Father and the Son. God the Father is the God of justice while God the Son is the principle of mercy. The appearance of Jesus, it seems, assures the triumph of mercy for those who believe in him. . . . The focus on Jesus is therefore the proclamation of the good news that the rigors of divine justice can be avoided. Through Jesus the mercy of God has triumphed over his justice. Judaism remains under the dialectic of justice and mercy. It is true that in the final analysis the mercy of God prevails over his justice. Israel has been told that it will be redeemed, that its election will never be withdrawn, and that while the anger of God is a passing phenomenon, his love and mercy endure forever.

"Judaism and Evangelical Christianity," chap. 2 in *Evangelicals and Jews in Conversation*, ed. Marc H. Tanenbaum, Marvin R. Wilson, and James A. Rudin (Grand Rapids: Baker, 1978), 49-50.

means of human language, has cognitive content, and is grasped in part through rational processes. One does not need to deny this in order to be wary of reductionist rationalism, which Rabbi Blumenthal rightly avoids in his opening remarks. When God revealed himself to Abraham, he did so in connection with a "word of promise." He said, "Look toward heaven, and number the stars, if you are able to number them. . . . So shall your descendants be." It was then that we read that Abraham "believed the Lord; and he reckoned it to him as righteousness" (Gen. 15:5-6). The immediate context favors the idea that 'emunah here does not emphasize Abraham's "faithfulness" but has more the idea of his acceptance and "trust" in God's divine word of promise concerning Isaac and a posterity. Elsewhere the word of promise includes the land and universal blessing to the Gentiles (Gen. 12:3, 7). While Abraham remained "faithful" to God's word of promise, he initially accepted it by faith in that he trusted in the God who could bring life out of Sarah's dead womb despite all empirical evidence to the contrary. It was at this moment that God "reckoned it to him as righteousness." This Genesis passage figures prominently in the great Pauline passages about grace and faith in God's economy (Rom. 4:1ff.; Gal. 3:6-14).

Perhaps this response may be closed by a few remarks concerning grace and faith in the New Testament part of the Bible. The Greek translation of the Hebrew Bible (LXX) most often translates ḥesed as "grace" (charis), although sometimes it uses "mercy" (eleos; cf. Luke 1:72), while 'emunah is translated as "faith" (pistis). In the New Testament the full range of ideas found in these words as expounded by Rabbi Blumenthal also occur (if we include 'emunah as "trust" and "trustworthiness"). However, in the New Testament the various aspects of both words are always linked to Jesus Christ as the fulfillment of God's covenant promises to Abraham. Thus Paul can use "faith" (pistis) in Romans 3:1-3 to refer to the unfaithfulness (or untrustworthiness) of man toward God and his word and at the same time of God's faithfulness to his word of promise to Abraham concerning the universal blessing to the Gentiles. Again Paul uses pistis to refer to the "faithfulness of Jesus" through which the manifestation of God's righteousness occurs, which brings forgiveness to all who have faith (pistis), the faith of Abraham (Rom. 3:21; 4:21-25). Furthermore, from the New Testament perspective God's supreme act of grace (compassionate love) is manifested in Jesus, the Messiah, in his life, sacrificial atoning death, and resurrection (Rom. 3:24-26). For the Christian, therefore, God's grace, his faithfulness, and man's trust and faithfulness all meet in the person of Jesus Christ. Here I am sure we will find our main difference, which will keep our dialogue both honest and frustrating and yet essential to us both.

Understanding the Chapter

1. What has contributed to creating the stereotype referred to by Johnson that Judaism is a "legalistic religion of law and good works in contrast to Christianity as a religion of grace and faith"?

2. How does Johnson suggest the "ultimate act of human grace" (burying the dead) might shed light on Jesus' words, "Follow me, and leave the dead to bury their own dead" (Matt. 8:21-22)?

3. Johnson points to a fifth way (in addition to Blumenthal's four ways) one may have faith in God. What is this way, and what passage from the Jewish Scriptures is used to support it?

4. What added perspective on grace and faith from the New Testament does Johnson point out that underscores the main difference between Jewish and Christian understandings of these doctrines?

11

The Place of Law and Good Works in Evangelical Christianity

WALTER C. KAISER, JR.

Evangelical Christianity can hardly be described as having a unified voice on the question of the place and use of the law and good works. There are few easy paradigms by which one can classify this group's standing on the matter of the law. Get any three evangelicals together in a discussion on the use of law and you will have four opinions.

However, there are some clear perimeters for evangelical discussion. All evangelicals will concede that the law to which we are referring here, in its more specific usage, is that legislation revealed from God to Moses at Mt. Sinai. Therefore, all evangelicals will readily acknowledge that this law has its source in God[1] and as such is an expression of the divine will. Consequently one may not easily shrug it off as being of little or no account or place it on a par with human legislations or observations.

Moreover, clear-headed evangelicals will likewise acknowledge that the character of this law is in itself "holy, righteous, and good" (Rom. 7:12). It is clear from both the *Tanak* (O.T.) and the later testament (N.T.) that if any fault was to be found in connection with the law, it was always located in the *users* of the law and not in the law itself.[2] Thus in both its source and its character, evangelicals place the highest level of respect and confidence in all law found in the *Tanak*.

---

1. This stance is also adopted in the New Testament: "God's law" (Rom. 7:22, 25; 8:7); "the commandments of God" (1 Cor. 7:19); and "the oracles of God" (Rom. 3:2).

2. Jer. 31:32: "not like the covenant I made [at the Exodus], which covenant *they* broke" (italics mine). Likewise, Heb. 8:8: "But God finding fault *with the people* said: ' . . . I will make a new covenant . . .'" (italics mine).

But to what extent should the law be used by evangelical Christians today? And to whom is it directed in all of its specifications? These questions introduce areas of deep debate. What makes this situation even more difficult are the numerous statements in the apostle Paul's writings that carry a negative flavor—at least on a *prima facie* reading of the text of the New Testament. However, before we introduce the Pauline formulas on the law, it would be well to see what the founder of Christianity had to say about it.

JESUS, THE LAW, AND GOOD WORKS

Jesus' statements in Matthew 5:17-20 about the continuing validity of the Torah are so strong that they have continued to cause great difficulty for many reluctant Christian interpreters. At first, they appear to be in direct conflict or contradiction to the teaching of Paul, the writer of Hebrews, if not also to Jesus' own practice on certain occasions.[3] Nevertheless, Jesus declared:

"Do not think [apparently some were doing so] that I have come to abolish the Law or the Prophets; I have not come to abolish them but to fulfill them. I tell you the truth, until heaven and earth disappear, not the smallest letter, not the least stroke of a pen, will by any means disappear from the Law until everything is accomplished. [Therefore] anyone who breaks one of the least of these commandments and teaches others to do the same will be called least in the kingdom of heaven, but whoever practices and teaches these commands will be called great in the kingdom of heaven." (Matt. 5:17-19, NIV)

An illustration of the way some Protestant interpreters read Matthew 5:17-20 is in the approach of Robert Banks[4] and the able critique of his views given by the evangelical David Wenham.[5] Banks concluded that the law had passed away for Christians except as it was continued or

---

3. Many would point to his "violation" of the Sabbath or Mark 7:19 as examples.
4. Robert Banks, *Jesus and the Law in the Synoptic Tradition* (Cambridge: Cambridge Univ. Press, 1975), 203-26.
5. David Wenham, "Jesus and the Law: An Exegesis on Matthew 5:17-20," *Themelios* 4 (1979): 93-96.

transformed in Jesus. He found the following three evidences for this line of argumentation in the passage:

1. The Greek word in verse 17, *plērōsai,* should not be interpreted to mean "establish," but instead "to fulfill" all that the law pointed to; thus Jesus "transcended" and actually replaced the law of the Old Testament.
2. The phrase "until all is accomplished" in verse 18 means that not one particle of the law (*jot* or *tittle*) would be phased out *until* Jesus came and replaced it with his teaching.
3. "Not one of the least of these commandments" in verse 19 cannot refer to the Old Testament Torah, but necessarily must refer to Jesus' commands.

David Wenham finds all three arguments to be wrongheaded:

1. *Plērōsai* cannot mean "fulfill and transcend" since the contrast in verse 17b favors the natural pairs: "abolish-fulfill/establish." This upholding of the Old Testament Torah easily leads to the practical "therefore" of verse 19.
2. The termination point set for the relevance of Torah is not the appearance of Jesus (*contra* Banks), but the end of time when "heaven and earth pass away" (v. 18).
3. The "commandments" of verse 19 are the Old Testament commandments and not Jesus' commands as Banks had argued, since verse 13 had just pointed to the Torah.

The context for this strong reaffirmation of the high standards of the Old Testament law was Jesus' call for "good works" in verse 16 and a standard of righteousness that surpassed that advocated in current practice of the first century C.E. (v. 20). According to Wenham, "It is not unlikely that Matthew (5:17-20) is answering a Jewish accusation that Jesus' way represented a departure from Jewish moral standards and a destruction of the law."[6] This charge Matthew and Jesus decisively deny. On the contrary, Old Testament law and its standards are endorsed and espoused.

But does such an endorsement mean that all of the Old Testament law

6. Ibid., 94.

is *equally* binding? No, Jesus taught (Matt. 23:23-24), as did the rabbis, that we must differentiate between the "lighter" and "heavier" commandments.[7] For him the "weightier matters" of the law were precisely those emphasized by the prophet Micah (6:6-8).

Many evangelicals, unfortunately, will balk at this point and will argue that the law is *one* and without any sort of weighting. In their view, with the collapse of the civil and ceremonial aspects of the law came the conclusion of obligation to all Old Testament law—including moral law in the Mosaic and prophetic revelations.

However, C. G. Montefiore contended that

the Rabbis . . . were familiar with the distinction between ceremonial and moral commands, and *on the whole* they regarded the "moral" as more important and more fundamental than the "ceremonial." . . . On the whole the "heavy" commands are the moral commands. . . . The distinction between "light" and "heavy" commands was well known, and is constantly mentioned and discussed.[8]

Gustaf Dalman agreed:

The Rabbis did not differentiate between the smallest and the greatest commandments but rather between "light" . . . (*qallīn*) and "heavy" . . . (*ḥamārīn*). . . . "Light" and "heavy" commandments are not those which are in themselves easy or difficult to keep, but such that cause the keeping of other commandments to be either light (*qōl*) or "heavy" (*ḥomer*).[9]

In my view, the moral law as witnessed by the Decalogue and the law of holiness in Leviticus 18–20 is "heavier" or "weightier"[10] because it

7. See W. C. Kaiser, Jr., "The Weightier and Lighter Matters of the Law: Moses, Jesus, and Paul," in *Current Issues in Biblical and Patristic Interpretation: Studies in Honor of Merrill C. Tenney,* ed. Gerald Hawthorne (Grand Rapids: Eerdmans, 1975), 176-92. See also my *Toward Old Testament Ethics* (Grand Rapids: Zondervan, 1983), 45-48.

8. C. G. Montefiore, *Rabbinic Literature and Gospel Teaching* (New York: Ktav, 1970), 316-17.

9. Gustaf Dalman, *Jesus-Jeshua: Studies in the Gospels,* trans. Paul P. Levertoff (London: SPCK, 1929), 64-65.

10. W. D. Davies, for example, denies this: "There is no essential difference in Paul between the Decalogue and the rest of the law" in "Law in the N.T.," *The Interpreter's Dictionary of the Bible,* ed. George Arthur Buttrick (Nashville: Abingdon Press, 1962), 3:97.

reflected the character, nature, and being of God. But the ceremonial and civil laws, while "lighter" in comparison to this standard, are nonetheless *authoritative* for evangelical praxis even though their specific *claim* is not addressed to us. To the degree that the civil and ceremonial laws illustrate the principles of the moral law, as they generally do, they contain normative teaching for evangelicals. Admittedly some of the civil and ceremonial legislation, especially related to the ministry and service of the tabernacle and its successor, the temple, had an expiration date attached to its original legislation. This built-in obsolescence is fairly served when the real to which its offices, services, and ministries pointed superannuated it. Thus, the word *pattern (tabnit)* in Exodus 25:9, 40 was one such signal to readers of all ages.

PAUL, THE LAW, AND GOOD WORKS

"Paul's attitude toward the Law," confides James A. Sanders, "has been one of the most puzzling and seemingly insoluble [issues] in biblical study."[11] The problem is a familiar one. On the one hand are those passages that appear to say that the law has been abrogated and transcended (Rom. 7:1-10; Gal. 2:19; 2 Cor. 3:4-17; Eph. 2:14-16). On the other hand, one can cite Paul as being just as certain that neither he nor any Christian has by any means abolished the law by means of faith. Instead, faith only establishes the law (Rom. 3:31) and, in fact, the law itself turns out to be "holy, just, good and spiritual" (Rom. 7:12-14). Likewise, Heikki Räisänen concludes that "Paul has two sets of statements concerning the validity of the law for Christians. According to one set the law has been abrogated once and for all. According to another the law is still in force."[12]

Most will also agree that "At the heart of the problem stands Rom. 10:4 which seems to belong to the first group of passages: 'Christ is the end of the Law.'"[13] However, this passage is precisely where Paul makes

---

11. James A. Sanders, "Torah and Paul," in *God's Christ and His People: Studies in Honor of Nils Alstrup Dahl*, ed. Jacob Jervell and Wayne A. Meeks (Oslo: Universitetsforlaget, 1977), 132.

12. Heikki Räisänen, "Paul's Theological Difficulties with the Law," in *Studia Biblica* (1978) and in *Papers on Paul and Other New Testament Authors*, Sixth International Congress on Biblical Studies, ed. E. A. Livingstone (Sheffield: University Press, 1980), 305.

13. Sanders, *Torah and Paul*, 132.

his strongest case for the fact that what he is preaching and teaching is exactly what Moses had taught in Leviticus 18:5 *and* Deuteronomy 30:12-14, and also what Isaiah (28:16) and Joel (2:32) had urged (cf. Rom. 10:5-13). We should not translate the *gar . . . de* construction of Romans 10:5-6 as "For [Moses] . . . *but*" (as if the two Mosaic citations were in opposition to each other), but instead as "For [Moses] . . . and"—even as all translators grant in a similar *gar . . . de* in Romans 10:10 ("For with the heart . . . *and* with the mouth").

Paul's argument, in this celebrated passage, begins with a contrast between a *righteousness* that comes from a faith the Mosaic law taught that was "in [our] mouth" and "in [our] hearts" (cf. Deut. 30:14 and Rom. 10:8) and a righteousness that had been turned into a law (Rom. 9:30: *nomon dikaiosunēs:* "[made] a law out of righteousness"—note the word order in Greek). But to turn righteousness into a law is to reject Moses' call to faith and to attempt to gain a right standing with God by works, "as if it were possible" (*all' hōs ex,* Rom. 9:32). The contrast for Paul, and for evangelicals, is so strong that it is the difference between a "righteousness that comes from God" and a "righteousness [that is] our own" (*tēn idian,* Rom. 10:3). This homemade righteousness resisted submitting itself to God's righteousness revealed in the law and the prophets.

Accordingly, we agree with C. E. B. Cranfield that much of our puzzlement over Paul's use of the word *law* comes from our failure to realize that he had no separate word-group or term to denote "legalism" and so he used the identical term for both his positive references to the Old Testament law (which he upheld) and his negative disparagements of the human tendency to make a "law out of righteousness" in order to devise "one's own righteousness," "as if it were possible," to improve or supplement what God had revealed in the *Tanak!*

In fact Paul, like Jesus,[14] appeared to have no objection to Jewish believers continuing to observe even the ceremonies of law as a mark of their solidarity with their kinsmen (Acts 16:3; 21:20-26; 1 Cor. 9:20-21). But, like Moses and the prophets, he was adamant on the point that a right standing before God never could be or ever had been established on the grounds of "the works of the law" (Rom. 3:21, 28).

In sum, Paul, it turns out, also is not against the Old Testament law.

---

14. See Robert Mackintosh, *Christ and the Jewish Law* (London: Hodder and Stoughton, 1886), chap. VI, pp. 115-32. Jesus recognized the authority of the ceremonial law in cleansings for lepers (Matt. 8:2; Luke 17:12), temple taxes (Matt. 17:27), cleansing of the temple (Matt. 21:12; John 2:13), and in tithes required (Matt. 23:23-26; Luke 11:41).

He only insists that law not be used as a substitute for faith when it comes to gaining that righteousness which can come only from God. Prior to faith, the law serves only to hold evil broadly in-bounds and to threaten us with judgment. But whenever there is a genuine repentance (*šûb,* "to turn") wherein men and women "turn" *from* their evil deeds and with their heart and mouth confess by faith the God of Abraham, Isaac, and Jacob, then good works and obedience to the law become both possible and personally satisfying and productive.

THE REFORMERS, THE LAW, AND GOOD WORKS

Two representative confessions of churches stemming from the Reformers make very similar distinctions. *The Thirty-nine Articles* states that

Although the Law given from God by Moses, as touching Ceremonies and Rites, does not bind Christian men, nor the Civil precepts thereof ought of necessity to be received in any commonwealth; yet notwithstanding, no Christian man whatsoever is free from the obedience of the Commandments which are called Moral. [15]

Likewise the *Westminster Confession,* though more expansive, agreed:

The "ceremonial laws are now abrogated under the new testament," the "judicial laws . . . expired together with" the "body politick" of Israel, "not obligating any other now, further than the general equity thereof may require," but "the moral law doth forever bind all, as well justified persons as others, to the obedience thereof; and that not only in regard of the matter contained in it, but also in respect of the authority of God, the Creator, who gave it. Neither doth Christ in the gospel any way dissolve, but much strengthen this obligation." [16]

John Calvin (1509–1564) was the clearest in his statements on the continuing significance of the law for Christians. His lucid discussions in his *Institutes of the Christian Religion* usually dominate evangelical Protestant expositions of the continuing significance of the law. For Calvin the moral law of the Old Testament has three main functions: (1) to show us God's righteousness while warning and condemning every form of man's

15. Article 7.
16. Chapter 19.

own righteousness (he cites Rom. 3:20; 4:15; 5:20; 7:7; 2 Cor. 3:7); (2) to restrain men who are otherwise unaffected by what is just or right with the dire threats of the law (he cites 1 Tim. 1:9-10; again Gal. 3:24); and (3) to provide instruction and stimulation to obedience for those in whose hearts the Spirit of God lives and reigns. [17]

This third use of the moral law is the principal use. It commands us (1) to worship God in sincerity and faith and (2) to love our fellowman with true devotion.

According to Calvin, while only the moral law, which normally denotes the ten commandments, remains without being changed or abrogated, the ceremonial and civil laws also reflect God's moral law. Thus the ceremonial practices and judicial regulations pointed away from themselves to a holiness and piety that could be separated from the regulations themselves. Therefore the piety, love, and holiness they enjoined or presupposed were perpetual and remained even when the formulas themselves were replaced. [18]

Martin Luther (1482–1546) was not as clear in his estimates of the place of the law for the Christian as was Calvin. The greatest differences between the two come in what traditionally has been called "the third use of the law" (*usus tertius legis*), that is, the use of the law as our adviser, teacher, and guide in the paths of righteousness and holy living. In fact, Luther probably never used this term at all. [19] The notion of the "three-fold use of the Law" first appeared in Philip Melanchthon's *Common Places (Loci Communes)* in 1535.

In fact, in the first edition of *Common Places* in 1521, Melanchthon (1497–1560) declared that freedom in the Spirit and place in the new covenant had abrogated the old covenant in every part just as Jeremiah 31:32 had promised. But the place he gave the third use of the law in 1535 was progressively enlarged by the time of the 1555 edition. In the context of his lengthy exposition of the Decalogue he affirmed that

> God has given his Church knowledge of his eternal and unchangeable law, which is called *lex moralis,* or the ten commandments, and he wants the Church to maintain it so that man may have a divine testi-

17. *Institutes of the Christian Religion* II.vii.6, 10, 12, 14.
18. Ibid., IV.xx.14-15.
19. We can point to only one passage in Luther (*Martin Luthers Werke: Kritische Gesamt-Ausgabe,* Weimar Ausgabe [1833–], 39.1, 485), and modern scholars regard it as a falsification.

mony of what is right and of what sin is; so that through the punishment of sin in all men the unconverted may be converted, and the
converted be strengthened in the fear of God.[20]

Thus, while Luther himself concluded that nothing Moses has com-
manded is binding for us[21] (unless it is also found in natural law),
Lutheranism nevertheless came to adopt the threefold use of the law in
The Formula of Concord of 1577:

> It is established that the Law of God was given to men for three causes:
> first, that a certain external discipline might be preserved, and wild and
> intractable men might be restrained, as it were, by certain barriers;
> secondly, that by the Law men might be brought to an acknowledge-
> ment of their sins; thirdly, that regenerate men, to all of whom nev-
> ertheless, much of the flesh still cleaves, for that very reason may have
> some certain rule after which they may and ought to shape their life.[22]

In sum, evangelicals like to claim the Reformers as their spiritual
ancestors; however, unfortunate as it may seem, the Reformers likewise
fail to speak with a unified voice on the place of the moral law for the
Christian. There still is a great need for this unfinished task to be re-
sumed.

A POSITIVE CASE FOR THE LAW AND GOOD WORKS IN EVANGELICAL CHRISTIANITY

At the heart of this problem lies the fact that "the Church has tended to
view its existence independently of Israel."[23] But the truth is, as Dan
Johnson warned in another connection, "In Paul's view any church which

---

20. Melanchthon, *Common Places* (1955).

21. See, e.g., Martin Luther, "How Christians Should Regard Moses," *Luther's
Works,* ed. E. Theodore Bachmann (Philadelphia: Muhlenberg Press, 1960),
35:161-74. Said Luther: "Moses has nothing to do with us. If I were to accept Moses in
one commandment, I would have to accept the entire Moses. . . . So then we will
neither observe nor accept Moses" (p. 165).

22. Article 6.

23. Dan G. Johnson, "The Structure and Meaning of Romans 11," *Catholic Biblical Quarterly* 46 (1984): 100.

exists independently of Israel ceases therein to be the Church as a part of God's salvation plan and becomes simply another religious society."[24]

The church must resist the temptation to divide the government of people into the famous two kingdoms of Luther (the temporal kingdom suggested at first, in his view, by Jethro, and the spiritual kingdom in which Christ rules in human hearts) with a middle kingdom, half spiritual and half temporal, constituted by Moses with commandments and ceremonies specifically and solely addressed to Israel.[25]

But such bifurcation of peoples and purposes was not part of the Pauline picture. In Romans 11, Paul has one overriding theme: God will save all Israel (v. 16) by means of a remnant (the "firstfruits"), just as there existed a similar believing remnant in the days when another prophet like Paul had bewailed the unbelief of Israel, that is, Elijah (Rom. 11:1-5).

Likewise, the "grafted-in wild olive shoot" of Gentile believers must not exhibit feelings of superiority, for we are completely dependent on the believing Jewish remnant: "You do not support the root, but the root supports you" (v. 18).

Therefore, to say that Moses' commands no longer bind believing Gentiles because the question of the *authority* of text is separate from the question of the *claim* of the text[26] places a division where Paul refused to make one. Luther wrongheadedly advised: "Leave Moses and his people together; they have had their day and do not pertain to me . . . we have the gospel."[27]

Space will not allow us to carry out this argument in detail, but one line of evidence will suggest that this antithesis is contrived and contrary to the purpose of God. The law and good works are set forth as "the third-use of the law" for evangelical Christians in the Epistle of James and his use of Leviticus 19:12-18.

---

24. Ibid. He correctly argued: "Whether they be exegetes such as Marcion, Harnack, or Bultmann who think the Church should rid itself of the Hebrew Scriptures or any number of pastors in the local church who see the church as the new Israel, whoever they may be, they have violated the clear claims of Paul's exposition [in Romans 11]."

25. Martin Luther, "How Christians Should Regard Moses," 164.

26. See W. C. Kaiser, Jr., *Toward Old Testament Ethics* (Grand Rapids: Zondervan, 1983), 47-48 for this distinction.

27. Martin Luther, "How Christians Should Regard Moses," 171.

James and Leviticus 19. For centuries now the letter of James, traditionally acclaimed as the brother of Jesus, has puzzled Christians. With
its stress on obedience as the proof or evidence that one who claimed to be
a believer actually was such, it just did not seem to fit the rest of the New
Testament.

But now we have evidence[28] that James may well have used Leviticus
19:12-18 as one of the sources for his paraenesis. What we can be certain
about is that James definitely knew and used the Septuagint or Greek
version of Leviticus 19, for he quoted 19:18b accurately from the LXX in
James 2:8. It is also noteworthy, as Luke Johnson points out so clearly,
that he placed this citation of 19:18b in the framework of a discussion of
not showing partiality when rendering a judgment, which also was a
clear allusion to Leviticus 19:15.[29] Thus James is well aware of the
Levitical context of the "Royal Law of Love."

But this is not all. James uses about six other thematic or verbal
allusions to this same section of the Law of Holiness (Lev. 18:20). Thus
from the heart of what many would regard as the ceremonial law came the
basis for ethical and moral nurture of believing Christians. We can only
briefly list the passages here in the order of the Torah text.

Lev. 19:12-18		*James*	
19:12	Do not swear falsely by my name and profane the name of your God	5:12	Do not swear . . . so that you will not be condemned
19:13	Do not hold back the wages of a hired man overnight	5:4	Behold, the wages you failed to pay the work-man who mowed your fields are crying out against you.
19:14			no parallel

---

28. See esp. the seminal article by Luke T. Johnson, "The Use of Leviticus 19 in
the Letter of James," *Journal of Biblical Literature* 101 (1982): 391-401, and P. W.
van der Horst, *The Sentences of Pseudo-Phocylides* (Leiden: E. J. Brill, 1978). Also note
O. J. F. Seitz, "James and the Law," in *Studia Evangelica,* vol. 2, part 1, *The New
Testament Scriptures,* ed. Frank L. Cross (Berlin: Akademie-Verlag, 1964), 472-86.
29. Johnson, "Use of Leviticus," 393.

19:15	Do not show partiality	2:1	Don't show favoritism
		2:9	If you show favoritism
	(*ou lempsē prosōpon*)		(*ei de prosōpolēmpteite*)
19:16	Do not go about spreading slander among your people	4:11	Do not slander one another, brothers
19:17b	Rebuke your neighbor frankly so you will not share in his guilt	5:20	Know that whoever turns a sinner back from his error will save him from death and cover a multitude of sins
19:18a	And your hand shall not avenge you and you shall not be angry with the children of your people	5:9	Don't take out your resentments on each other, brothers
19:18b	You shall love neighbor as yourself	2:8	You shall love your neighbor as yourself

Four of these six verbal and thematic allusions appear to be fairly certain, while only two are less likely (19:17b; 19:18a). It may even be, as Johnson suggests,[30] that the apodictic commands of Leviticus 19:11 are embraced, at least in their substance, in James 3:13–4:10.

The fact that calls for special attention is not what is meant by the *basilikos* of James 2:8, but the relation that existed in his inspired mind between "fulfilling the law" and "according to the Scripture" (*kata tēn graphēn*). Furthermore, if the Greek particles (*mentio*, v. 8 and *de*, v. 9) are used here as correlatives and the "law" of verse 9 ("you are convicted by the law as lawbreakers") corresponds to the "royal law" of verse 8, then evangelical Christians are obliged to render obedience to the law or be found guilty of sin.

Johnson has stated the case well:

Keeping the law of love involves observing the *commandments* explicated in the Decalogue (2:11) and Lev. 19:12-18 in the entirety.

30. Ibid., 399 n.29.

. . . For James, Lev. 19:12-18 provides an accurate explication of the
law of love which should be obtained in the Church.[31]

CONCLUSION

Thus we conclude that evangelical Christians can and ought to use the
Mosaic law, for as Paul affirmed, "The law is good if we use it rightly"
(1 Tim. 1:8). The Old Testament "law is holy, just, good, and spiritual"
(Rom. 7:13-14); that is not where the problem ever existed, for Israel or
the church: the problem always was with people, not the law.

If some complain that it is impossible for any mortal, Jewish or
Gentile, ever perfectly to fulfill the law of God, we will ask only that two
kinds of "impossibility" be defined. There is the impossibility due to the
nature of a thing (e.g., it is impossible to make square circles or one-
ended ropes) and there is the impossibility of the *degree* of a thing (every
degree of success attained invites us to go on). It is not the first type of
impossibility that one should complain about, for after all we were
endowed with such strength to keep the law at our creation and so there
was no unfairness in God. But we have grown weaker and unable to
measure up to the standard set by the character and nature of God since
Adam involved all of creation in the Fall.

What good works and types of obedience, then, are evangelicals called
to when they read Moses today? They are called to the same type of
obedience that springs out of true love for God and wholehearted faith in
him ("the obedience of faith"; Rom. 1:5; 16:26). This first obedience
presupposes the right condition of the heart toward God as a precondition
for the second obedience of action. These two uses of "obedience" and the
priority of one to the other can be seen in Deuteronomy 8:2; 30:5, 11-14.
In the scope of one verse (Deut. 30:16), both types of obedience appear.
But in its more narrow usage, the obedience of action is just as necessary
for evangelical Christianity as it was for Mosaic Judaism (e.g., Deut.
10:12: "to serve him by keeping his commands"; notice the Hebrew
syntax here).

Evangelicals would be well advised to "fulfill the law" "according to
the Scriptures" rather than seek some new displacements for either the

---

31. Ibid., 400.

Mosaic law or, for that matter, Israel herself! The principles for correctly interpreting just how such an observance is to be accomplished are, for the most part, contained in the *Tanak* and in Moses' legislation. Both evangelicalism and Judaism have erred in not knowing the law. We have both built up our own traditions around the law so that often the message of the inspired prophet was muted or silenced. For this we must repent and return to the law and the prophets.

Understanding the Chapter

1. Kaiser states that both testaments teach that "if any fault was to be found in connection with the law, it was always located in the *users* of the law and not in the law itself." Do you agree with this statement? If so, do you feel this concept has contributed in any way toward the history of anti-Judaism?

2. What, according to Kaiser, was Jesus' relation to the law?

3. Does Kaiser believe that all of the Old Testament law is *equally* binding for the Christian? Why?

4. What, in Kaiser's argument, are the "heavy" commands ("weightier matters") in distinction from the "light"?

5. According to Kaiser, to what degree do the civil and ceremonial laws of Moses contain normative teaching for evangelicals?

6. How does Kaiser resolve Paul's apparent ambivalence about the law?

7. In general, what view of the law did the Reformers take?

8. According to Calvin, what are the three main functions of the moral law? Which use did Calvin call the principal use?

9. Luther taught, "Moses has nothing to do with us." Though Luther also made many anti-Semitic statements about Jews and Judaism during one period of his life, how did Lutheranism come to regard the law of Moses?

10. In what sense is the Christian bound by Mosaic law, according to Kaiser? What added light does a study of the Epistle of James and Leviticus 19 throw on this question?

12

A Response to Walter C. Kaiser, Jr., by Gordon Tucker

It is difficult to structure an adequate response to Professor Kaiser's scholarly, forthright, and highly persuasive paper. There are, of course, the inevitable minor points scattered here and there that elicit some comment, but such textual notes would hardly do justice to the striking thesis he has put before us. The questions that, it seems to me, ought to be raised flow rather from the broad components of that thesis, and from assumptions and premises that constitute their underpinnings. I will therefore attempt, in a necessarily constricted space, to direct attention not to fissures or lacunae in Kaiser's arguments, for these are not apparent, but rather to the issue of what the argument as a whole demonstrates for Jewish-evangelical dialogue. To the extent that the comments to follow indicate specific points of difficulty or disagreement, that will essentially be to allow us to formulate the more general question.

The reflections on Matthew 5:17-19 take up the issue of the "least of the commandments" as well as the related notion of "lighter" and "weightier" commandments referred to in Matthew 23:23-24. While it is true that these texts, as well as rabbinic literature, distinguish between the "light" and "heavy" commandments, care must be taken to differentiate between a distinction based on some external category and one with respect to authority and claim. External categories might include such things as sanctions accompanying the commandments, or the difficulty in complying with them; those categories could well determine a division between "light" and "heavy" commandments for purposes of human analysis. Indeed, they did give rise to such a division for the rabbis and in the texts from Matthew cited. Two examples will suffice to illustrate this: (1) The very end of the Mishnah tractate Hullin (12:5) states that the Torah promises reward for both light and heavy commandments, and the representative of the "light" class is the requirement to send away the mother bird before taking chicks or eggs from a nest (Deut. 22:6-7). It is "light" because it requires little effort and expense. (2) The Mishnah tractate Yoma (8:8) tells us that repentance atones for "light" transgressions, while repentance plus Yom Kippur atone for "heavy" transgres-

134

sions. The Talmud there (85b-86a), as well as Maimonides ("Laws of Repentance" 1:4), makes it clear that the light/heavy distinction hangs on the severity of punishment exacted for violating the commandment.

Indeed, Robert Johnston has cogently argued[1] that Matthew 5:19 must be referring to the law of the bird nest in speaking of the "least of the commandments." That was the Jewish cliché.

The fact of the light/heavy distinction having been established, however, it must be said that there does not appear to be a meaningful distinction in terms of *authority* or *claim*. On the contrary, the rabbis only raise the distinction to stress that it does not carry over into the area of authority or efficacy. For the rabbis, the law was a unity (as it was for the Hebrew Bible), and distinctions were only the products of human conceptualization. The Babylonian Talmud (Yebamot 47a-b), in describing procedures for proselytization, makes it clear that the convert must be instructed in some of the "light" and "heavy" commandments. They are equally binding.[2]

Nor is there any real distinction for the rabbis along the lines of "moral" and "ceremonial" to the extent that they made any such nominal distinction at all, it did not even coincide with the light/heavy distinction. The conversion ceremony mentioned in Yebamot 47a-b seems to illustrate the "light" commandments by the "moral" commands pertaining to gifts to the poor, and the "heavy" commands by the "ceremonial" prohibition against eating suet.

If Johnston is correct, then Jesus too uses "least of the commandments" to refer to the *morally* compelling requirement pertaining to the mother bird. And Brice Martin[3] has constructed an argument that makes the strong claim that all of Matthew 5:17-48 intends to uphold the law in its unity, and in fact to complete it by deriving its most radical and far-reaching consequences.

The point of all of this is that for rabbinic Judaism, and quite possibly for the Matthean community as well, God's law was conceived of ho-

---

1. Robert Johnston, "The Least of the Commandments," *Andrews University Seminary Studies* 20:3 (Autumn 1982).

2. Among other rabbinic passages that make this unity quite clear are Mishnah Avot 2:1; 4:2, and the Babylonian Talmud Erubin 21b.

3. Brice Martin, "Matthew on Christ and the Law," *Theological Studies* 44:1 (March 1983). Martin follows to some extent the thesis propounded by John Meier before him.

listically,[4] and its authority, as it extended to human beings, was unitary. I
I cannot find persuasive support for the notion that there is "weighting"
in the law with respect to authority or claim. Indeed, Kaiser's distinction
between "authority" and "claim" in connection with the "ceremonial and
civil law" is hard to follow, in light of the reflections given above.

My dissension on this point helps to answer a question that recurred in
my mind as I followed the unfolding of Kaiser's thesis, namely: "What
then really divides evangelicals and Jews, apart from the obvious division
in the *form* their eschatologies take?" The tendency to subdivide the law
is, I believe, one of those factors.[5] Moreover, it is related to another
important phrase employed by Kaiser: "whenever there is a genuine
repentance . . . then good works and obedience to the law become both
possible and personally satisfying and productive." What is missing in
that last phrase, from the perspective of rabbinic Judaism, is that the law
is, in addition, *binding* on us as a whole, even though it may be susceptible to divergent interpretations.

This brings me to what may be the most interesting point of diver-
gence between Kaiser's program and a Jewish one. He speaks of the law as
being an "expression of the divine will" and also says that "evangelicals
place the highest level of respect and confidence in all law found in the
Tanak." I don't know what his (or another evangelical) stance would be
concerning morally problematic sections of the *Tanak*, such as the command to wage genocidal war against the Canaanites (Deut. 20). A Jewish
stance is ready at hand thanks to the classical rabbinic notion that there *is*
no direct communication of the divine will any longer, not even through
God's text. That is an indirect communication over which we, in our
progressive wisdom and moral development, are custodians. There is
only a *presumptive* will of God, and it is *precisely* for that reason that the
totality of the law takes on such immense proportions for classical Judaism. If the logic of that point is somewhat rarefied, it is nonetheless quite

4. C. G. Montefiore, *Rabbinic Literature and Gospel Teaching,* cited by Kaiser at
note 8, makes it clear at p. 331 that the rabbis would never have considered tithing to
be "light." And even Matt. 23:23 makes it clear that no law should be neglected.

5. I am speaking here of rabbinic Judaism. There are, to be sure, varieties of
Judaism that do subdivide the law categorically, notably Reform Judaism. Indeed,
the passages from the *Thirty-nine Articles* and the *Westminster Confession* quoted by
Kaiser sound remarkably like the so-called "Pittsburgh Platform" of American Reform Judaism (1885).

authentically rabbinic. Rabbinic theology does not have confidence in the ultimacy of our moral categories, since they are necessarily *ours*. The law became for Jews the vehicle through which to develop, through interpretation and exegesis, ever closer approximations to the divine will. Individual interpretations may change, but the law as a unitary, organic system with its own history remains authoritative, because it is our only way to approach God's will. If Kaiser's suggestion that evangelicals and Jews must "return to the law and to the prophets" means returning to the Bible, then we have indeed exposed a major point of difference in the two traditions. For the ironical truth is that a return to the Bible, as has been pointed out by Solomon Schechter, and for reasons only sketched above, would be for Jews both ill-advised and illegal!

Understanding the Chapter

1. According to Tucker, what distinguishes a "light" commandment from a "heavy" one? What example does he cite from the law of Moses?

2. What does Tucker say about the question of *authority* or *claim* in regard to the "light" and "heavy" distinction? How does this compare with Kaiser's argument?

3. Does Tucker believe the rabbis subdivided the law or made any real distinction between the "moral" and "ceremonial" laws? If not, how *was* God's law conceived in rabbinic Judaism?

4. What does Tucker mean when he asserts that for Judaism there is only a "presumptive will of God" enshrined in the Bible and that it is through the custodial care of the Jewish community that "ever closer approximations to the divine will" are achieved? Do you find any parallel here to the Roman Catholic concept of authority and how the will of God is divulged?

5. Tucker raises the question of "morally problematic sections of the *Tanak,* such as the command to wage genocidal war against the Canaanites (Deut. 20)." Discuss both Jewish and evangelical approaches to solving such difficult issues as this one of "Holy War." How do the approaches differ, if at all? Why?

6. Discuss the implications of Tucker's final statement that "a return to the Bible . . . would be for Jews both ill-advised and illegal."

13
American Evangelicalism: Today and Tomorrow

VERNON C. GROUNDS

I

"Give me a place to stand," Archimedes cried, "and I can move the world!" I have no illusions whatsoever about my ability to move the world—or, for that matter, adequately to handle my current assignment to appraise the present status and predict the possible future of the American religious movement designated as evangelicalism. But at least I am one up on Archimedes, since I am not crying out for a place to stand. I have my *pou stō,* as the Greeks might put it. I have my standpoint, my Archimedean point, from which I view the swirl of events in which I am a participant-observer.

I myself am an evangelical whose perceptual grid has been ideologically formed by a WASP background and a myriad of influences, including a conversion experience, a theological education at a militantly anti-ecumenical seminary, and a long relationship with separatist fundamentalism. So I am firmly planted in the evangelical camp; and it is from this standpoint that I will attempt, with questionable objectivity, to survey the evangelical scene.

Like any other "ism," this descendant of the Reformed faith is difficult to define precisely. For instance, there are Roman Catholics who claim that in the truest sense they are evangelicals. More than that, I recall some English Christians of several generations back who insisted that they were evangelical liberals. I remember too that Karl Barth and Emil Brunner, stigmatized by many evangelicals as the standard-bearers of neoorthodoxy, claimed to be authentically evangelical. Indeed, one of Barth's shorter works is entitled *Evangelical Theology: An Introduction.* Thus I admit that to explain evangelicalism is to grapple with an elusive semantic ell. Let me therefore call for help. What is evangelicalism? Donald Bloesch, in his praiseworthy book-length analysis of the very subject I am discussing, *The Future of Evangelical Christianity,* provides an insightful definition. Aside from sincere subscription to the core tenets of biblical faith, an evangelical, according to Bloesch, is

> one who affirms the centrality and cruciality of Christ's work of reconciliation and redemption as declared in the Scriptures; the necessity to appropriate the fruits of this work in one's own life and experience; and the urgency to bring the good news of this act of unmerited grace to a lost and dying world. It is not enough to believe in the cross and resurrection of Christ. We must personally be crucified and buried with Christ and rise with Christ to a new life in the Spirit. Yet even this is not all that is required of us. We must also be fired by a burning zeal to share this salvation with others. To be evangelical therefore means to be evangelistic. . . . If asked to list the key elements in a vital Christian faith, an evangelical in the classical sense might well reply: biblical fidelity, apostolic doctrine, the experience of salvation, the imperative of discipleship, and the urgency of mission. Holding firm to the doctrine taught by the prophets and apostles in Holy Scripture, evangelicals stress the need for personal experience of the reality of Christ's salvation as well as the need to carry out the great commission to teach all people to be his disciples and to call all nations to repentance.
>
> Undergirding this whole pattern of discipleship and mission is a further element in the evangelical vision: the eschatological hope. Evangelicals affirm as belonging to the essence of faith not only belief in the first advent of Christ but also hope for his second advent. While this messianic kingdom is already present in the community of faith, this kingdom is yet to be consummated and fulfilled in the kingdom of glory.[1]

That definition catches, I think, the essence and spirit of evangelicalism as adhering to traditional Christian beliefs objectively and highlighting personal experience and responsibility subjectively.

Helpful, also, is the affirmation Bloesch makes in an exchange of letters with Vernard Eller, who has faulted him for using evangelicalism as an overly constrictive and exclusive category. Agreeing with Eller that the "word 'evangelical' belongs to the whole church," Bloesch nevertheless points out that

> many segments of the church have lost sight of the very meaning of the gospel: that Christ died for our sins according to the Scriptures and rose

---

1. Donald Bloesch, *The Future of Evangelical Christianity* (New York, 1983), 17-18.

from the dead for our justification and redemption. There are various theological schools that reduce the gospel to a system of ethics. There are others that call into question the reliability and even the normativeness of the biblical witness concerning the gospel. With the Reformers and their Puritan and Pietist descendants, I affirm that the integrity of the gospel cannot be maintained without holding to the divine authority, inspiration and infallibility of Holy Scripture. The divine content of the Bible cannot be divorced from its historical form, from what Barth calls "the language of Canaan." This is why (with Barth) I reject *Sach* criticism (a critique of the substance or message of Scripture in the light of an extra-biblical criterion) but make a place for literary and historical criticism . . . evangelicalism as an ideal type is brokenly reflected on the cross, his glorious resurrection from the dead, the outpouring of the Holy Spirit, salvation by grace, justification by faith alone, the divine authority and primacy of Holy Scripture and the urgency of evangelicalism are themes that unite all of these movements. In addition, the blessed hope of Christ's second appearing figures prominently in this evangelical heritage, though it was somewhat muted in the Reformation itself because the polemics of the time were directed to other issues.[2]

That forthright yet irenic explanation satisfies me. If a further taxonomy is asked for, however, perhaps that suggested by Richard Quebedeaux will suffice.[3] He has discovered these five subgroups within contemporary evangelicalism:

1. *Separatist Fundamentalists.* Isolate themselves from all they consider to be liberal or modern.
2. *Open Fundamentalists.* Similar to #1, though not quite as extreme and vocal. They will engage in self-criticism and often dialogue with others they consider to be orthodox.
3. *Establishment Evangelicals.* Seek to evangelize outsiders, but attempt to break away from the separatist mentality and absence of social concern of #1 and #2.
4. *New Evangelicals.* Claim an intellectual transformation in grasping the Scriptures. As a result, they oppose dispensationalism and its

2. Donald Bloesch, "Evangelical: Integral to Christian Identity? An Exchange Between Donald Bloesch and Vernard Eller," *TSF Bulletin* (Nov.-Dec. 1983), 8-10.
3. Richard Quebedeaux, *The Young Evangelicals* (New York, 1974), 18-45.

apocalyptic speculations, consider ethical living to be as important as correct doctrine, cultivate dialogue with nonevangelicals, and are acutely interested in the social dimension of the gospel.
5. *Young Evangelicals*. Lacking a well-defined theology, they advocate an interest in human beings as whole persons, sociopolitical involvement, creative worship forms, ecumenicism, combating civil religion, and opposing the attempt to equate spirituality with religious customs.

In my opinion, even five subgroups are excessive, tending to overlap as they undeniably do. Yet Robert Webber has actually classified evangelicals into fourteen—yes, fourteen—identifiable entities.[4] Allow me simply to run through his categories as if they comprised a sort of litany: fundamentalist evangelicalism, dispensational evangelicalism, conservative evangelicalism, nondenominational evangelicalism, Reformed evangelicalism, Anabaptist evangelicalism, Wesleyan evangelicalism, Holiness evangelicalism, Pentecostal evangelicalism, charismatic evangelicalism, black evangelicalism, progressive evangelicalism, radical evangelicalism, and mainline evangelicalism.

Well, I suspect no additional taxonomic hairsplitting is needed and therefore I move on to consider the resurgence of evangelicalism in recent years.

II

Pietism, revivalism, and evangelicalism have been major influences in American religion from colonial days to the 1980s. Now fused into a somewhat homogeneous dynamic, they are making a powerful impact nationally. Eschewing the role of a historian, let me highlight some aspects of evangelicalism's development over the past few decades.

With the death of the renowned doyen of evangelicalism, William Jennings Bryan, in 1925, and the dominance of liberalism in seminaries and churches, there was, in Robert Handy's phrase, "a time of religious depression." To be sure, we must not forget the individuals, agencies, and denominations that continued to lift high the evangelical torch during this period of relative darkness. But to fix a date quite arbitrarily,

4. Robert E. Webber, *Common Roots* (Grand Rapids, 1982), 32.

starting in the 1940s evangelicalism enjoyed an ongoing renaissance it is still enjoying. The ensuing years saw the organization of the National Association of Evangelicals; Fuller Theological Seminary opened its doors; *Christianity Today* began publication; Billy Graham emerged from obscurity to gain worldwide attention. Meanwhile, evangelical institutions of higher education, some of them with roots in the nineteenth century, were burgeoning. And as the years have kept rolling along, evangelical radio and TV programs have been phenomenally successful. New translations of Scripture have proliferated. The cause of global missions has been thriving, sparked by, to mention one stimulus among many, the trememdous Urbana Conferences of the Inter-Varsity Christian Fellowship, which have been drawing together thousands of college students to face the challenge of the Great Commission. Professional societies such as the Christian Association for Psychological Studies, the American Scientific Affiliation, the Christian Medical Society, and the Christian Legal Society have been increasingly active. Youth for Christ, Campus Crusade, World Vision, the Christian Businessmen's Committee, Bible Study Fellowship, Prison Fellowship—all these, together with hundreds of other agencies, have been leavening American society.

On the political scene such influential individuals as Mark Hatfield, John Conlan, Jesse Helms, Paul Simon, and Reuben Askew have been articulating their spiritual convictions. And recall that in 1976 all three candidates for the presidency were self-avowed evangelicals. In addition all sorts of once rather ignored issues have come out of the evangelical closet since the 1973 Chicago Declaration of Social Concern was drafted. More recently the Moral Majority, headed by Jerry Falwell, has persuaded evangelicals that politics and fundamentalism are compatible bedfellows.

To mention one more fact, though statistics are notoriously undependable, today between forty and fifty million Americans identify themselves as evangelicals, most of these alleging a born-again experience. Little wonder, therefore, that a mood of triumphalism prevails within this now sizable segment of Christianity, especially when so distinguished a luminary as George Gilder pays it a high compliment:

By 1985 evangelical religion will be seen as the most positive force in American intellectual life as it moves to challenge directly the secular humanist predominance in the universities and the media. It will dispel the current dark age in American culture, epitomized by the near-depravity and intellectual fatuity of much of the average Ivy League curriculum, network television schedule, and Hollywood film, all of which are resorting to shocks of sex and violence to make up for the emptiness and banality of secular thinking. . . . Intellectuals will come to understand that the Moral Majority is a sensible and moderate response to the great evils it is combating, pressures that are destroying American families and thus unleashing waves of criminality in American cities.[5]

If it could be said in the nineteenth century that evangelicalism was "the single most widespread influence in Victorian England," the same boast can no doubt be made concerning evangelicalism in late twentieth-century America.

III

Perhaps so. Perhaps not. Kenneth Kantzer, whose editorials are featured in *Christianity Today,* declares that evangelicalism is weaker than it was fifteen years ago. He suspects that, when evangelicals numbered only one in ten of our population, their influence on the nation was, in his words, "infinitely greater than the evangelical influence today." Kantzer is right, evangelicalism has no cause for self-congratulatory triumphalism.

To be sure, it is immensely influential, but so far it has seemingly been ineffective in changing the moral climate of American society. Abortion, crime, pornography, alcoholism, drug use, divorce (America has eleven and a half million single-parent homes), mental illness, family disintegration, two and a half million unmarried adults in our country are cohabiting—ethical problems like these cry out for solutions, and those espoused by evangelicals are not being eagerly embraced and implemented.

Turning to another matter that is obviously related to what I have said thus far, no spirit of self-congratulatory triumphalism is warranted in the light of evangelicalism's disunity. Think back to the fourteen different brands Robert Webber asserts are available in the marketplace of American evangelicalism. I wince as I hear Sheldon Vanauken remark that Jesus Christ spoke of his church in the singular, not in the plural of ten thousand sects. I wince again, even though I manage to smile weakly,

5. George Gilder, cited in "Brief Case," *Eternity* (Apr. 1981), 12.

when someone revives that hoary joke about the six GIs shipwrecked on a
desert island in the South Pacific, two of them Catholics, two Jews, and
two Baptists. After a while, concerned that their spiritual life be nour-
ished, the two Catholics organized the Church of the Holy Virgin. Not to
be outdone, the two Jews organized the Beth Israel synagogue. And also
not to be outdone, the two Baptists organized the First Baptist Church—
and the Second Baptist Church! Alas, that evangelicalism is cursed with a
fissiparous propensity, tending to magnify doctrinal molehills into theological mountains! That is why we are an embattled brotherhood. We
have hardliners vs. the softliners; Calvinists vs. Arminians; premill-
lenarians vs. postmillenarians, immersionists vs. paedobaptists; charismatics vs. anticharismatics; propositionalists vs. existentialists; fundamentalists vs. neo-evangelicals; separatists vs. ecumenists; biblical
inerrantists vs. noninerrantists; and social activists vs. privatistic pietists. Can we blame outsiders for being perplexed and bemused by our
disunity?

Take the last three antitheses in the catalog of conflicts I have just
rehearsed, beginning with the antagonism between separatists and ecumenists. Most evangelicals denounce serious efforts to bring about
ecclesiastical togetherness as a diabolical strategy designed to sabotage
the gospel. Any allusion to the World Council of Churches or the National Council of Churches (both of which in my judgment deserve
stringent criticism) causes the typical evangelical to bridle in righteous
wrath. Yet such staunch evangelicals as Arthur Glasser and Richard
Lovelace attended the Sixth Assembly of the World Council in Vancouver last summer and issued a letter signed by over two hundred of
their fellow-believers. Its conclusion must be of interest to evangelicals
everywhere, even the most ardent separatists.

Our experience at Vancouver challenged stereotypes some of us have
had of the WCC. And our involvement in WCC processes and programs made us realize anew the distortions in the popular evangelical
understanding of them. Hence, we feel pressed to declare publicly our
determination to be more actively involved in all efforts seeking the
unity and renewal of the church. Because we have seen evidence of God
at work here, we cannot but share our growing conviction that evangelicals should question biblically the easy acceptance of withdrawal,
fragmentation and parochial isolation that tends to characterize many
of us. Should we not be more trustful of those who profess Christ's

lordship? Should we not be more concerned with the peace, purity and unity of the people of God in our day? And if God thereby grants the church renewal for which many pray, shall this not forever demolish that all too popular evangelical heresy—that the way to renew the body of Christ is to separate from it and relentlessly criticize it?[6]

Simultaneously, however, with the release of that letter a smaller group of evangelicals, including Peter Beyerhaus of Germany and Arthur Johnson of the United States, released a letter that took precisely the other position, ending with this warning:

All these observations contribute to our apprehensions that the WCC is in danger of becoming a mouth-piece of false prophecy to Christianity. Until these shortcomings and distortions are recognized and disavowed publicly in favor of a new affirmation of the Bible as God's infallible revelation, we cannot, with good conscience, encourage our fellow evangelicals to actively participate in the structures and programs of the WCC. Rather we should channel our contributions through truly Christian alternative organizations. Otherwise, we would become responsible for bringing evangelical believers and churches under the influence of such deceptive ideas as we encounter them at this Assembly. We do not state this in a judgmental spirit nor with a divisive attitude, but out of our loving concern for the maintenance of biblical truth in all churches inside and outside the WCC, that truth, without which the world cannot find the life which is in Jesus Christ.[7]

Thus the tension between separatists and ecumenists remains unrelaxed. Thus, too, the effectiveness of the evangelical witness is diluted and nullified:

Consider also the tension between social activists and privatistic pietists. In the wake of the fundamentalist controversy any openly expressed concern for political and economic issues on the part of an evangelical was liable to render him suspect of being a covert disciple of Walter Rauschenbusch and a believer in the social gospel. But today a Jerry Falwell, reversing the shibboleth thundered from most fundamentalist pulpits

6. Arthur Glasser and Richard Lovelace, "Evangelicals at Vancouver: An Open Letter," *TSF Bulletin* (Sept.-Oct. 1983), 18-19.

7. Peter Beyerhaus, Arthur Johnston, and Mying Yuk Kim, "An Evangelical Evaluation of the WCC's Sixth Assembly in Vancouver," *TSF Bulletin* (Sept.-Oct. 1983), 19-20.

that religion and politics don't mix, has been spearheading involvement in governmental policy. Evangelicals of less privatistic orientation than Dr. Falwell—for example, Ron Sider—though applauding the social activism of the Moral Majority, voice their distress over the sorts of issues that Falwell and his followers stridently insist are of primary importance while they ignore other issues that appear to be more crucial and substantial. Yet I must report that Bob Jones III castigates Dr. Falwell as "a pseudo-neofundamentalist" and "the most dangerous man in America"—an appraisal motivated, I assume, by Jones's intense opposition to some of Falwell's social and political positions. Listening to such rhetoric—which, tragically, is all too commonplace within evangelicalism— I bow my head in shame. Why must we berate our brothers and sisters so vituperatively in public?

Furthermore, think of the sharp difference between the late Francis Schaeffer and Norman Geisler in this area. Schaeffer, rather surprisingly, in his *A Christian Manifesto,* advocates civil disobedience and even, if a state commands participation in evil, reluctant resort to force. Geisler, *per contra,* in an article contributed to the *Fundamentalist Journal,* contends that obedience to Paul's teaching in Romans 13—really, God's directive—rules out absolutely any disobedience to a *de jure* state. Under no circumstances, he avows, must any state be disobeyed.

Third, consider the clash between inerrantists and noninerrantists. In a thought-provoking essay, "Inerrant the Wind: The Troubled House of North American Evangelicals," Robert Price reviews the internecine struggle precipitated by the publication of Harold Lindsell's *The Battle for the Bible.* He discusses the stance of the International Council on Biblical Inerrancy and its 1978 *Chicago Statement on Biblical Inerrancy.* Because his article appeared in July 1983, Dr. Price could not of course comment on the forced resignation of Robert Gundry from the Evangelical Theological Society in December 1983, an action demanded by a majority of the society's members at its annual meeting in response to Gundry's commentary on Matthew. Gundry in that very scholarly work has allegedly repudiated inerrancy; Gundry himself, however, emphatically denies that charge. In any case, Price maintains—and I think does so irrefutably—that

the more consistent group is willing to identify with a particular church tradition. Some of the Orthodox Evangelicals had already begun to identify with the "New Oxford Movement" in the United States and the United Kingdom. The movement which expresses its concerns in *The New Oxford Review,* was already Anglican in orientation and has begun to flirt conspicuously with Roman Catholicism, thus threatening to follow the original Oxford Movement of John Henry (Cardinal) Newman out of separate existence, and into the papal fold. Another body of American Evangelicals, disenchanted with their sectarian past, has formed a new denomination called "The Evangelical Orthodox Church," which intends to disappear into unity with the (formerly Russian) Orthodox Church in America. So via these various routes, a number of evangelicals seem to have given up hope of a viable doctrine of exclusively biblical authority, in favour of apostolic succession and ecclesiastical authority.

In the current North American debate over biblical inerrancy and authority, it has become apparent that we cannot speak simply of two sides, as if one group affirmed inerrancy and the other denied it. That would not be even half of the story, since among non-inerrantists, we may distinguish five different emphases, some of which actually represent entirely different and opposing views. Furthermore, it looks as if each of these positions reflects the hermeneutical stances of other (Catholic or Protestant) theological camps. Either a given non-inerrantist view unwittingly tends in the same direction as a non-evangelical view (e.g., Jewett parallel Bultmann's demythologizing and content-criticism); or the non-inerrantist view willingly emulates the non-evangelical view (e.g., Rogers and Bloesch echo the "Biblical Theology Movement"; Webber *et al.* move toward catholic ecclesiasticism). This being so, there would seem no longer to be anything distinctively hermeneutical defining these emerging paths (or anyone treading them) as "evangelical."[8]

Whatever one's own judgment as to Price's probing analysis, it is incontestably plain that evangelicalism even with respect to the watershed issue of biblical authority fails to speak with one voice. Instead, Price at least hears a babble of conflicting voices as do, I suspect, many of the outsiders who overhear our in-house conversations.

In summary, therefore, I as an evangelical must confess that, despite some encouraging signs of a willingness to keep doctrinal molehills from

8. Robert M. Price, "Inerrant the Wind: The Troubled House of North American Evangelicals," *The Evangelical Quarterly* (July 1983), 143-44.

being magnified into faction-splitting mountains, evangelicalism in 1984 continues to frustrate our Lord's plea to our Father: "That they may all be one as we are one."

IV

What, then, about the future of this divided but dominant and dynamic form of Protestantism? Will evangelicalism become even more dominant and dynamic while, we hope, less and less divided? Will it surge on into the twenty-first century as the wave of the future? Or has the wave already crested and is it slowly, perhaps imperceptively, receding? Will evangelicalism overcome its fissiparous proclivity and in doing that slough off its tendencies toward cultural ghettoism, biblical obscurantism, narcissistic individualism, otherworldly indifferentism, uncritical nationalism, selfish materialism, and impossible antiquarianism?

But what about the future of evangelicalism? Is Episcopal bishop John Shelby Sprong a discerning prophet? He chides traditional Christianity, and hence evangelicalism, for failing to read the signs of the times:

> To be catapulted into a world beyond tribal identity is also to be catapulted beyond every religious definition into a world of dreadful religious insecurity that cries out in the darkening void in the hope that there will be a responding divine voice. In that place the interdisciplinary religious conflicts of the past, differences among Christian groups that still seem so important to so many, the ecumenical movement that seeks to address these differences, will all seem like irrelevant carryovers from a pre-modern conscientiousness. They will all finally be ignored as unworthy of much human energy, for larger issues will confront us. Christianity's future life may well depend on the Christian ability to respond to those larger issues, for that response will force a degree of change which will give us the possibility of achieving the evolutionary expansion that is the key to survival.[9]

Is that the future of evangelicalism? Is it doomed to disappear at best or remain as an impotent hangover of outmoded mythology, pushed to the periphery of culture as civilization moves on toward the kind of syncretistic faith Arnold Toynbee envisioned? Who can foretell? I for one confess

9. John Shelby Sprong, *Into the Whirlwind* (New York, 1983), 189.

my utter inability to prognosticate. But I flatly reject the pessimism of many fellow-evangelicals who are persuaded with Hal Lindsay that we are living in *The Terminal Generation* and that therefore apostasy must inevitably grow worse and worse with no hope of spiritual revival or cultural renewal. Whatever one's eschatological stance—and I have confessed myself to be a premillenarian—there is no need to despair over the prospects of Christianity. After all, God is still alive. He rules in loving sovereignty, and his perspective on history is no doubt astonishingly different from my own myopic vision. I believe that the future is amazingly malleable and in God's omnipotent hands, and he, I know, delights in miraculous surprises. Thus Malcolm Muggeridge marvels at the wonders of personality-transformation that have been occurring—of all places!—in the Soviet Union. Listen to what he writes:

A wonderful sign has been vouchsafed us, one of the great miracles of the story of Christendom. This sign is the amazing renewal of the Christian faith in its purest possible form in, of all places, the countries that have been most drastically subjected to the oppression and brainwashing and general influence of the first overtly atheistic and materialistic regime to exist on earth. This is a fact. I should say myself that it is the most extraordinary single fact of the twentieth century. . . .

If when I was a young correspondent in Moscow in the early thirties you had said to me that it would be possible for the Soviet regime to continue for sixty years with its policy of doing everything possible to extirpate the Christian faith, to discredit its record and its originator, and that after this there would emerge figures like Solzhenitsyn speaking the authentic language of the Christian, grasping such great Christian truths as the cross in a way that few people do in our time, I would have said, "No, it's impossible, it can't be." But I would have been wrong. . . .

Recently, we were making a television programme about the anti-God movement in the Communist countries and were filming a selection of their propaganda posters. The early ones all showed old peasants, old has-been people. But the latest posters showed young people as the ones being foolishly deluded by religion. So contrary to what might be expected, this fantastic steamroller trying to destroy every trace of Christian faith has failed. All the efforts of the most powerful government that's ever existed in the world, in the sense of taking to itself the most power over its citizenry, has been unable to shape these people into the sort of citizens it wants them to be. Of all the signs of our times, this is the one that should rejoice the heart of any Christian most, and for that matter of anyone who loves the creativity of our mortal existence. [10]

Pondering the sovereign outworking of God's grace in human affairs, ancient and contemporary, I join with Richard Lovelace in prayerful hope and hopeful prayer. He discerns signs of spiritual renewal and sees Christians of every theological orientation taking tentative steps toward unity. Hence in optimistic anticipation of another Great Awakening, he encouragingly declares:

> The body of Christ is closer to organic working order. These are not just my own positive scenarios for the church's future; they are things that are happening now. If we extrapolate a line from these points, we reach toward a worldwide spiritual awakening at a depth and breadth never before attained. This presupposes a wide knowledge of the biblical principle of life in the Spirit, along with the core of the gospel, but we are gaining the instruments to promote this. It also assumes a widespread hunger for deeper spiritual vitality, but this is now appearing. [11]

Listening to Muggeridge and Lovelace I am reminded of G. K. Chesterton's remark: "At least five times the faith has to all appearances gone to the dogs. In each of these five cases it was the dog that died." This prompts me to exclaim as a relative pessimist whose pessimism is wrapped in an ultimate optimism, "The future is as bright as the promises of God," and our Lord promised that the gates of hell shall not prevail against his church.

Understanding the Chapter

1. According to Grounds, aside from core doctrinal tenets of Scripture, what commitments and practices comprise the essence and spirit of evangelicalism?

2. What five subgroups of evangelicals mentioned by Quebedeaux does Grounds point to as indicative of the plurality within evangelical-

10. Malcolm Muggeridge, *The End of Christendom* (Grand Rapids, 1980), 38-42.

11. Richard Lovelace, "Future Shock and Christian Hope," *Christianity Today* (Aug. 5, 1983), 16.

ism? Discuss these and other possible classifications of evangelicals. Can you offer your own classification?

3. List some of the signs, starting in the 1940s, that point to an ongoing renaissance that evangelicalism has still been enjoying.

4. Why and how does George Gilder, as quoted by Grounds, argue that "By 1985 evangelical religion will be seen as the most positive force in American intellectual life"? Do you agree with Gilder's assessment?

5. Discuss Grounds' observation that "evangelicalism is cursed with a fissiparous propensity, tending to magnify doctrinal molehills into theological mountains! That is why we are an embattled brotherhood." Is the same true for modern Jewry? Why or why not?

6. Grounds discusses three main conflicting groups among evangelicals that divide them: separatists and ecumenists, social activists and privatistic pietists, inerrantists and noninerrantists. Considering these divisions, is there any consensus that unites them?

7. Discuss the following negative tendencies, given by Grounds, characteristic of evangelicalism: cultural ghettoism, biblical obscurantism, narcissistic individualism, otherworldly indifferentism, uncritical nationalism, selfish materialism, impossible antiquarianism. In your opinion, which of these are most damaging to the unity of the church?

8. What does Grounds see as the future of evangelicalism?

9. Explore what appears to be the future of evangelicalism against G. K. Chesterton's remark, "At least five times the faith has to all appearances gone to the dogs. In each of these five cases it was the dog that died."

14
Evangelicals and Jews: Shared Nightmares and Common Cause

HILLEL LEVINE

The dialogue between Jews and evangelicals, on the local and national levels, both formally and informally, is a relatively new and positive development. For Jews, prudence alone would support this dialogue in consideration of the growing visibility and numerical and political strength of the evangelicals. Yet, for many Jews, an increasing sense of compatibility with evangelicals on important issues provides the moorings for new alliances, which may transcend former political identities of left/right or Democrat/Republican.

A growing number of more savvy and more thoughtful Jews can no longer be seen as knee-jerk liberals. The traditional alignments have become too tenuous, the packages of issues too complex, and the means by which policies have been pursued too ambiguous for the Jewish vote to be "in anyone's bag."

The Democratic party, which has provided a political home for the majority of American Jews, at least since the days of the New Deal, has undergone major transformations. The shift in emphasis in the perennial and tragically irreconcilable antinomy between liberty and equality and the concomitant shift in concern from rights of individuals based on achievement to entitlements of social categories based on deprivation and past suffering comes just at the moment when Jews are enjoying the sweetest fruits of success. They have made half-hearted attempts to compete along these new lines by displaying their wounds and underscoring the fact that not all Jews have "made it." But on the whole, American Jews are too confident in the American dream and too proud of their own accomplishments to dispense with merit. This new philosophical base to the Democratic party, insofar as there is one, the flirtation with quotas in its party planks, and even in its party organization and rules, would be enough cause for Jews to reconsider their political affiliations. Resentment among ethnic groups, which these policies foster, has occasionally been aimed with particular sharpness against Jews, further weakening their commitment to the Democratic party and the liberal agenda. Stalwart Jewish liberals have even resorted to name-calling, describing their neoconservative coreligionists as "Jews without mercy." Yet a growing number of Jews are prepared to surrender their self-image of being progressive and high-minded for a more pragmatic approach, in which political issues are confronted on their own merit.[1]

The recognized rightward drift of the Jews, therefore, should come as little surprise. In fact, if there were surprises, they would be found in the residual attachment of Jews, against what would be expected based upon their socioecomonic attainments, to issues supported by those to the left of center.

At the same time, there may be even more reason to assume a basis of political compatibility between Jews and evangelicals. There is mounting evidence of broader distribution of evangelicals along the political spectrum. While we cannot underestimate the influence of the New Christian Right within the evangelical camp, more "born-again" Christians than heretofore anticipated identify their positions on important issues as centrist and even left of center.

Yet despite the apparent increase in dialogue and political compatibility between the two communities, there is still a palpable standoffishness among Jews toward alliances with evangelicals. Some of this reticence is due to the size and heterogeneity of the evangelical camp, whose internal organization and ability to achieve consensus are likely to be exaggerated by outsiders. Thus, a Key '73 or the much publicized statement of the Reverend Bailey Smith regarding God's inattentiveness to the prayers of Jews, despite the criticism and dissociation from both by prominent evangelical leaders, are likely to be experienced by some Jews as characteristic and representative of the "true" position of all evangelicals. Even those Jews closest to the dialogue are likely to harbor a degree of suspicion toward some evangelical activity, which can be clearly harmful to Jews, experiencing it as regressive and a betrayal of a new and emerging alliance. Jews must come to terms with the political realities of

1. Sarah Bershtel and Allen Graubard, "The Mystique of the Progressive Jew," *Working Papers* (March-April 1983): 19-25.

evangelical Christianity as a mass movement—with leaders who must deal with reluctant followers, energetic challengers, and ideological cross-currents and eddies that often, but not always, lead into the mainstream.

What are some sources of evangelical reticence toward Jews? Two abiding myths about American Jews have had a powerful influence upon the way Christian conservatives and evangelicals view them: that Jews are not only liberal, but radical to the point of being unpatriotic and espouse what are considered to be modern causes at the expense of traditional, time-proven values; and that Jews are secularists opposed to the religious roots of American society. These myths often merge into the image of the secular humanist, against which evangelicals are prepared to lambast with heightened enthusiasm.

As with all myths, there is more than a grain of historical truth in these characterizations of Jews. From the late eighteenth century, the period in which Jews began to attain civic rights, they were most often among those who questioned traditional ideas and undermined the conventional social order. In many areas of Europe, it was their activity as Court Jews or entrepreneurs that contributed to the transformation and development of modern society at the expense of traditional power holders, like the aristocracy and the clergy. Insofar as their incorporation into modern society did not proceed as an irreversible process, Jews, in their impatience and frustration, were often most prone to radical ideas.[2] Most American Jews, of East-European origin, immigrated at the time of the downfall of Russian feudalism. Some, moving from the old world barricades to the new world ghettos, channeled their revolutionary fervor into the economic achievement made possible by the freedom and openness of American society. But the Jews' strong involvement in early American socialism and labor organization, although short-lived, is long remembered. Also, their more recent and prominent involvement in the New Left and antiwar movement of the sixties connected them with protest movements whose patriotism was questioned by their detractors.

Nevertheless, American Jews had a romance with America that cannot be overlooked. In my grandfather's synagogue, in the New York suburb where I lived as a child, the more pious congregants would gather late Saturday afternoons to usher out the holy Sabbath with the *Seudah*

2. For a survey of the transformations that took place among Jews, see the work of Jacob Katz, particularly *Out of the Ghetto* (New York, 1978).

Shlishit, the third Sabbath meal, also known as the feast of the Messiah. At this moment of transformation from the sacred day of rest, thought of by the rabbis as "a taste of the world to come," to the thoughts of everyday mundane life, the old Jews would ponder the future and ultimate redemption. During this beautiful moment, they would break into a thronging rendition of "God Bless America." As they would sing, their eyes drifted back to their not so dim childhood memories of old world homes, pogroms, prejudice, persecution, and uncertainty. With enthusiasm and in thanksgiving, they sang of their adopted homes.

Three decades later, the overwhelming majority of native-born American Jews, by every standard comfortable in America and privileged to have spent their formative years during a golden age of Jewish security, sang "God Bless America" with equal fervor. The occasional critical position, with which a large segment of the Jewish community has been identified on certain controversial issues, in no way should preclude the recognition of what Jews feel for this unique experiment in pluralistic democracy and multicultural existence that has endured for over two centuries. If anything, with another generation passed since the immigrant experience, Jews are more integrated economically, socially, and politically, and by any indicator are more active in civic life on community, city, state, and national levels. The romance with the American experience has deepened, but is now expressed in political action: the stuff from which good citizenship is created. The messianic associations with the American experience prompt Jews to focus on the renewal of that experience. That evangelicals might ever call this into question can lead only to intensified misunderstanding.[3]

An even more pervasive generalization made by evangelicals regarding Jews is that they are secular. Again, there is more than a grain of historical truth in this. The same historical forces that placed them in this position and made it in their interest to undermine the traditional privilege of the aristocracy made it seemingly in their interest to promote the removal of religious authority, associated with the state in Europe, from politics. But the American experience is quite different and prompts a different reaction from Jews. As Robert Bellah stated, "The American solution to the problem of church and state is unprecedented, unique and confused."[4] While Jews may be regarded consistently as the most secular

3. Henry Feingold, *Zion in America* (New York, 1974).
4. Robert Bellah, "Civil Religion: The American Case" (1980).

group in American society, as measured by such questionable indicators as attendance at religious services, it is an ambiguous issue for most Jews, and as evangelicals have recently been discovering, there is no consensus among different Jewish subgroups on the major church/state issues. What must be made clear to evangelicals, however, is that for Jews, a vote on any of the growing number of issues, which seemingly support a strong separation of church and state, is not a vote for a secular, godless, and valueless American society, any more than the concern voiced by evangelicals for enduring values in comtemporary society should be taken as a vote for a Christian theocracy.

Discourse on Christmas crèches and Hanukkah displays trivialize what is really at stake. Beyond the principled position that many Jews have taken lies an intense fear of the vision of a Christian America. The activities of many evangelicals have done little to allay this well-founded fear. Evangelicals, with their multiple visions and competitive church organizations, should be the same zealous guardians of pluralism and enemies of theocracy as any nonevangelical or non-Christian. Notions of Christian love and brotherhood have not prevented internecine blood-baths; the secularism evangelicals struggle to overcome is a product of irresolvable Protestant sectarian wars in seventeenth-century England. America itself has had its share of religiously inspired conflict, such that the means of religious influence, resorting to Madison Avenue, the legis-latures, the courts, and even terrorism, must receive the utmost con-sideration from those who are most fearful of the effects of secularization and are seeking to restore public virtue.

Dreams of a Christian America cannot tame the nightmares evangeli-cals share with Jews. The twentieth century has produced modes of divinized politics and political messianism that, when making use of modern technology, can become particularly insidious. The most dan-gerous movements of the right and left, though in their own terms antireligious, self-consciously used the language of religion to mobilize the masses and eliminate contending loyalties based on faith, political ideology, or even family ties.[5] Monistic belief systems legislated from the top make total demands upon adherents promising to resolve the confu-sion and conflicts engendered by life in the modern world. They devalue the variety of personal and collective endeavors outside of their politics;

5. Uriel Tal, "Political Faith of Nazism Before the Holocaust," Annual Lecture of the Jacob M. and Shoshana Schreiber Chair of Contemporary Jewish History (Tel Aviv, 1978), 5-44.

to their politics they grant the claims of exclusive truth. They eliminate the boundaries between those spheres in which ultimate values, including religious, should be influential, and those which should be governed by political norms allowing trial, error, and compromise. They press their messages with a greater literalness and often with far greater brutality than religious movements that do not expect to achieve their dominion before the ultimate redemption.

Jews and evangelicals share other nightmares. The last decades of the twentieth century have witnessed the unleashing of religious passions that undermine any semblance of civic society. While the religiously prompted civil wars have generally been contained within a comfortable distance in underdeveloped regions of the Third World, when we examine such countries as Northern Ireland, and even to some extent Lebanon and Iran, where a degree of modernization does not inhibit political chaos and wanton murder, we have reason to be concerned with some of the religious responses to the "postmodern" discontents, as they become manifest in our own country.

Max Weber's frightening description of the modern world has been realized in part. The modern economic order with its technical and economic conditions of machine production and rational modes of social organization, as manifest in the hierarchical bureaucracy and its markets providing capital, have had an enormous effect on the lives of contemporary Americans. The machine has not been running so smoothly, however, nor has it determined all spheres of life. It has broken down in wars, social conflict, and business cycles, prompting unemployment and creating pockets of the "Religion of the Oppressed." Beyond that, secularization theory did not foresee nor account for the growing leisure time, the greater possibilities of boredom, and the underinstitutionalization of many sectors of contemporary life, leaving important openings for religious influence. Recent American history has been riddled with fads, many involving transcendental cravings, such as cults, drugs, and fascination with oriental religion. But many of these fads respond to and are prompted by more elusive religious needs. Seemingly contradictory fashions in health and gourmet food, ascetic exercise and unrestrained sensuality, absorbed by segments of the population in a cyclical manner but with intense seriousness, illustrate, perhaps, some of this diffused religious passion. Litigiousness, beyond greed and ethical confusion, perhaps expresses the need to know "whodunit?!"[6] Beyond the enclaves of

6. Hillel Levine, "Whodunit?: Religious Intolerance and the Secularization of Law," *Humanities in Society* (Spring 1979), 2:95-103.

the patently devout, there is overwhelming evidence of an unsecular America. Against this unstable religious background, shifting from extremes and evolving new forms, civic virtue, republicanism, and civil religion lose plausibility. The foundations of public order through consent and consensus become weakened and yield to coercion. The delicate balance between civil liberties and communal values is offset.[7] Isolated individuals are prime candidates for totalitarian mobilization. Single issue advocates, formerly of the left but now more consistently of the right, have occasionally been successful in using government to legislate abstract rights of the individual, often at the expense of communal values. By incautiously weakening viable communities that are the very matrices of values and participation, they win the battle and lose the war. Of some of these responses to anxiety and uprootedness and the loss of certainty, which is so characteristic of our time, both Jews and evangelicals have ample reason to be fearful.

Historians and sociologists have demonstrated the historical links between secularization and pluralism.[8] Only with the decline of formal religious authority and influence could divergent values and ideas receive a hearing; only with the separation of the religious community of the saved from the community of citizens could pluralistic democracy take root. But secularity has its costs, as we have seen, and is eschewed in one form or another by a growing segment of Americans. Can a nonsecular, even an antisecular, ethos have affinities with the pluralism and tolerance so integral to the American experience? This is the great challenge shared by Jews and evangelicals. Beyond tactical agreements and *quid pro quo,* can they develop a new outlook on American society that is both salutary and the basis of common cause?

A new pluralism, which does not necessitate the spiritual attenuation of life or a wishy-washy ecumenism that does not lead anywhere, must emerge. This pluralism must do more than make the best of a demographic dilemma: it must lead toward principled commitment. It must infuse political life with more virtue than zeal and train self-disciplined citizens in the theory and mechanics of pluralistic democracy, creating consensus where possible, but preserving the sacredness of communal domains where differences that do not endanger nor impinge upon the

7. Peter L. Berger and Richard J. Neuhaus, *To Empower People: The Role of Mediating Structures in Public Policy* (Washington, 1977), 40-45.

8. Peter L. Berger, *The Sacred Canopy* (Garden City, N.Y., 1967), 134ff.

larger collectivity and its values are deemed legitimate. We face a dangerous situation in which, with the politicization of the American economy (as manifest, perhaps, in the real estate boom in Washington, D.C., caused by the needs of every industry and cluster of industries to maintain a lobby to deal with regulatory agencies and the like), what might be called organic communities, natural communities, religious groups, or ethnic groups must work harder to maintain their collective influence and support for the special issues of particular communities.

What do we share? Where do we differ? How can we bargain it out? Against this background of an inspired pluralism, the internal Jewish agenda takes on a new vitality. For Jews, it is important to face our nightmares and what are essentially the nightmares of all of western civilization—the Holocaust. The historical record is by no means complete; we have some explanations for this tragedy, but our understanding is still lacking in many ways. In the wake of the Holocaust, there can no longer be, in the words of William James, "Once Born Souls." We are all Twice Born in realizing the potential of large-scale brutality, of which the Holocaust was unfortunately not the last instance. Understanding the Holocaust is not, at least initially, within the rubric of Jewish-Christian dialogue or ecumenism. Our respective communities have different relationships to those events and must face them as part of our internal religious dialogue. Christians must face Christian history. Christianity is that which in a presecular world preserved Jews by defining their religious-symbolic purposes in Christendom and assigning them certain functions. At the same time, Christianity was the most important carrier of antagonistic attitudes toward Jews. It is only when Christians and Jews begin to understand their histories that both communities will be able to stress what they share rather than what separates them. Part of the understanding of that history must lead to a greater respect for pluralistic democracy, the political processes upon which it is based, and a realization of the dangers of utopias in this unredeemed world, either in their theocratic versions with their Bibles and books of sayings or in their rabidly secular versions with their game-plans and cost/benefit analyses.

The new experience for all Jews—the existence of a sovereign Jewish state—alters the basic terms of Jewishness. Jews are grateful for the support we have received from Christians, particularly from evangelical Christians. Because of our appreciation and hope that it will continue, we are baffled when it is not forthcoming. We turn to our Christian brothers and sisters to help and support us with the spiritual as well as the political changes which have occurred in our generation. With a sovereign state, Jews must now deal with issues of power and responsibility that they have not confronted for millennia. We hope that the Jewish values that have thrived under different circumstances, in which Jews lived as minorities, can be applied in an exemplary way to the Jewish experience in Israel. We turn to our Christian friends for support in this. It is your dependable political support of Israel that will deter the aggressiveness of Israel's enemies and encourage them to respond constructively to Israel's initiatives in making peace. It is your understanding that will ensure that Israel does not succumb to the frustrations of isolation and to the sense that "the whole world is against us," which have had deleterious effects on the political and the spiritual growth of that young nation.

Two religious leaders, living in the early period of the respective encounters of Judaism and evangelical Christianity with modernity, foresaw the dangers of secularism and anticipated a principled pluralism that would provide the spiritual moorings for a society in which Jews and Christians participate. Shneur Zalman of Lyady, who lived during the end of the eighteenth and beginning of the nineteenth century in eastern Europe, is the founder of the Lubovitch Hasidic movement. Still thriving today with its center in Brooklyn, New York, this movement has made an interesting adjustment to the modern world, not unrelated to its founder's thinking. Shneur Zalman lived in the wake of the French Revolution and observed the Napoleonic conquests with their unbridled enthusiasm for enlightenment and secularity. He reflected upon Napoleon who, among other fatuous claims, wanted to restore Jerusalem. Shortly before his death, Shneur Zalman wrote the following epistle to his disciple:

> During the Mussaf services on Rosh Hashanah they showed me that if Bonaparte is victorious, the horn of Israel will be exalted and wealth will increase in Israel. But the heart of Israel will be separated and removed from their father in heaven. And if our master Alexander, the Czar, is victorious, even though the horn of Israel may be brought low and poverty increased to Israel, the heart of Israel will be joined to their father in heaven.[9]

Why did Shneur Zalman of Lyady, who had himself been arrested by the Czar, support the Czar? He knew the brutality of the Russian offi-

9. Abraham S. Heilman, *Bayt Robi* (Tel Aviv, n.d.), 92-93.

cials. Why did he choose the Czar over Napoleon, whose victory, as Shneur Zalman himself recognized, changed the situation of Jews in Russia and may have increased their dignity and prosperity? Did he really believe, as might be implied by the manner in which he presents the alternatives, that poverty and suffering are more conducive to piety? There is little in the volumes of Shneur Zalman's profound theological writings that would support this interpretation.

In a letter that Shneur Zalman's son wrote shortly after his father's death, he notes that his father favored the Czar because he went to war carrying icons; his Russian Orthodox priests would sprinkle the holy waters on the Russian forces. Napoleon, on the other hand, was an arrogant and godless man who represented brutality.[10] If the son reported accurately, the Hasidic master made a rather striking assessment of the Czar's spirituality and the dangers of secularity. Even though Shneur Zalman was far from being ecumenically inclined and would hardly attribute sacred significance to those icons, the Czars' unexceptional display of religiosity, even at the moment of going to war, which would inspire pious feelings in the greatest atheists, impressed Shneur Zalman with the sense that God's presence would be more plausible under the feudal tyrant than under the enlightened despot. As we pray to be spared of such tragic choices between the Czars and the Napoleons, we must marvel at the wisdom of this Hasidic master whose insight has been supported by nearly two centuries of experiences with totalitarian democracies.

The Reverend Adoniram Judson Gordon, a nineteenth-century premillennialist preacher who lived most of his life in Boston, and in many ways was a spiritual soulmate of Shneur Zalman of Lyady, had similar keen insight into modernity and its discontents.[11] He was a man of seeming contradiction, but not of inner conflict. In the robustness and wisdom he displayed in living his life, he defies the categories we would like to impose upon him. He was an ardent evangelist, a talented preacher, and a man of deep Christian faith. At the very moment his colleagues were turning to other modes of Christian piety, seeking to resolve their spiritual confoundedness through good work and the social gospel, the

10. Ibid., 95-103.
11. This too-brief assessment of Adoniram Judson Gordon follows from a preprint of an article my colleague, Professor Russell, generously shared with me. See C. Allyn Russell, "Adoniram Judson Gordon: Nineteenth Century Fundamentalist," *American Baptist Quarterly* (1985).

Reverend Gordon protested that we must walk in the spirit and be filled with it. For him, as for Shneur Zalman, in a world hostile to spirituality, the supreme challenge was to make God's presence plausible. All the rest will spontaneously and inevitably follow. Election by grace or faith did not, for Gordon, exclude the need for election by works. At a time when his colleagues sought to accommodate biblical teaching to new concepts of evolution and progress, at a time when the new theology or progressive orthodoxy, as it was called in the late nineteenth century, sought to embrace the spirit of the times by applying the teachings of Jesus to economic and political problems, A. J. Gordon, as he was lovingly known, sought the spirit to respond humanly and modestly to poverty, disease, overcrowding, unsafe working conditions, and political corruption. For the Reverend Gordon, it was not the vision of a secular city, but the repentance, on the one hand, and the regeneration, on the other, that would create an appropriate place for those who are to become the children of God. With his usual eloquence, he once declared that new Jerusalems are not evolved from municipal Babylons by improved drainage systems and sanitation.

What advice and legacy did these two spiritual leaders have for those of us who are still struggling with the problems of secularism, who want to live in the modern world but not entirely of it? The earth is the Lord's. That is the reality we must sustain and that is our view from the hinterland of the municipal Babylon in which we dwell. We need universal support for the sense that the earth is the Lord's, as Shneur Zalman seemed to have found in the Czar but not in Napoleon. But having affirmed that spiritual perspective and committed ourselves to the modesty that should ensue, we must be able to establish those areas in life in which we can particularize, privatize, and create our own meaning without pressure from without. Perhaps that is what the blessed inefficiency of the Czarist polity vouchsafes to Shneur Zalman. The Napoleons and the Czars both make their demands. The Napoleons want totally and wholly to enlist our hearts and souls in their drainage and sanitation systems. They promise us not only clean streets and orderly homes, but pure hearts, pure souls, pure air, right thinking, and freedom from cognitive dissonance. Napoleon's vision, although beautiful and enthusiastic, is worldly, monistic, and covers over intrinsic contradictions, often with brutality, and therefore, in its humanism, is a contradiction. The alternative may have been the order under which the trains do not quite run on time, sanitation is not as efficient, the pride of Israel might be

lowered, and certain sacrifices would have to be made. But, if there is to
be freedom, the hearts of Israel might be joined and again attached to
their father in heaven. This is what Shneur Zalman thought he saw in the
Czar. Unfortunately, as it turned out, he was more correct about his
pessimism in regard to Napoleon than he was in his cautious optimism
about the Czar and his heirs.

Adoniram Judson Gordon understood the limits of progress. He did
not eschew improved drainage and sanitation, but he knew that there was
an unbreachable gap between the municipal Babylons in which we live
and the new Jerusalems for which we strive. In his ardor as a premillennialist, he was very Jewish, for he knew that the Napoleons, in their
spiritualistic or technocratic versions, would never disappear. They
would continuously be opening the gates to their new Jerusalem. But the
Reverend Gordon, in the spirit of Isaiah, knew that on that day an event
not predicted by any progressivist computer printout would take place.
The nations would go up to the mountain of the Lord; that would be a
step different from all other steps. And what both Adoniram Judson
Gordon of Boston and Shneur Zalman of Lyady understood quite well was
that the new Jerusalem may be approached by different gates.

Understanding the Chapter

1. What reason does Levine give to support his contention that "there
is still a palpable standoffishness among Jews toward alliances with
evangelicals"?

2. What "two abiding myths about American Jews" have distanced
evangelicals from Jews and proven to be sources of evangelical reticence
toward Jews?

3. What historical, cultural, and economic factors in European Jewry
from the late eighteenth century to the early part of the twentieth have
influenced current Jewish involvement in more liberal, radical, and protest causes often set against the conventional social order?

4. What does Levine mean when he states that American Jews have
had a "romance with America" that has deepened over the years?

5. Misperceptions and misunderstandings continue to persist between evangelicals and Jews. Discuss the implications of the following
statement by Levine: "What must be made clear to evangelicals . . . is
that for Jews, a vote on any of the growing number of issues, which
seemingly support a strong separation of church and state, is not a vote

for a secular, godless, and valueless American society, any more than the concern voiced by evangelicals for enduring values in contemporary society should be taken as a vote for a Christian theocracy."

6. Levine states, "Evangelicals, with their multiple visions and competitive church organizations, should be the same zealous guardians of pluralism and enemies of theocracy as any nonevangelical or non-Christian." Do you agree with Levine? Why or why not?

7. What are some of the "nightmares" that Jews and evangelicals share?

8. Levine calls for the emergence of a "new pluralism" today. What does he mean? Do you agree that such a pluralism is necessary?

9. What kind of evangelical Christian help, support, and understanding does Levine call for and encourage regarding the State of Israel?

10. Were Rabbi Shneuer Zalman's and the Reverend Adoniram Judson Gordon's appraisals of modernity prophetic or were they narrow and backward-looking? Discuss.

15
An Evangelical View of the Modern State of Israel

JOHN N. OSWALT

How does an evangelical Christian view the modern State of Israel? Of special interest, I suppose, is the right of such a state to exist. This issue could be approached from several points of view, among which might be history, social justice, political expediency, and so forth. But none of these possesses any final degree of authority, each being susceptible to the wishes of the interpreter. Finally, each takes on the aspect of rationalization for the ancient dictum "Might makes right." On that basis one would be saying that since the Israelis have been strong enough to establish a bridgehead in that part of the world there must be some reason to justify their action.

However, the evangelical Christian does not accept the fact that the world is the result of such cynical relativisms. For him or her, all events have their meaning by reference to the saving purposes of God, the Father of our Lord Jesus Christ. Thus all things are either in line with his will or in temporary defiance of it. In this light such issues as historical precedent, apparent social justice, political expediency, and the like must take on a distinctly secondary aspect. They may not, and must not, be ignored, for they can provide valuable correctives to our interpretations of God's will. However, determination of those points does not provide the final basis for our judgment.

The question is, then, is there reason to believe that the modern State of Israel exists as an expression of God's saving purpose for the world? Answers to such a question could range from a flat "No" to an all-inclusive "Yes" that would see all Israeli political and military activities as a direct extension of the divine will. My own position, which I will express in the remainder of this chapter, lies somewhere midway between these extremes. On the one hand I believe that the presence of a Jewish state in Israel today is an expression of God's will and is a partial fulfillment of his purposes for the world. As such, I believe evangelical Christians should support Israel's right to exist and should use their influence to thwart all attempts at the destruction of that nation.

On the other hand, I see no reason to conclude that all of Israel's policies and actions are direct expressions of the divine will. The great majority of Israelis would classify themselves as nonreligious and would explicitly disavow the idea of seeking God's will in relation to national policy. Thus, while I believe that Israel has a right to exist and to devise policies and strategies to secure that existence, I do not feel constrained to endorse all those policies and strategies as being necessarily God's will to achieve that end.

Now let me tell you the biblical bases from which I derive such a position. At the outset we must remember that until the last century no significant section of the church looked for the physical return of the Jewish people to the land of Israel. The church saw itself as the new Israel to whom all the promises were given (Rom. 9:8) and into which the believing Jewish nation would be integrated at the end of time (Gal. 3:28). To be sure, the fact that the church took this position for so long does not prove it was correct and we are wrong (after all, neither did any significant part of the church look for the premillennial return of Christ), but it should induce in us a bit of humility regarding the absolute certainty of our own position.

Nonetheless I am convinced that the Bible does look forward to a physical return of the Jews to Israel. I base this belief upon two groups of texts. The first speaks of God's giving of the land to his people. Virtually all of these passages are well known; I include here some of the best known:

> Then the Lord appeared to Abram, and said, "To your descendants I will give this land." So he built there an altar to the Lord, who had appeared to him. (Gen. 12:7)

> On that day the Lord made a covenant with Abram, saying, "To your descendants I give this land, from the river of Egypt to the great river, the river Euphrates." (Gen. 15:18)

> "The land which I gave to Abraham and Isaac I will give to you, and I will give the land to your descendants after you." (Gen. 35:12)

> "This is the land of which I swore to Abraham, to Isaac, and to Jacob, 'I will give it to your descendants.'" (Deut. 34:5)

Similar passages are found in Deuteronomy 4:38; Joshua 1:12; 24:13; 1 Chronicles 16:14-18. Beyond these representative references is the whole concept of the land as the property of God that he distributes according to his sovereign will (e.g., Exod. 15:17) and that may not be redistributed at will by the fief-holder (cf. 1 Kgs. 21:23-24).

What these texts do for one who takes the authority of the Bible seriously is to establish God's intent for his people to possess the land of Canaan at least during the time of the Hebrew kingdom. What they do not necessarily establish is the duration of the time "descendants" (as in Gen. 15:18) is intended to cover. Is it not possible that this gift was for a limited time only? Could not the gift be annulled or even forfeited?

In my mind the second group of texts deals with this potentiality. These texts relate to the return from exile. To be sure, God did annul his promise; the people were ejected from the land, as Deuteronomy 28:15-68 forecasted so graphically and terribly. However, the very ejection demonstrated the durability of God's promise, for along with the ejection were first the promise and then the reality of the return. Not only was God's gift applicable during the kingdom period, it was so deep and of such a permanent nature as to be reinstated after the horror of exile. Again, many of these passages are well known; again, I quote some of the key ones:

> And the Lord your God will bring you into the land which your fathers possessed, that you may possess it; and he will make you more prosperous and numerous than your fathers. (Deut. 30:5)

> And there will be a highway from Assyria for the remnant which is left of his people, as there was for Israel when they came up from the land of Egypt. (Isa. 11:16)

> And they shall bring all your brethren from all the nations as an offering to the Lord, upon horses, and in chariots, and in litters, and upon mules, and upon dromedaries, to my holy mountain Jerusalem, says the Lord, just as the Israelites bring their cereal offering in a clean vessel to the house of the Lord. (Isa. 66:20)

> And after I have plucked them up, I will again have compassion on them, and I will bring them again each to his heritage and each to his land. (Jer. 12:15)

These passages demonstrate the trans-temporal nature of the promise for the Old Testament period. However, the Christian cannot escape asking whether all of that comes to a close at the end of the Old Testament era. So much of the Old Testament is composed of physical or material object lessons intended to teach spiritual truth that, having done so, no longer had significance. The most obvious case in point would be the ceremonial and sacrificial law. Is this also true regarding the promise of the land?

This question has two answers. One relates to the nature of the promises of the return; the other relates to the continued existence of the Jewish people in the New Testament economy. On the one hand the promises seem to speak of much more than that which was fulfilled in the returns of the sixth and fifth centuries B.C. They are too sweeping and too glowing for those historic events. Of course it may be argued that this is merely apocalyptic or proto-apocalyptic language and not to be taken too seriously. However, that is a one-sided view of the significance of apocalyptic and, regarding the return of the Jews, one which the events of our own times call into question. Beyond this, such references as Isaiah 66:20-21, which is normally taken to be addressed to the postexilic community, and Isaiah 11:11, which speaks of a second return in the messianic age, make it apparent that Isaiah, at least, specifically foresaw a further return from exile.

The second answer to this question relates to the New Testament vision of the Jews. Does it see them as having fulfilled their historic function when the church comes into existence and ceasing to be of interest to God? The answer is clearly "No." That most Gentile of all New Testament writers, Paul, gives the clearest statement of this principle in Romans 9–11. He makes it plain that Israel is not cast away (11:1) and he foresees a day when Israel as a whole will receive her Messiah (11:26-28). Finally, the Book of Revelation makes it clear that the representatives of the twelve tribes will take their places alongside the twelve apostles, demonstrating that Israel is not merely replaced by the church (21:12-14) but has a continuing significance in all ages.

In the light of all of this I conclude that God's promise of the land to Israel is for all time and that Israel has significance to God through all time. It is on this basis that I support the existence of a Jewish state in Israel today. However, the mere fact of Israel's presence in her land again does not guarantee that her policies and practices are God's policies and practices any more than they were in Old Testament days. Even a David or a Hezekiah, let alone an Ahab, was capable of proud, cynical, self-serving acts that were in fact an affront to God. That Israel's presence in her land is a fulfillment of prophecy does not remove her actions from the scrutiny of God's Word and Spirit. As an evangelical Christian I look forward to a day when Israel will, as a nation, turn to God and become the light to the nations Isaiah foresaw.

Understanding the Chapter

1. How does Oswalt argue that the State of Israel signifies an expression of the divine will? What are the implications of this argument for Christians?

2. Does Oswalt believe that all of Israel's policies and actions are direct expressions of God's will?

3. "Until the last century no significant section of the church looked for the physical return of the Jewish people to the land of Israel," states Oswalt. Considering this fact, what lesson does Oswalt say Christians can learn about the dilemmas and difficulties of biblical interpretation?

4. Oswalt does not believe the New Testament teaches that the Jews fulfilled their historic function when the church was born. What scriptural support does he give for this position?

16
An Evangelical Christian View of Israel

MARVIN R. WILSON

Evangelicals, like Jews, have been described as "People of the Book." That label is apt in that the Bible and biblical authority are pivotal in the thinking of evangelical Christians. As a community, we tend to approach almost everything from a biblical or theological perspective. The question of Israel is no exception. Historically, many Christians world-over have been deeply influenced in their viewpoints and attitudes on Israel and modern Zionism as a result of studying the Scriptures. To be sure, Zionism, the Jewish people's national liberation movement, has deep roots in the Hebrew Scriptures, no less than in the painful history of the Jewish people.

Teddy Kolleck, present mayor of Jerusalem, once said, "If you want one simple word to symbolize all Jewish history, that would be Jerusalem." The long history of Christianity, however, reveals a propensity toward understanding the word *Jerusalem* in terms of otherworldliness. This has sometimes obscured the rich, this-worldly meaning of the place name about which Kolleck and his biblical ancestors, David, Jeremiah, and others write. By transmuting Jerusalem into a spiritual or "heavenly" concept, Christian literature and hymnology have greatly truncated its meaning. For to remove Jerusalem from the concrete world of flesh and blood is to remove what has been the heart and soul of the Jewish people for nearly three thousand years. Jerusalem has neither parted this world for the heavenlies, nor does it presently lie in silence as a buried *tell,* mute testimony of a dead civilization. To the contrary, the golden city is a pulsating modern city; Israel is real: *am yisrael chai* ("the people of Israel lives").

Though there are notable exceptions, the primary basis of concern for Israel on the part of Jews has usually been historical, cultural, and economic, whereas the main concern of evangelicals has usually derived from a theological starting point. I will begin then with the question of theological interpretation, the place where many evangelicals start to formulate their understanding of Israel. Far from monolithic on this subject, two main schools of interpretation have characterized evangelical Christian thought toward Israel. Many evangelicals identify—at least broadly—with one of these, while others fall somewhere between the two.

One school of theological interpretation sees the church as the new and "true" Israel. In this view, Judaism is often referred to as a dead and legalistic religion. With the destruction of the temple in the year 70 and rejection of the Christian message, Israel has been cast off by God, exiled from her land as a wanderer among the nations. Replaced by the church, Israel has had no theological validity as the "people of God" for the last nineteen hundred years. As the second stage of God's "salvation rocket," the church has superseded Israel. Prophecies in the Hebrew Scriptures concerning Israel and her future have been fulfilled, or are now being "spiritually" fulfilled, in the life of the church. Those evangelicals who hold to some form of this position have sometimes been chided by their theological opponents for, as it were, viewing Mayor Kolleck more as the "curator of a museum" than as a civil servant in touch with a living people for whom certain covenant promises yet hold deep and permanent meaning.

A second view of Israel popular among many evangelicals makes a clear distinction between God's program for Israel and that of the church. Prophecies concerning Israel—down to the very details of her future— are interpreted literally. God has a bright and glorious future for Israel on this earth. With a rebuilt temple, Jerusalem will be the focal point of future world redemption as Israel is restored to her land under Messiah in peace, prosperity, and divine blessing.

To be sure, the concepts of "land of promise" and "return to Zion" are deeply grounded in biblical literature. The very last word in the Hebrew Bible (2 Chron. 36:23) is a call to "go up" to Zion. But the term is more complex. In the Hebrew Bible, "Israel" first has reference to a person (Gen. 32:28). The nation came into existence in the desert before it had land. The Holy Land was the historic fulfillment of the sons of Israel, not their origin.

In the New Testament, *Israel* occurs some sixty-eight times, and virtually all these uses do not refer to a land but to a people, the covenant people of God. In writing to the church at Rome, the apostle Paul uses the metaphor of the olive tree. He refers to the people of Israel as "the root that supports" Gentile Christians (Rom. 11:18). The sum of my point is this: to understand Israel as land, one must first grasp the idea of Israel as peoplehood; to talk about the State of Israel's survival is first to understand Jewish survival.

As for myself, I believe that the prophets of Israel had the supernatural ability to reveal certain truths about the future and destiny of God's covenant people. I also believe that the remarkable preservation of Israel over the centuries and her recent return to the land are in keeping with those many biblical texts which give promise of her future.[1] But my concern and support for Israel only begins with predictive prophetic texts; it does not end there. The more relevant prophetic texts, to me personally, are those which speak to Israel's present situation by calling men and nations to practice justice, righteousness, kindness, and brotherhood in their dealings with one another.

The State of Israel was brought into being by an affirmative vote of the United Nations. Such a vote was sustained on far more than any marshalling of numerous predictive prooftexts; it was established on a historical and contemporary understanding of what justice and morality demand. In their eagerness to witness the fulfillment of prophecy in the life of contemporary Jewry, evangelicals must never lose sight of the importance of the sociological, humanitarian, political, and cultural factors involved in the birth and present sustaining of that state. When prophecy is seen by some evangelicals to be little more than prediction or prewritten history, and when Israel is seen to be little more than the key piece of some gigantic eschatological jigsaw puzzle, the Bible is divested of its burning concerns of justice and compassion, of ethical and social righteousness, directed to our day.

In general, evangelicals score very high on their knowledge of the first two thousand years of Jewish history; on the last two thousand years, however, they score very low. This fact is tragic, for so much has happened during these years to affect the understanding of Jewish peoplehood, survival, and the desperate need for a homeland. Why do I support the idea of a Jewish state in the Middle East and the on-going need for Christians to help sustain its qualitative survival? The Crusades, Inquisition, pogroms, Holocaust, and painful history of anti-Semitism over

---

1. For a listing of these texts, see my article "Zionism as Theology," *Journal of the Evangelical Theological Society* (March 1979): 27-44.

these years ought to give every person—especially Christians—reason to pause before giving assent to the proposition that "Zionism is racism." At the close of the last century, Herzl, the father of modern Zionism, saw the Jews of the diaspora to be outsiders of history; they were a persecuted minority with nowhere to call home. He envisioned a place where a scattered and powerless people could find self-determination and a refuge from victimization. On May 14, 1948, Herzl's dream came true.

The tangible and growing support of Israel by the evangelical community in recent years is worth noting. Evangelicals account for more tourist dollars than any other Christian group. Evangelicals are also contributing to the growth of the land by planting trees and by working on kibbutzim. A number of evangelical organizations are located in Jerusalem, including the Institute of Holy Land Studies, Bridges for Peace, and the International Christian Embassy. The newly formed Center for Judaic-Christian Studies (Austin, Texas) works closely with evangelical and Israeli Jewish scholars in its efforts to publish and promote outstanding biblical research on the Jewish origins of the Christian faith.

Despite these positive signs of evangelical involvement in Israel, a number of issues of concern remain for future discussion. In particular, I speak of evangelical-Israeli relations, certain theologies held about Israel, and reaction to the political situation there today. The following observations deal with several matters that need further clarification, thought, and action:

1. More effort should be made to sponsor joint evangelical-Jewish study tours of the Holy Land. This can become a strong tool for impressing evangelicals with the necessity for a conscious commitment to the principle of religious pluralism. For evangelical visitors to Israel, it may be the first time they experience what it means to be a religious minority in another religious culture.

2. The Bible is Israel's national genius and treasure. As such, evangelical biblical scholars could profit immensely from establishing extended periodic conferences on biblical and archaeological studies in Jerusalem with their Israeli Jewish counterparts. A foundation could be incorporated to encourage and sponsor this unique interchange.

3. Many evangelical leaders must give more attention to overcoming a spirit of disinterest or apathy regarding a visit to Israel. Some are frightened away by the political and military unrest in the area. Others are repelled by stories of the commercialism surrounding holy sites. Still others stress that making a pilgrimage to a particular shrine is far less

important than the spiritual transaction within a human heart. To coun-
teract this apathy, evangelical seminaries and colleges must give more
attention in their curricula to biblical geography, archaeology, and Hebrew and Jewish backgrounds to the New Testament.

4. Evangelicals must maintain a tentativeness about the interpretation
of certain predictive prophecies about Israel's future. The evangelical
must learn how to distinguish between sheer speculation and sensational-
ism on the one hand, and sound biblical exegesis on the other. The reason
for this tentativeness is at least twofold: (1) the poetical literary genre of
much of the prophets, which includes many figures of speech, and (2) the
hermeneutic employed by the writers of the New Testament is such that
they frequently reinterpret various texts from the Hebrew Bible in terms
foreign to the expectation and understanding of the original hearers.

5. Evangelicals should not read biblical promises concerning the land
as they would a real estate deed. If Israel were to seek to annex the West
Bank by "divine right," or if any people were to perform a given political
or military action based on the words "God has willed/prophesied it," it
would likely be on very precarious and dangerous grounds. Should the
Israelis annex the East Bank (the western third of the State of Jordan) on
the grounds that God swore this land to Israel as evidenced by the fact
that the tribes of Reuben, Gad, and half of Manasseh settled there? I
think not. The sanction of any action should center on justice. It is
unfortunate, but so often true, that politics may prove far more compassionate and humane than theology.

6. Evangelical friendship and concern shown to Jewish people must
always be unconditional, without prerequisites or hidden agendas. Evangelicals should be candid with their Jewish friends as to what motivates
them to do such things as to come to Jerusalem each year by the thousands to celebrate the Feast of Tabernacles (cf. Zech. 14:16-19) or to
provide financial and other support toward efforts to build a third temple
in Jerusalem (Dan. 9:26, 27?; Matt. 24:15?; 2 Thess. 2:4?). Perhaps
some evangelicals suppose they are "helping God out" by taking an active
part in what they perceive to be the "fulfillment" of some prophecy. At
any rate, evangelicals should realize that most Jews are likely to take
umbrage at any Christian attempts to make them the cooperating partner
of some Christian devised "end times scenario of redemption."

7. No government is sacred and no government's policies are beyond
criticism. The State of Israel is not the kingdom of God; it was not so even
in biblical times. Its present fallible human rulers, however, must not be

held to a standard of morality and conduct different from that applied to all other nation-states. Some evangelicals assume that to "fight" Israel is to "fight" God (cf. Zech. 2:8), and hence usually give the impression of endorsing every action Israel makes in the Middle East, whether right or wrong. Another group of evangelicals—equally committed to the support of Israel—is concerned about how one might sensitively criticize an individual policy or act of the Israeli government without coming across as an anti-Semite or anti-Zionist. The whole question of criticism of Israel—whether by Jews or evangelicals—needs much greater thought on the part of both groups.

8. Evangelicals must refrain from easy, quick-fix solutions to territorial and political disputes between the Israelis and Arabs. There are Palestinian Jews and there are Palestinian Arabs; neither is going to leave the land. Instead of pontificating facile answers to complex, millennia-long problems, we must encourage each group to negotiate jointly a solution. Israel wants recognition within clearly defined and secure borders; the Palestinian Arabs want self-determination, a homeland, and legitimate rights. Only when bitterness, hostility, and hatred give way to a spirit of compromise, friendship, and mutual recognition will the residents of the land know peace.

9. Missionary work conducted by evangelicals among Palestinian Arabs poses a particular problem—especially for those evangelicals who also believe in supporting the State of Israel and the objectives of Zionism. How can evangelicals serving in the Arab world speak out firmly on behalf of legitimate Palestinian rights without being charged with anti-Zionism? Is it practically possible for an evangelical to champion the cause of justice on both sides, particularly when moderate Palestinians who denounce terrorist acts are involved? We must remember that the continuing conflict in the Middle East is not so much a struggle between right and wrong, good and evil; it is a conflict between two rights, between two peoples who have occupied the same territory for several thousand years and consequently have a deep devotion to this land of the Bible.

10. Evangelical support of Israel need not mean the Palestinian is automatically cast into the "demonic" role, the object of divine rejection. God's love and concern for all people is constantly affirmed in Scripture.

The people of God are individually called to be a *rodef shalom*, "one who pursues/chases after peace." The prophet Isaiah envisioned a day when a highway would connect Arab nations to Israel and each nation would know the blessing of the true God of the prophets as they worship him together (Isa. 19:23-25). Evangelical and Jew are called to "pray for the peace of Jerusalem" (Ps. 122:6). But we must do more. We must not desist from working toward that day when all descendants of Isaac and Ishmael will be able to embrace each other and echo, *"Shalom"* and *"Salam."*

Understanding the Chapter

1. Why is the spiritual or "heavenly" concept of Jerusalem, so much a part of the history of Christian thought, in reality a foreign concept to Jews? Discuss what steps the church might take to eliminate this gap between the two communities.

2. What two main schools of biblical interpretation have characterized evangelical thought toward Israel?

3. To what biblical concerns, other than predictive prophecy, must contemporary Christians turn in order to grasp the full reality of the meaning of the State of Israel?

4. What practical words of exhortation does Wilson bring regarding evangelical support of Israel and the need to understand Israel's present political situation?

5. Discuss Wilson's position on Arab-Jewish coexistence in Israel. Do you agree with this view?

17

A Jewish Understanding of the State of Israel

JOSHUA O. HABERMAN

As everyone familiar with Genesis 12 must know, God's covenant was extended to Abraham not as an individual but as the ancestor of a nation: "I will make of thee a great nation . . . and in thee shall all the nations of the earth be blessed." This nation was to be in possession of a land. Though not yet named and delineated in the call to Abraham, the promised land was the first step in the fulfillment of the covenant and caused the patriarch to depart immediately to follow God's guidance in locating and possessing the land: "Get thee forth from thy country, from thy kindred, from thy father's house unto the land which I will show thee" (Gen. 12:1).

In subsequent reaffirmations it is made abundantly clear that the covenant applies to all the people of Israel collectively and not selectively to only some individual Israelites.

In Moses' final restatement of the covenant all future generations of Israel are included: "Neither with you only do I make this covenant and this oath; but with him that standeth here with us this day before the Lord our God and also with him that is not here with us this day" (Deut. 29:13-15).

Isaiah sees the nation of Israel collectively serve as "a light unto the nations" and "a covenant of the people" (Isa. 42:6)[1]—a model nation

---

1. Note the word order; one would expect "*people* of the covenant." What is the meaning of "*covenant* of the people"? A covenant that had been put in writing will now be embodied, "incarnated," in the people of Israel through whom the nations of the world would receive spiritual light and be bound to God in a covenantal relationship. What Torah, which was given to Israel, did in tying Israel to God, now Israel as a nation will be doing for humankind: expanding the covenant with God to embrace all peoples. This interpretation of the function of Israel among the nations leaves open and, in my view, acceptable, the signal role of Jesus as a son of Israel, in the universal extension of the covenant.

whose just and compassionate society would lead the world toward freedom and righteousness.

This people is defined not merely as a community united by faith and ritual but as a sovereign nation, governed by divinely revealed principles and laws of Torah. Adherence to Torah law is to be Israel's chief distinction among the nations of the earth:

> Observe therefore and do them; for this is your wisdom and your understanding in the sight of the peoples, that, when they hear all these statutes, shall say: "Surely this great nation is a wise and understanding people." For what great nation is there, that hath God so nigh unto them, as the Lord our God is whensoever we call upon Him? And what great nation is there, that hath statutes and ordinances so righteous as all this law, which I set before you this day? (Deut. 4:6-8)

Nearly two thousand years of Jewish diaspora existence have been a mixed bag of triumph and tragedy. On the positive side, these two millennia demonstrated the miracle of Jewish survival and internationalized the Jewish people, enabling us to encounter every nation, every race, and every civilization. On the negative side, diaspora life deprived the people of Israel of their sovereignty and made it largely impossible to fulfill those parts of covenantal law that can be carried out only by a self-governing nation.

With the emergence of the State of Israel a new opportunity has been given to the people of Israel to live up to the covenant without any restrictions.

However pressing the immediate political, socioeconomic, and cultural problems of the state may be for us, the most important question is: How does the State of Israel relate to God's covenant with Israel?

The answer depends on our perception of the meaning of Jewish peoplehood. There are two options. In the first place, we can define the Jewish people in purely secular terms. Accordingly, we can speak of our diaspora communities as ethnic minorities whose national center is the State of Israel. In this perspective, the State of Israel boils down to an essentially political concern. No one could fault Israel for acting purely in terms of its political self-interest as do other nations. Israel would then be a nation just like other nations and of no particular significance as a model of Jewish values.

The other option is to include the State of Israel within a theological concept of Jewish peoplehood. As a matter of fact, the Jewish people in their identification with Zionism never abandoned the historic self-image as a worldwide *religious* community. We see the Jewish people, here and in Israel, as both creator and creature of the religion of Judaism. A wholly secular view of Jewish statehood would do violence to our sense of Jewishness. This fact challenges us to think through the religious significance of the State of Israel. In this light, the most timely theological issues for contemporary Jews are the covenant, the election, and messianism. All hang together. What, then, is the religious significance of the State of Israel within this theological triangle?

The religious importance of the State of Israel lies in its preeminent role as the Jewish community best equipped to express Judaism at all levels. It follows that Israel must be the standard-bearer of Judaism.

What about Jewish messianic hopes, which encompass the whole world, and the State of Israel? Jewish sovereign existence in a state of their own is not incompatible with a world-saving task enunciated in prophetic Judaism. Indeed, Judaism's relevance to the shaping of a better society can best be tested in a setting where Jews have both political power and full responsibility.

Zionists of various ideologies and parties overwhelmingly believe that the Jewish state must be somehow expressive of Judaism and must become a major factor in its preservation of certain sanctities. Solomon Schechter, a foremost thinker of Conservative Judaism in America, summed up a consensus among all branches of Judaism in a statement as true today as when originally written in 1906:

> The selection of Israel, the indestructibility of God's covenant with
> Israel, the immortality of Israel as a nation, and the final restoration of
> Israel to Palestine, where the nation will live a holy life on holy ground,
> with all the wide-reaching consequences of the conversion of humanity
> and the establishment of the Kingdom of God on earth—all these are
> the common ideals and the common ideas that permeate the whole of
> Jewish literature extending over nearly four thousand years.[2]

What will be the long-range impact of the State of Israel on Jewish-Christian relationships? Will it widen the gap and raise new barriers between us, or will it bring us more closely together?

Among all the issues that have in the past embittered Jewish-Christian

---

2. As quoted by Arthur Hertzberg in *Being Jewish in America* (New York: Herzl Press, 1979), 249.

polemics, two stand out as especially divisive: the supercedence doctrine and the debate on particularism versus universalism.

I believe that the restoration of Jewish statehood will hasten the demise of the supercedence doctrine. Based on certain ambiguous New Testament passages (and contradicted by other, perhaps also ambiguous, passages in the New Testament), the supercedence doctrine regards the covenant with Israel abrogated, its role in history terminated, and the people of Israel superceded by the church with respect to the election. In the many centuries of Jewish-Christian polemics the church cited the destruction of the temple and Israel's loss of land and sovereignty as evidence for this doctrine. But restoration of the Jewish state on May 14, 1948, necessitated a reassessment of the doctrine. Vatican II formally broke with this age-old doctrine by leaning heavily upon Romans 9:4-5 in acknowledging that the Jews still "have the covenant . . . and the promises" and affirming with Romans 11:29 "that God's gifts are irrevocable."

Another major development in the Jewish-Christian dialogue on which the State of Israel has had a favorable impact is the gradual resolution of the conflict between particularism and universalism, as a non-issue. The notion that particularism and universalism in religion are opposites is part of the pernicious legacy of the fallacious abstractions of German idealistic philosophy. In reality, Israel's universal mission and Jewish particularity are not opposites but interdependent characteristics of Judaism. Particularism is the means to Judaism's universal ends.

The German-Jewish theologian Leo Baeck put it well: "Everybody who is in possession of the truth feels a peculiar responsibility bestowed upon him which separates him from other men." When a people becomes conscious of a distinctive message, such as the unique conceptions of ethical monotheism held by the Jewish people, the message becomes a mission and justifies—even requires—self-segregation. "Exclusiveness," says Baeck, "has the same significance for the community as the command to segregated holiness has for the individual."[3] As the sacred must be separated from the profane, so a people committed to certain sanctities must remain apart from those not sharing its commitment. Such exclusiveness is not egocentric but idealistic.

This leads Baeck to the conclusion that, in Judaism, particularism and universalism are related as are the means to the end. He asserts, "Israel's

---

3. Leo Baeck, *The Essence of Judaism* (New York: Schocken, 1948).

distinctive existence thus became a consciousness of its service for mankind's future." In his view, Jewish universalism and particularism are truly complementary. Essentially, Baeck's is a contemporary reformulation of the age-old biblical concept of the Covenant People, people singled out by God to do his work among the nations.

We welcome the fact that Christian thinkers, including some in the mainline denominations, have revised their harsh judgment on religious particularism. A study guide published by the United Presbyterian Church in the USA makes the following comment:

> The particularity of this covenant is striking: it is a promise of a land and a people. . . . Throughout the history of ancient Israel the nation failed repeatedly to fulfill the will of God, yet the covenant relationship was never irrevocably severed. While Israel was temporarily separated from the land (as in the Babylonian exile), the promise of the land lived on in its hopes, its prayers and its worship. In this perspective, the current conjunction of land and people in the State of Israel may be viewed as a sign of the continuing relationship of God with the Jewish people.

What follows is especially important. It is a statement that suggests that a reaffirmation of the particularistic implications of Israel's covenant with God may be of great importance also in upholding certain particularistic aspects of the Christian faith that previously had not been identified as such.

> Not only is Israel a reminder of the vitality of Judaism but it also reminds us of the particularism of Biblical faith. We are often inclined to assume that God reveals himself through abstract principles and universal categories. The "scandal" of particularity is manifest in Jewish identification with Israel in a way which parallels the "scandalous" claim of Christianity that the full and decisive revelation of God to man is Jesus of Nazareth. The questions of why God works through this people or why He sends His son into a certain culture at a certain time are not answered. That he has in fact done these things is an affirmation of the Bible and the church.[4]

Roy and Alice Eckardt, who have probably gone further than other Protestant theologians in the development of a Christian theology of the

4. *Peoples and Conflict in the Middle East—A Preliminary Report for Study*, General Assembly of the United Presbyterian Church (1973), 32.

land and people of Israel, stressed in their book *Encounter with Israel* the interdependence of universalism and particularism as it relates to the land and the people of Israel:

> [Judaism's] unique and indispensable contribution to the human family is through the persuasion (in opposition to all forms of other-worldliness) that prophetic spirituality and morality demand rootage in "ordinary" space and time. The very essence of Israel lies in her relating of the great heritage of the Jewish people and Judaism to normal political and social life. Without universal demands and responsibilities, particular human communities become self-centered, exclusivist, and subject to the corruption of power. But without any application to concrete human problems, universal principles remain empty dreams.
>
> Particularity is the home that keeps universality from flying away into abstract ideals; universality is the adventure that judges particularity and lures it away from self-concentration.[5]

Note that Roy Eckardt's commitment to the State of Israel is rooted in something much deeper than compassion or social idealism:

> We, who are Christians, are part of the Jewish people—by the very nature of our Christian faith. We do claim membership in the Jewish family. Therefore, Israel grasps us in our very existence, not merely as human beings (as men, we will simply try to be humanitarian), but as Christians. It is by virtue of our Christian existence that Israel can never be just another country for us . . . through its indissoluble bond with the Jewish people and the Jewish faith, the Christian faith is yoked spiritually to Eretz Israel.[6]

If Roy Eckardt is truly representative of a significant number of Christians, I have no doubt that such a spirit of solidarity and Christian concern for Jewish survival and the State of Israel will change radically the Jewish perception of Christianity from a rival to a partner faith.

---

5. Alice and Roy Eckardt, *Encounter with Israel: A Challenge to Conscience* (New York: Association Press, 1970), 254.

6. A. Roy Eckardt, *Your People, My People: The Meeting of Jews and Christians* (Quadrangle Books, 1974), 182-83. Note also such statements as: "Living today, Jesus would be called an Israeli," 181-82.

Understanding the Chapter

1. How does Haberman define Israel's role as "a covenant of the people"?

2. What was to be Israel's chief distinction among the nations of the earth?

3. What is the relationship between covenant and land? Between covenant and statehood? How is Zionism related to Judaism?

4. Haberman believes the long-range impact of the State of Israel on Jewish-Christian relationships will be positive and favorable in two particular ways. What are these?

18
Jewish Attitudes Toward Israel: A Précis

A. JAMES RUDIN

It has been said that when a person loves someone, the lover can easily list a thousand reasons for his or her affection. Whether this is true in our personal relationships I leave to those more qualified to judge than I. However, when it comes to the Jewish people's love and passion for the land and the State of Israel, there can be no doubt about the validity of the statement.

That intense love and passion has been well expressed in countless Jewish prayers, poems, sermons, midrashim, speeches, books, and songs. And that same love and passion has been tested in countless battles, attacks, and wars—all filled with suffering and agony.

The poet Yehudah Ha Levi poignantly wrote "My Heart Is in the East," but many men and women also named Levi have had to die to maintain Jewish existence and, since 1948, Jewish sovereignty in the "East," the land of Israel. So, at the outset, it is important to remember that Jewish love and passion for Israel, while deeply rooted in religious, cultural, and historical traditions, is continually being played out on the stage of real time, real place, real life, and sometimes real death.

Since the record of Jewish attachment to the land of Israel is so well documented and so well known, especially to those concerned with the evangelical-Jewish relationship, my task is to recount, albeit briefly, some facts about that passion that are not always recognized. I want to look at the forces within Jewish life that were extant before 1948, the year of Israel's rebirth, and to indicate that these same forces are extant today, though in somewhat different form; and that these factors, attitudes, beliefs, and commitments remain today a potent component of contemporary Israel and the diaspora. They are potent in their power to influence men and women, and they remain, in my opinion, unresolved questions thirty-five years after Israeli independence.

The amalgam that brought the Jewish state into being was a combination of political, cultural, spiritual, and psychological forces, all coalescing within a century, seemingly united to outside observers, yet often in intense competition with each other within the Jewish community. Zionism, the national movement that supplied the élan and the organization for Jewish rebirth, is often viewed solely as a labor socialist movement combining the idealism of Judaism with the platform of late nineteenth-century and early twentieth-century European socialism. And indeed it was. The now legendary figures of Chaim Weizmann, David Ben-Gurion, and Golda Meir have long dominated the imaginations of several generations of Jews and Christians. For Israel's first twenty-nine years, this part of the Zionist movement dominated and actually controlled to a large degree the government, institutions, and indeed the rhythm and cadence of Israeli life. But we do a disservice to reality if we believe that this form of Zionism, of Israeli nationalism, exhausts the total picture of modern Israel. Labor Zionism, and I use this term to describe the extraordinary range of opinion within that sector of Israeli life, never had a monopoly on the Israeli mind and collective heart. It was only one of myriad expressions of Jewish love and passion for the land and the State; an important one, of course, but not the only one.

The religious Zionist movement is also a picture of that reality, another of the thousand ways of love. Rav Kook, the charismatic and influential leader of this form of Zionism, is also a parent of today's Israel. His all-encompassing love for the Jewish land and people transcended the borders of his own Orthodox Judaism, and his power in pre-state Israel, the power to reach out across the lines and parties, and his ability to exclude no Jew, to include all Jews in the redemption of the land, is a model that needs to be repeated today. Rav Kook's Zionism was no parochial expression, no narrow view; for him the very act of residing in the land was part of redemption itself. Unfortunately, the institutionalization of charisma is often unsuccessful, and Rav Kook's broad vision, his true love for his people, is missing from some of today's Israeli society. Yet the compelling vision of Rav Kook is one more reality of contemporary Israel.

And there is another facet as well. It is said that the winners, or apparent winners, write the officially accepted history. Because of this, the Zionism of the minority, the self-styled Revisionists, the Zionism of Vladimir Jabotinsky, and that of his most famous disciple, Menachem Begin, was given short shrift until 1977. Yet Revisionism is also part of the reality of modern Israel. Its powerful call on Jewish history, its inextricable link with the Jewish religion (often without the universal vision of Rav Kook), its continuing evocative call for strength and physical prowess, and its absolute claim on the land—all this and more has made Jabotinsky, Begin, and others also into legendary Founders of Israel, and at least in the past two elections they have emerged as narrow victors over the labor socialists. To dismiss Revisionism as a "fraction within a fraction," as "extremists," is to miss the point and again to deny reality. This form of Zionism is also one of the thousand ways Jews have expressed their love. "How do I love thee, let me count the ways . . ." Revisionism, with all of its claims, is one of the ways.

Timothy Smith mentioned Judah Magnes. Magnes, while he was president of the Hebrew University in pre-state Israel, was also active in the binational Zionist movement with Martin Buber. The Magnes-Buber attempt to share power with Arabs and Jews, its quest for a peaceful solution to the conflicting claims to the land called Israel by the Jews and Palestine by the Arabs, is now seen, by historians, as a failure because Magnes and Buber could not find an Arab partner in dialogue, even though it was Buber who taught us all that a partner is necessary in any successful dialogue. Still, the passionate quest among Israelis to find an Arab negotiating partner remains part of the reality of Israel. The voices of cooperation and moderation and reconciliation heard in today's Israel are reaffirmations of the Zionism of Judah Magnes and Martin Buber—not the call for a binational state, but the yearning for a permanent, just sharing of the land between two peoples, Jews and Arabs, with a maximum of justice and a minimum of injustice. Can it be done? Can it succeed? Will it take place during our lifetime? Only God knows, but it is part of the reality of the Jewish passion and love, one of the thousand ways of expressing it, a significant strand in the Israeli tapestry, which Magnes and Buber so clearly articulated some five decades ago.

Finally, there is the question that Henry Feingold so brilliantly raised about American Jews. I give that question an Israeli coloration. The sacrifice of blood, treasury, and talent has gained, maintained, and, I pray daily, guaranteed Israeli survival and security as a nation-state. Space, sovereignty, and security have been gained, but what shall be planted in Israel by its 3.4 million Jews? Is it to be another Sparta as some of Israel's enemies have charged? God forbid! Is it to be a nation of Hebrew-speaking citizens devoid of Jewish values (however broad that elusive term is defined)? God forbid! Is it to become a state of religious zealotry, intolerant of those of its citizens who express a non-Orthodox religious view of Judaism? God forbid! What, then, shall be planted in that sacred space?

This is the question another school of Zionist thought has raised. Led by Ahad HaAm (Asher Ginzberg, who died in 1927), "spiritual Zionism" asks the fundamental question, What kind of Israel shall it be? Because of the overwhelming concerns of the past fifty years, the Holocaust, the creation of the Jewish state, the unending battle to remain alive, the need to assist Jews in other lands (lands of oppression), the concern about Jewish continuity—because of these factors, Ahad HaAm's questions have been deferred, not answered. Now a new generation of Israelis has come to the fore, Israelis born in the land, whose native language is Hebrew. Chilled by wars with their Arab neighbors, unsatisfied with the answers given them by their legendary elders the Goldas and the Begins, the Weizmanns and the Jabotinskys, they now return to Ahad HaAm's question: "Will the Jewish State be . . . a ball tossed between the Great Powers?" The answers are not given, but part of the thousand ways a Jew shows love and passion is to ask these questions with great seriousness. This, too, is part of the reality of modern Israel.

To summarize this all too incomplete and brief overview is to state the obvious. Zionism is a great "Tent of Meeting" for the Jewish people. Magnes and Jabotinsky, Buber and Begin, Ahad HaAm and Golda Meir, Rav Kook and David Ben-Gurion—all are legitimate and authentic expressions of the reality that is Israel. Zionism, Israeli nationalism, is *not* monolithic, nonpluralistic. Like so much else in Jewish life, it is diverse, often conflicting, intensely passionate, and never dull! Jews no less than Christians need to be reminded of this mosaic reality of Israel. Christians need to know our in-house debates, our internal divisions, our diverse approaches to Zion, just as much as they know and experience the reality of Jewish unity and solidarity when it comes to Israel's survival and security. Indeed, Israel, the Jewish people, and the entire Christian-Jewish encounter and strengthened, not weakened, when we affirm Zionist/Israeli/Jewish pluralism. We love those who are complex, multi-splendored, unpredictable, profoundly and constantly changing, who sparkle even as a diamond sparkles in the sunlight with many prisms radiating the beams of the sun. So too we love Israel for all it is—complicated, contradictory, complex. Christians, too, can share in that love. Yehudah Ha Levi was, of course, quite right; all of our hearts and souls *are* in the East, and although the light from the East radiates differently for each of us, we rejoice and give thanks to God for that light coming, even shining, from Zion.

Understanding the Chapter

1. Enumerate and discuss some of the ways in which Jews love Israel.

2. Rudin writes that Zionism is a great "Tent of Meeting" for the Jewish people, illustrating the great pluralism found in Israeli nationalism. Briefly distinguish the different emphases brought by each of the following Zionist leaders: Ben-Gurion, Rav Kook, Jabotinsky, Magnes, Ahad HaAm.

3. What are the implications of the pluralism within Zionism?

4. What are the similarities between the Jewish love of Israel, discussed above, and the Christian love of Israel? What are the differences?

19
Church and Synagogue at the End of the Twentieth Century

KENNETH A. BRIGGS

Now that the last meaning possible has been extracted out of George Orwell's 1984, we can safely turn our attention to the much more religiously symbolic year of 2000. Religiously symbolic, at least, to a number of very important groups. For some members of the Pentecostal and evangelical families, it signals an apocalyptic age pregnant with possibility. Premillennialists, postmillennialists, all those who think about the final destruction and the beginning of the age of peace, the messianic age, are almost inevitably attracted to the year 2000 and all that it portends in so many minds and imaginations. That is, among one group.

And then we have those among the mainline Protestant and Orthodox groups, such as Lewis Mudge within the Consultation on Church Union, who have proposed that by the year 2000 the Christian community should make a striking advance in the form of some kind of joint creed they might be able to utter together. I do not think we have yet heard the last from this group; in fact, I believe there is some potential for that kind of unity to occur. The Baptist Eucharist Ministry statement by the World Council of Churches, I think, begins to head hopefully in that direction.

Even Pope John Paul II speaks repeatedly and more often than you might believe of the portentousness of the year 2000, the end of this millennium. This, fortunately, was called to my attention by scholars who know the pope's work better than I, and have read it in Polish as well as in some of the translations. The pope speaks eloquently in urging the church to proclaim its mission and to carry that mission to the far corners of the world. He speaks as though under an apprehension that the eschaton may indeed be upon us and that the work must be accomplished. He speaks with urgency about the end times. He speaks of destruction and fulfillment, often within the same paragraph.

There is no exact equivalent to this feeling or concept within Judaism, but in somewhat different terms we hear the agony over survival as yet another way of looking at the significance and the ominous possibility that the conclusion of this century could mark the demographic danger point for the Jewish people. Modernity has posed the haunting and frightening message that the continuation of the Jewish nation and Jewish faith is under one of its severest tests. The outcome is far from assured.

With that in mind, I wish to turn to some analysis of what I see as the present situation that anticipates the year 2000. The kind of world we can expect is intimated and hinted at in many ways. One is the joke about the rabbi who was sitting on the roof of the synagogue as the floodwaters were rising. A helicopter flies over and the pilot says, "Rabbi, won't you join us?" to which he replies, "No, my belief is in Torah—I will be safe." As the water rises farther, a boat comes by with the same request, "Rabbi, won't you join us?" and he says, "No, I believe in the God of Abraham, Isaac, and Jacob—I will be safe." The water keeps rising, and finally he's gone. He reaches heaven, where he asks God, "Why didn't you do something about this?" And God replies, "I sent you a helicopter and a boat."

I mention this story not essentially for its comic possibilities, though it has that, but to let you know that that joke is extremely popular among nonreligious people. And what makes it funnier among them than it might be among you is precisely that it says how really improbable is such divine interaction with humankind. For those people the joke has a surprise ending. How amazing that something like that could take place, even conceptually. There is a sense among many, many of our brothers and sisters that God's intervention in any of life's affairs is inherently impossible.

This is largely the tone and context in which we are now working. Setting aside for the moment the hypothesis of the secular humanist conspiracy, let us at least concede that cultural conditions do not appear to be conducive to the growth of large-scale institutions of religion. They have not been for a while, and I would forecast, along with most of you I suspect, that they would not be in the immediate future. The flow is, in fact, away from organized religion rather than toward it.

We can—and many spokespeople do—attribute this to many factors.

Maybe this drift away is because of human orneriness and apostasy; maybe it is because of radical "this-worldliness"; maybe it is because of capitalist decadence; maybe it is because of Marxist atheism, or material sloth, or idolatry aided and abetted by technology, and so on and so on and so on. But whatever the cause, we can wisely listen to the insights of Louis Dupré of Yale, that indeed we live in a world of functional atheism. His thought follows in the trail of the death of God theologians. The death of God movement in my judgment disappeared too quickly, before its significance was understood. Its significance remained though the discussion went by the boards.

According to Dupré, if I understand him correctly, if we are to light the lamp of faith we must endure the climate of polemical unbelief that encompasses us all. And in order to arrive at a position of belief, we do have to, in fact, pass through that valley of the shadow of death and unbelief. This requires exceptional rather than common effort. Few will endure. In pragmatic terms, this means, I suspect, that self-conscious Christians and Jews will live farther and farther on the periphery and without social legitimacy.

It is all headed in that direction, I think—headed that way now in some ways that we did not even see a decade ago. Christianity, after all, was disestablished at the birth of the nation called America. The implications of this revolution are only now beginning to be realized. Jews were disenfranchised, if we can ever say Jews were truly enfranchised, with the destruction of the second temple; thus, they have had a lot more practice. Christians can learn a great deal from Jews about what it means to be an alien community of believers among the heathen. Call it spiritual endurance in the broadest sense—refining the phenomenon of living as strangers among those who have no regard for you. It is indeed living in the face of hideous trials.

Even now every believer experiences this pain and suffering to a certain extent—a certain social embarrassment, particularly in urban areas in this country, for being attached to a religious organization or congregation. A few years ago, there seemed to be a parade to church on Sunday morning and you almost had to answer for not going. Now more often you have to answer why you do go. In any event, the stark challenges of pluralism and separation of church and state, the mass appeal of cabbage patch dolls and CDs are upon us and, I venture to say, will relegate religion increasingly to marginal status. People calling themselves Christians and Jews will have to make a greater effort to do so. It is no longer a birthright, per se. Religious communities will be called upon to define themselves over against society, and in the process facing the greatest opportunities and dangers.

Let us now turn to the best case scenario for the years ahead for the church and the synagogue.

I have a vision of the church and synagogue as places of the Book. As each congregation becomes a living affirmation that is a tradition, it stands under the Book. They become communities whose self-understanding derives from the authority of sacred texts as the groundwork of a total spiritual life, with a centrality of divinely revealed wisdom pervading those who call themselves Christians and Jews. I am speaking about Scripture, sacred texts, as being a reliable guide to the profound transformation of lives.

Second, I would envision the church and the synagogue as places of the heart—in the broadest possible sense. The heart is seen here as the totally encompassing aggregate of human spiritual attributes and has nothing to do with sentimentality or emotionalism of any sort. These are the places where the heart can truly flourish in such a way as to enable persons to grow into full humanity as sons and daughters of God. I see the church and synagogue as places where the heart leads to the kind of personal journey that is described by the theologian John Dunne at Notre Dame, or the blossoming of prayer intimated by Henry Nouwen, or outlined within the existentially embodied scholarship and life of Rabbi Adin Steinsaltz. The journey moves toward full, human spiritual growth; toward the restored idea that life is not complete without a spiritual, physical, and emotional dimension.

I was reminded a couple of weeks ago of the relatively inhospitable climate in which such an idea arrives these days. A certain religiously founded school, a prep school, four years ago decided to return to its roots, though it had always been in name a religious private school, by hiring someone whose agenda was explicitly religious. Faculty and students, I learned, have been fighting the move ever since it occurred because the headmaster has said, in effect, you are not complete, boys, without a full spiritual dimension in your lives. The teachers do not like standing up with him and the students say it is irrelevant.

The church and synagogue I envision, however, are places of the heart.

Third, I envision the church and synagogue as places of joyous, continuing revelation, where divine messages are received through the secular sphere, enlightening and unfolding religious truth. I cannot think of this whole subject without harkening to the issue of feminism. It is one expression of something that is still too harsh and shrill for many to hear, yet calls us inevitably to a confrontation with a compelling message. The feminist movement has an inexorable quality that suggests a wider reality than ever generally understood in human history. It is inviting and sweet to foresee a broad coming to grips with this and other clues to the whereabouts of God within history.

Fourth, I like to envision the church and the synagogue as places for upholding the common good, in a day when it is attacked from every direction. In an age of fragmentation and specialization, this becomes a special concern. Perhaps the church and the synagogue are, in fact, the only places where one might feel and sense and experience a comprehensive concern for the welfare of all souls. The contrast, again, is the increasing fragmentation of life in other areas. I speak of a place of practical theology that can serve as a platform for the prophetic word in a world of unbelief; reason and faith, where those can be joined in a confident statement, being held together to witness to the comprehensive and total life of the whole world.

I was fortunate recently to hear someone expound very expertly and wisely on this very subject; those of you at the Jewish Theological Seminary certainly do—David Weiss Halivny. He is a man of wisdom and insight, and I was privileged to hear him give one vision of what that model of faith and reason in comprehensive fashion might look like. He was proposing a means of answering the question, "How can a modern mind reconcile belief in the divine origins of Scripture and Halakhah, on the one hand, and the fruits of rational, historical, and form criticism on the other?" His answer, I believe, can be instructive to all of us. This man, the lone survivor of his family from the camps at Auschwitz, proposes what he calls "creative parallelism," receiving gladly the enhanced, scholarly understanding of Bible and Talmud through the process of human experience.

Of course there are other approaches to reconciling and resolving the same problem. My point is to pose the church and the synagogue as places where ancient faith and the modern critical mind can coexist, places that address the world in many dimensions from an assured position.

If these visions are what I hope for, where do I see danger? Well, for each right possibility I have mentioned, there is an enormous peril lying in the way like an underwater explosive device threatening the safe conduct of the ship.

First, if the church and the synagogue are to be places where the people of the Book take root and witness, they must avoid the extremes that threaten to undermine scriptural authority, both the radical demythologizing of the far left and the rigid inerrancy of the far right. The battle for the Bible is far from over. It isn't as visible now, but the fighting is still hot and heavy. There is renewed interest in the whole subject, and the subject is important—even sometimes to those who are the least lettered among the congregations. Everyone is moving in on it, and the ground is shifting even among those who think their minds are already made up. It sometimes astounds me how much the terms of discussion have changed among those who think they are standing in the same spot that they were five decades ago. So there is a danger to the status of the people of the Book, inasmuch as there is danger to the authority of Scripture. And unless that is resolved in some way across lines in some comprehensive fashion, the problem will continue to raise havoc.

Second, the potential of the church and synagogue to be grand places of the heart can be crippled by a resort to spiritual sentimentality on the one hand, or collapse into religious narcissism on the other. It is no accident that the "me" generation corresponded to the wave of personal pietism. The choice is ever before Christianity and Judaism: Will their vision respond to the all-encompassing, embracing call to compassion and sacrifice, or retreat into pockets of self-righteousness and defensiveness? There are strong pressures on many individual congregations and communities to embrace one form or other of the "church growth" movement, which brings yields only through spiritual infertility and myopia. I think we are at a very crucial point at this hour, inasmuch as many who began within the evangelical movement as born-again Christians, especially in the last ten to fifteen years, have reached the point of potential spiritual and human maturity. They can go either way.

Third, there is a threat also to the possibility that the church and synagogue can be the locus of interpreting continuing revelation. On one side is the institutional hardness that denies the premise that in fact there is such a thing as continuing revelation, assuming that all that needs to be said has been said; on the other side is such confusion, disarray, and dilution of the historic faith that congregations cannot read the signs of the times. They will be unwilling or unable to separate the wheat from the chaff. There is again a possibility of opening up the church and the synagogue evermore to what those signs of the times are. There is no infallibility in picking them. Holding the Bible in one hand and *The New York Times* in the other does not guarantee your ability to judge the import of world events.

Fourth, rather than stake out a destiny on the vision of the common good, I fear that churches and synagogues will become more captive of the forces antithetical to the Spirit. They will become another form of cultural or civic religion. The church as a place of narrow self-centered concern along the force lines of petty self-interest will experience that same caving in to cultural forces that earned the scorn of many religious people four decades ago under the Third Reich. There is plenty of evidence that this low road is crowded with travelers at the moment. And yet we hope for a breakthrough. We hope for more breakthroughs than we have seen. The categorical and decisive issue here, I believe, is the tremendous tension and struggle between left, middle, and right in both Christianity and Judaism. Among Protestants in the seventies the Christian right asserted itself as never before, and reopened questions that many Protestants believed had been closed—inerrancy, the relation between theology and ethics, and so on. There is among Protestants a situation of diversity, hostility, indifference, and alienation marked by an almost total lack of communication across lines.

For several reasons, I have been an advocate of increased communication and development of dialogue particularly among those I would consider moderate evangelicals and mainline Christians. Faced with the challenge that Christianity is encountering in this country, both from the underside where religious motivation seems to be subsiding in the rising competition for the soul, and in the overside where the threats to the Protestant establishment are readily identified, there is a greater need for this kind of dialogue than ever before.

Among Catholics, there is at the present time a very serious and potentially fruitful tension over the issue of the Americanization of the Roman Catholic Church. As the church has become more and more indigenously settled into the environment of America, it has begun to take the democratic ethos of its cultural and political surroundings. This flies in the face of a good deal of understanding of the way the church itself works as a hierarchical organization. The tension, much of which is relatively underground, is how far the American church is going to go, or be allowed to go, before a de facto schism would take place. There is great resistance from the Vatican at this point. The pope is not enthralled by the idea that American Catholics are reflecting their cultural values more than the Vatican ethos.

In Judaism, the tension is rising and becoming more serious. Judaism is wracked by its own severe divisions. The rise of Orthodoxy, particularly right-wing Orthodoxy, has posed a threat to those who consider

themselves modern Orthodox. Meanwhile, the left in Jewish life, the
Reformers, those who consider themselves left of the center, are becoming more and more estranged from all elements of Orthodoxy. One issue
that illustrates the severity of this tension is the fate of a joint conversion
program in Denver, Colorado, which was ended quite sadly after seven
years. It was stopped not because Reform, Conservative, and Orthodox
Jews in Denver disagreed basically with the program, which responded
to an alarming intermarriage rate, but because of pressure from outsiders
who discovered what was going on. The pressures are engendered by the
very deep sense of unfinished business over basic religious legitimacy.
That tension runs painfully through Judaism.

The significance of these struggles is that they represent crucial efforts
to define the character of major traditions in the face of highly challeng-
ing secular opponents. The goal cannot be religious unanimity but toler-
able diversity both among Jews and Christians. That is the meaning of
much unpublicized local relationships among churches and synagogues
such as took place in Denver, where in the rough-and-tumble of daily
experience something was worked out that seemed to be better than what
had existed before.

Finally, I wish to point to what I believe to be a good sign. As I travel
about, I am encouraged by the growth, the creativity, and the spirituality of actual congregations. Many have returned to basics, have
become alive without forgetting their wider social and religious mission.
They are places where attention to liturgy and prayer go hand in hand
with efforts for peacemaking and works for the poor. I spoke with a rabbi
last week in a very prosperous area of New York, who recently began
taking homeless men into his synagogue every night of the week. He told
me of the transformation that had gone on in him and in members of the
congregation as they met with an element of people with whom they
normally would have had no contact.

I am encouraged by this—I am encouraged by churches and synagogues where the particularity of a tradition can coexist with an ecumenical and/or universal spirit. I am encouraged by real-life congregations where, in practical terms, reconciliation among theological and
ethical points of view has become a fact of life and can serve as an example.
In the great circle of events, finally, I am encouraged and am heartened to
hear, as I did from a seminary president recently, that seminarians themselves are seeing the parish, the local congregation, as the grand locus of

that interaction between God and the people. It is a word of encouragement. I think that as the months and years unfold toward that year 2000, we may look hopefully toward a regeneration of congregational life, an inspiration for others to follow.

Understanding the Chapter

1. Briggs points out that there are those within mainline church groups such as the Consultation on Church Union who have proposed some kind of joint creed by the year 2000 that Christians might be able to recite together. Discuss the prospects of doctrinal unity within the church.

2. "Cultural conditions do not appear to be conducive to the growth of large-scale institutions of religion," says Briggs. He adds further that "the flow is, in fact, away from organized religion rather than toward it." Do you agree with Briggs? If so, what do you feel are the main factors that contribute to this present phenomenon?

3. What can Christians learn from Jews about living as a religiously committed minority in a hostile culture?

4. What is Briggs' fourfold vision for the role of church and synagogue in the future? Is this shared role a basis for Jewish-Christian dialogue?

5. What dangers, inherent to both Judaism and Christianity, could subvert the growth of their respective institutions into "places of the Book and of the heart"?

A Selective Bibliography

Most of the following works fall into one of four broad categories: (1) evangelical Christian thought, (2) Jewish thought, (3) Christian-Jewish relations, or (4) works authored by contributors to this present volume on themes related to the above.

Ahlstrom, Sydney E. *A Religious History of the American People*. New Haven: Yale University Press, 1972.

Askew, Thomas A., and Peter W. Spellman. *The Churches and the American Experience*. Grand Rapids: Baker Book House, 1984.

Baeck, Leo. *The Essence of Judaism*. New York: Schocken Books, 1948.

――――. *Judaism and Christianity*. New York: Harper & Row, 1966.

Banki, Judith H. *What Viewers Should Know about the Oberammergau Passion Play*. New York: The American Jewish Committee, 1980.

――――. *The Image of Jews in Christian Teaching*. New York: The American Jewish Committee, 1980.

Baron, Salo. *A Social and Religious History of the Jews*. 16 vols. Philadelphia and New York: Jewish Publication Society and Columbia University Press, 1952.

Berger, David. *The Jewish-Christian Debate in the High Middle Ages*. Philadelphia: Jewish Publication Society, 1979.

Bivin, David, and Roy Blizzard. *Understanding the Difficult Words of Jesus*. Austin: Center for Judaic-Christian Studies, 1984.

Bloesch, Donald G. *The Evangelical Renaissance*. Grand Rapids: William B. Eerdmans, 1973.

――――. *Essentials of Evangelical Theology*. 2 vols. San Francisco: Harper & Row, 1978.

――――. *The Future of Evangelical Christianity*. Garden City, N.Y.: Doubleday & Co., 1983.

Blumenthal, David R. *Approaches to Judaism in Medieval Times*. 2 vols. Decatur, Ga.: Scholars Press, 1985.

――――, ed. *Emory Studies on the Holocaust*. Atlanta: Witness to the Holocaust Project, 1985.

Buber, Martin. *Two Types of Faith: The Interpenetration of Judaism and Christianity*. New York: Harper & Row, 1961.

————. *I and Thou*. Translated by Walter Kaufmann. New York: Scribners, 1970.

Cohen, A. *Everyman's Talmud*. New York: Schocken Books, 1949.

Cohen, Martin A., and Helga Croner. *Christian Mission—Jewish Mission*. New York: Paulist Press, 1982.

Croner, Helga. *Stepping Stones to Further Jewish-Christian Relations*. New York: Stimulus Books, 1977.

Davies, William D. *Paul and Rabbinic Judaism*. New York: Harper & Row, 1948.

Dayton, Donald W. *Discovering an Evangelical Heritage*. New York: Harper & Row, 1976.

Dimont, Max. *Jews, God and History*. New York: American Library, 1964.

Donin, Hayim H. *To Be a Jew*. New York: Basic Books, 1980.

Eckardt, Arthur Roy. *Elder and Younger Brothers*. New York: Scribners, 1967.

Eckstein, Yechiel. *What Christians Should Know about Jews and Judaism*. Waco, Tex.: Word Books, 1984.

Falk, Harvey. *Jesus the Pharisee: A New Look at the Jewishness of Jesus*. New York: Paulist Press, 1985.

Feingold, Henry L. *The Politics of Rescue: The Roosevelt Administration and the Holocaust, 1938–1945*. New York: Schocken Books, 1980.

————. *A Midrash on American Jewish History*. New York: State University of New York Press, 1982.

Fisher, Eugene. *Faith without Prejudice*. New York: Paulist Press, 1977.

Flannery, Edward H. *The Anguish of the Jews*. Rev. ed. Mahwah, N.J.: Paulist Press, 1985.

Gade, Richard E. *A Historical Survey of Anti-Semitism*. Grand Rapids: Baker Book House, 1981.

Gager, John G. *The Origins of Anti-Semitism: Attitudes toward Judaism in Pagan and Christian Antiquity*. New York: Oxford University Press, 1983.

Goldin, Judah. *The Living Talmud*. Chicago: University of Chicago Press, 1957.

Harrington, Daniel. *God's People in Christ: New Testament Perspectives on the Church and Judaism*. Philadelphia: Fortress Press, 1980.

Heschel, Abraham Joshua. *God in Search of Man*. New York: Farrar, Straus, Giroux, 1955.

————. *Israel: An Echo of Eternity*. New York: Farrar, Straus and Giroux, 1969.

Hunter, James Davison. *American Evangelicalism*. New Brunswick, N.J.: Rutgers University Press, 1983.

Jacob, Walter. *Christianity through Jewish Eyes*. New York: Hebrew Union College Press, 1974.

Kaiser, Walter C. *Toward an Old Testament Theology*. Grand Rapids: Zondervan Publishing House, 1978.

———. *Toward an Old Testament Ethics*. Grand Rapids: Zondervan Publishing House, 1983.

Kantzer, Kenneth C., ed. *Evangelical Roots*. Nashville: Thomas Nelson, 1978.

Klein, Charlotte. *Anti-Judaism in Christian Theology*. Philadelphia: Fortress Press, 1978.

Klenicki, Leon, and Geoffrey Wigoder, eds. *A Dictionary of the Jewish-Christian Dialogue*. New York: Paulist Press, 1984.

Koenig, John. *Jews and Christians in Dialogue: New Testament Foundations*. Philadelphia: Westminster Press, 1979.

Küng, Hans, and Walter Kasper. *Christians and Jews*. New York: Seabury Press, 1975.

Lapide, Pinchas. *Israelis, Jews and Jesus*. Garden City, N.Y.: Doubleday & Co., 1979.

———. *Hebrew in the Church: The Foundations of Jewish-Christian Dialogue*. Grand Rapids: William B. Eerdmans, 1984.

Lapide, Pinchas, and Ulrich Luz. *Jesus in Two Perspectives: A Jewish-Christian Dialogue*. Minneapolis: Augsburg, 1985.

Malachy, Yona. *American Fundamentalism and Israel*. Jerusalem: Hebrew University of Jerusalem, 1978.

Marsden, George M. *Fundamentalism and American Culture*. New York: Oxford University Press, 1982.

———, ed. *Evangelicalism and Modern America*. Grand Rapids: William B. Eerdmans, 1984.

McGarry, Michael B. *Christology after Auschwitz*. New York: Paulist Press, 1977.

Mittleman, Alan. *The New Testament and the Jews: A Background Sketch*. New York: The American Jewish Committee, 1986.

Moore, George Foot. *Judaism in the First Centuries of the Christian Era*. 3 vols. Cambridge: Harvard University Press, 1948.

Neusner, Jacob. *Judaism in the Matrix of Christianity*. Philadelphia: Fortress Press, 1986.

Oesterreicher, John. *Anatomy of Contempt*. South Orange, N.J.: Seton Hall University, 1975.

Olson, Bernhard E. *Faith and Prejudice.* New Haven: Yale University Press, 1963.

Opsahl, Paul, and Marc Tanenbaum, eds. *Speaking of God Today: Jews and Lutherans in Conversation.* Philadelphia: Fortress Press, 1974.

Packer, James. *Fundamentalism and the Word of God.* Grand Rapids: William B. Eerdmans, 1958.

Pawlikowski, John T. *Sinai and Calvary: A Meeting of Two Peoples.* Beverly Hills: Benziger, 1976.

————. *What Are They Saying about Christian-Jewish Relations?* New York: Paulist Press, 1982.

Peck, Abraham J., ed. *Jews and Christians after the Holocaust.* Philadelphia: Fortress Press, 1982.

Quebedeaux, Richard. *The Young Evangelicals.* New York: Harper & Row, 1974.

Ramm, Bernard L. *The Evangelical Heritage.* Waco, Tex.: Word Books, 1973.

————. *After Fundamentalism: The Future of Evangelical Theology.* San Francisco: Harper & Row, 1983.

Rausch, David A. *Zionism within Early American Fundamentalism, 1887–1918.* New York: Edwin Mellen Press, 1980.

————. *A Legacy of Hatred.* Chicago: Moody Press, 1984.

Rosenberg, Stuart E. *The Christian Problem: A Jewish View.* New York: Hippocrene Books, 1986.

Rosenstock-Huessey, Eugen. *Judaism Despite Christianity.* University, Ala.: University of Alabama Press, 1969.

Rudin, A. James. *Israel for Christians.* Philadelphia: Fortress Press, 1983.

Sachar, Abram L. *A History of the Jews.* New York: Alfred A. Knopf, 1964.

Sanders, E. P. *Paul and Palestinian Judaism.* Philadelphia: Fortress Press, 1978.

————. *Paul, the Law, and the Jewish People.* Philadelphia: Fortress Press, 1977.

Sandmel, Samuel. *We Jews and You Christians.* Philadelphia: Lippincott, 1967.

————. *Anti-Semitism in the New Testament?* Philadelphia: Fortress Press, 1978.

————. *Judaism and Christian Beginnings.* New York: Oxford University Press, 1978.

————. *We Jews and Jesus.* New York: Oxford University Press, 1978.

Silberman, Charles E. *A Certain People: American Jews and Their Lives Today.* New York: Summit Books, 1985.

Silver, Abba Hillel. *Where Judaism Differed.* New York: Macmillan, 1956.

Smith, Timothy L. *Revivalism and Social Reform: American Protestantism on the Eve of the Civil War.* Baltimore: The Johns Hopkins University Press, 1980.

Steinberg, Milton. *Basic Judaism.* New York: Harcourt, Brace & World, 1947.

Steinsaltz, Adin. *The Essential Talmud.* New York: Bantam Books, 1976.

Stendahl, Krister. *Paul among the Jews and Gentiles.* Philadelphia: Fortress Press, 1976.

Stott, John R. *Basic Christianity.* Grand Rapids: William B. Eerdmans, 1958.

Strober, Gerald S. *American Jews: Community in Crisis.* Garden City, N.Y.: Doubleday & Co., 1974.

Tanenbaum, Marc, Marvin R. Wilson, and A. James Rudin, eds. *Evangelicals and Jews in Conversation on Scripture, Theology and History.* Grand Rapids: Baker Book House, 1978.

————. *Evangelicals and Jews in an Age of Pluralism.* Grand Rapids: Baker Book House, 1984.

Thoma, Clemens. *A Christian Theology of Judaism.* New York: Paulist Press, 1980.

Trepp, Leo. *Judaism: Development and Life.* Belmont, Calif.: Wadsworth, 1982.

Van Buren, Paul. *Discerning the Way.* New York: Seabury Press, 1980.

Vermes, Geza. *Jesus the Jew: A Historian's Reading of the Gospels.* Glasgow: Fontana, 1973.

————. *Jesus and the World of Judaism.* Philadelphia: Fortress Press, 1983.

Wells, David F. *Reformed Theology in America: A History of Its Modern Development.* Grand Rapids: William B. Eerdmans, 1985.

Wouk, Herman. *This Is My God.* New York: Pocket Books, 1970.

Yaffe, James. *The American Jew.* New York: Paperback Library, 1968.

Yaseen, Leonard C. *The Jesus Connection.* New York: Crossroad, 1985.

Zeik, Michael, and Mortin Siegel, eds. *Root and Branch: The Jewish-Christian Dialogue.* New York: Roth, 1974.

75676

Lincoln Christian College

261.26
R917